Kathy And Donald Porges
7062 Veneto Dr
Boynton Beach, FL 33437

The Nonprofit Imagineers

The Nonprofit Imagineers

Infuse Disney-Inspired Creativity Into Your Organization

Benjamin Vorspan

Leader in applied, concise business books

The Nonprofit Imagineers:
Infuse Disney-Inspired Creativity Into Your Organization

Cover design by Benjamin Vorspan

Interior design by Exeter Premedia Services Private Ltd., Chennai, India

First published in 2023 by
Business Expert Press, LLC
222 East 46th Street, New York, NY 10017
www.businessexpertpress.com

ISBN-13: 978-1-63742-457-5 (paperback)
ISBN-13: 978-1-63742-458-2 (e-book)

Business Expert Press Human Resource Management and Organizational Behavior Collection

First edition: 2023

10 9 8 7 6 5 4 3 2 1

For Elana, Evan, and Judah
Always remember that "it's kind of fun to do the impossible."
(Sometimes what Walt Disney says is worth repeating ...)

Description

What do Disney Imagineering and nonprofit organizations have in common? More than you think! Although nonprofit organizations are rarely known as creative powerhouses, once you understand how innovation and creativity work, you quickly realize that it's possible to use the same principles that make Disney Imagineering the gold standard of imaginative thinking to transform any nonprofit organization into an equally innovative environment.

The Nonprofit Imagineers explores how more innovation can happen at nonprofits, no matter how small the budget, how meager the staff, how tight the board oversight, or how limited the time commitment. Using more than 100 real-life examples from theme parks, movies, and Walt Disney's life, the reader will come away inspired to experiment with Disney Imagineering principles such as blue sky meetings, storytelling, creative intent, kinetics, plussing, and weenies. Yes, weenies.

In a refreshing break from traditional business books, Ben Vorspan uses a clever and amusing narrative to help illustrate the importance of storytelling in communicating ideas, and how innovative and creative concepts might be applied in a real nonprofit setting, while also adding levity and entertainment.

This book is perfect for employees, managers, board members, and volunteers at schools, faith-based organizations, community centers, and similar organizations of all sizes looking to use creativity to improve their facilities, programming, fundraising, and relationship with their families, members, and donors.

Keywords

nonprofit; not-for-profit; creativity; innovation; leadership; management; marketing; fundraising; communications; business; school; church; synagogue; community center; Disney; Imagineer; blue sky; plussing; creative intent; storytelling; weenies; forced perspective; hidden mickey; adjacent possible; mission statement; Innovator's Dilemma; motivation; ideation; brainstorming

Contents

Acknowledgments..xiii

The Preshow.. xv

Chapter 1   Removing Limitations 1

Chapter 2   Addressing Concerns 19

Chapter 3   The Truth About "Innovation" 45

Intermission 63

Chapter 4   Find New Ideas Through Blue Sky Dreaming.................65

Chapter 5   Connecting With a Story..................................91

Chapter 6   Imagineering Principles 123

Chapter 7   Yes, But How Do We Actually Do It? 149

Chapter 8   Did I Ever Tell You You're My Hero? 183

The Postshow..195

Inspirational Resources (aka The Bibliography).......................203

About the Author..207

Index 209

Acknowledgments

First and foremost, this book is inspired by and written for all of you underpaid, overworked nonprofit professionals that I have crossed paths with over the past 20 years, whether in a shared office suite, over e-mails, phone calls, and instant messages, or through an online discussion board or Facebook group. If you think I'm talking about you, I probably am. If you've ever used the phrase "hashtag nonprofit life" while griping about frustrations, I definitely am. The stories and challenges in this book belong to you, as do our communal successes and the difference we make.

Thank you to my parents, Bonnie and David, and my sisters, Alisha and Shaina, whose innovative, do-it-yourself spirit, as seen in so many of our creative family ventures (with varying levels of success), keeps me motivated to continue coming up with projects and ventures of my own (also with varying levels of success). And thank you to so many other family members (with a special shout out to my wife, Elana), almost all of whom currently or have at one time dedicated yourselves to working in the nonprofit community, and somehow still wonder why we aren't all millionaires…. My only advice is to invest in real estate.

Thank you to Scott Isenberg, Michael Provitera, Charlene Kronstedt, and the entire team at Business Expert Press for taking the chance on this first-time author, and for your guidance and insights throughout the very long process of publishing a book.

Thank you Walt Disney and all of the Imagineers who, for 70+ years, have shown us that "all our dreams can come true, if we have the courage to pursue them." If it wasn't for you, this book would have been 14 pages.

And, in an effort to future-proof this acknowledgments page, I would like to thank the tens of millions of you readers who helped propel this book to the bestsellers lists and keep it there for so many months; Walt Disney Imagineering, for the amazing job offer that you sent after reading this book; the folks who determine the Nobel Prize for Literature—I really wasn't expecting that one!; the Studio, for your generous offer to buy the film rights to this book; and the Emmy/Oscar folks—I know it's cliche, but it really is an honor just to be nominated.

The Preshow

In a perfect world, this book would begin with a musical number. Something reminiscent of the opening scene from *Book of Mormon*. Or *La La Land*. Something that starts off nonchalant. Unassuming. Lulls you into a false sense of doldrum.

Then, BAM—it picks up! A bunch of very tone, very pretty people, in solid-colored shirts, with a snappy bounce in their step, start emerging from their offices one by one, cha-cha-ing in unison to a beat that'll be stuck in your head for at least a few chapters. It starts off small and grows with each iteration of the melody. First in the hallway of the office suite, then the lobby, and before you know it, volunteers with their preschoolers have joined the spontaneous flashmob that spills out into the parking lot. Yes—preschoolers dancing in unison! That's how good this book-introduction-musical-number is! Never before have you seen an assemblage of professionals, lay leaders, and preschoolers with such a sense of rhythm and presence all in one organization before.

There's something special happening here.

Not just the dancing—the lyrics on their own are masterful. There is a sequence of lines in the fundraising stanza of the song that, in the down-beats, rhyme "maintain," "sustain," "preordain," "capital gain," and "annual campaign!" I know, right?!? This is *Hamilton* level!

And here's the best part—at least in my opinion.… Some people won't notice it, but it's one of those small details that makes a difference to me—It's all one continuous shot! (Yes—this book-intro-musical-number also has camera direction.) From the steadicam in the office, to the dolly in the courtyard, to the drone a hundred feet above the parking lot—somehow, it's all one continuous shot! How the heck did they do that?!? I'll tell you this much—it couldn't have been cheap.

But then, before you know it, and way before you're ready for it to be, it's over. The dancers are gasping for air, the parents resume their excruciatingly slow quest for the early drop-off room, and the tone for the rest of the book has been set. This clearly isn't your average nonprofit guide to effective postpandemic fundraising. It's better than that! It's better than all other instructional business books. It's genuinely interesting! You're not drudging through dry, 50-word sentences about proactive board management, just to be able to gloat to your boss that you've read it. You're reading it for fun!

It seems excessive—why does a book for nonprofit professionals need a musical opening number? And such an ambitious one at that? I can't imagine the bar for business book opening numbers is so high that this couldn't have been handled with traditional camera work. But it also makes you wonder—why don't all books for nonprofit professionals start with musical numbers? It's just so much better this way.

It's almost as if a very wise, handsome, and humble author put extra effort into analyzing and perfecting the book-reading experience, so as to instantly form a strong and lasting connection with you. He wrote the book he'd want to read, or "wore his guest's shoes," as one of *Mickey's Ten Commandments* says. What a novel approach (yes, pun intended)!

Why don't more authors of instructional materials aim for this sort of "love at first sight?" Why don't more people in general do that—regardless of what they're producing? And, of particular interest to you and me, why don't more nonprofit leaders prioritize that goal more than anything else—to make people fall in love with their organization from the very first moment of contact, and then make them fall in love over and over again with each connection thereafter?

I might as well ask you that question too ... right? Whether you're an executive, an employee, a board member, or a volunteer, what are you doing to help your nonprofit seduce its supporters at every interaction? Yes—literally *every* interaction.

That's what I thought. Maybe it's time to change the way we think about our nonprofits.

Burn the Box

The CEO of a large investment firm was handed several clippings from a financial magazine. He laid the pages on a table and, with all identifying information obscured, was asked to select the advertisement from his institution. After analyzing the graphics and copywriting for a few minutes, he realized that the only real difference between the ad that his company was running, and those of his competitors, was their logo. Without their logos, they were completely interchangeable.

This is the problem with classic "inside the box" thinking—everything's the same. Obviously, we aren't going to touch anything inside the box. If you're looking for "fundraising best practices" and "cutting-edge social media strategies" that analyze what everyone else in the industry is doing, and offer suggestions to help you rise to their level, you'll need to look elsewhere (I suggest you do—there absolutely is value in having that knowledge under your belt).

The goal of this book isn't to help you be as good as the top organizations by mimicking them—it's to train you to think for yourself in ways you never have before—in ways *no one* ever has before—and come up with brand new ideas that don't conform to any lists of best practices. We're not here to design a better print ad—we're here to gain the knowledge and courage to slash print ads from our marketing budgets and find entirely new ways to better connect with our people.

In fact, we aren't even going to be thinking "outside the box!" As Disney historian Jim Korkis said, "Walt would say, 'No! Don't think outside the box! Once you say that, you've established that there is a box.' Walt would refuse to accept the existence of the box."

So, let's rip the box to pieces to use as kindling and focus on what we're really talking about here: Disney-level creativity.

I'm going to introduce you to an entire world of creative thinking and discussions about what true innovation is (here's a hint: "Innovation" doesn't mean what you think it means). We aren't just going to be inspired by innovators like Steve Jobs, Thomas Edison, and, of course, Walt Disney; we're going to take a deep dive into how innovation happens, and what stands in the way of our creativity. We're then going to use that knowledge as a base on which to build, as we explore Disney's Imagineering process, and see how we can use those concepts to improve our operations.

A Blank Sheet of Paper

In a time when amusement parks were noisy, dirty venues, Walt Disney had a vision for a clean, family friendly theme park. When Walt, a man who enjoyed remaining on a first-name basis, wanted to migrate the concepts from his imagination into tangible drawings for what would become Disneyland, he first approached his friend and accomplished architect Welton Becket for advice on where to find the right architect to turn his vision into a buildable plan. Becket responded, "You'll use architects and engineers, of course, but Walt—you'll really have to train your own people; They are the only ones who will understand how to accomplish your idea."

This quote from Marty Sklar in the foreward to *Walt Disney's Imagineering Legends and the Genesis of the Disney Theme Park* illustrates a problem most businesses and nonprofits face when trying to unleash creativity in an environment that isn't set up to work that way. We hire people for specific, preexisting jobs with the expectation that they perform those exact jobs. The foundation of our business practices is that each person has a specific expertise. We hire bookkeepers to do the bookkeeping, program directors to plan programs, and communications managers to send e-mails. It makes sense. But it also restricts us from truly exercising our creative muscles. When was the last time your bookkeeper was asked her opinion on how to better reach millennials? When was the last time your janitor was asked to help plan your next big event?

We stay in our lanes because that's what we were trained to do and is expected of us. But is that the way it should be? Within our jobs, we each accumulate vast knowledge that might help a co-worker form a better plan. And outside of work, each of us has an array of hobbies and experiences that can help that plan flourish. I can't tell you how many times I've run an idea by our head of maintenance and received feedback about crowd flows, acoustics, and which appetizers are always left in the walk-in fridge the next day because no one likes them, leading me to completely change my plans. Why shouldn't he be involved on some level other than as an afterthought?

It's not easy to convince an accountant to share her thoughts on adult education, and it's even harder to convince an executive director that 10 percent of that accountant's time should purposely be diverted to anything and everything other than accounting. But just as Walt's neighbor explained, you need to train your people to think like you. It won't come naturally.

"Any ride engineer can design parts," Don Hilsen, Disney Imagineer, said. "But it is a unique kind of engineer who can blend a creative story and theme with practical technology.... You have to be a big thinker, a 'blank sheet of paper' person."

The truth is there are more than 100 Imagineering disciplines at Disney, including project managers, writers, and accountants—just like the crew at your organization. Imagineers aren't trained by the Disney company to be accountants or writers—they come to the organization with that skill set and then are trained to think and interact differently, from within their chosen field. This has been the case dating back to the original Imagineers, who were animators and artists that Walt borrowed from his studio to help him with an experimental theme park project. They had no training in ride design and had never planted jungles or erected castles—they worked together, used the skills they had, and figured it out!

Deep down, we all have the ability to imagineer! The Walt Disney Imagineering website describes its team as "the creative engine that designs and builds all Disney theme parks, resorts, attractions, and cruise ships worldwide," in addition to many other creative endeavors. Similarly, we Nonprofit Imagineers will be the driving force that will bring creativity and innovation to our individual organizations, and to our industries as a whole. We will combine "imagination" and "engineering" to come up with brilliant new ideas and put them into action.

Somewhere, there's a blank sheet of paper inside each of us. When given the right motivation and flexibility, and provided with the proper tools to be creative, we can do what Walt once did, and what Disney Imagineers do every day—change the way we perform our jobs and build something brilliant!

I'll go out on a limb here and say that at the time of writing this book, no nonprofit in history has ever hired someone to be in-house imagineer. That's because, unless you're the Disney company, you wouldn't hire imagineers (well, except for Alcoa—the company credited with first coining the term *imagineering* as a way of encouraging creative uses for their aluminum products during World War II)—but you *can* hire bookkeepers, program directors, and communications managers and train them to imagineer!

The Nonprofit Imagineers

Walt was a cartoonist for the first few decades of his life. When he decided to build his first theme park, his challenge was to give people the opportunity to experience walking, touching, breathing, and tasting what it would be like inside a cartoon—to take two-dimensional art and transform it into a three-dimensional world. In many ways, I see that as a primary goal of this book. Many nonprofit employees work in two, or sometimes, one dimension. They are hired for a specific job, and day after day, they do that single job.

Nonprofit Imagineers, on the other hand, need to look at all dimensions. Our job is to prioritize one of Walt's cardinal rules—"Know what the people want and build it for them." We need to understand how to emotionally connect with those who we support, and those who support us, in order to further our mission and make the greatest impact in our marketing, communications, fundraising, programming, and so much more.

With a view from 1,000 feet up, we need to see the Candyland-style map that ties together the sequence of events from the first point of contact to moments far in the future, making sure the entire interaction is well choreographed and leaves our guests wanting more. We must see how an event fits into a campaign, and how the campaign fits within our mission. We must make sure that every piece of collateral and every interaction gives our guests exactly what they want and need. And, often without anyone realizing just how many dominoes we've precisely set up, we execute the chain reaction that might continue for months or years in the future. The chain reaction with a single goal that is always in the back of the Nonprofit Imagineer's mind: to make our supporters fall in love with our organization over and over and over again.

"Guests?" "Choreographed?" "Candyland?" We're a nonprofit…. We don't "choreograph guest experiences." We "meet an important need for our members/clients/community." We are a serious business!

Fair enough—maybe we can't look at religion or poverty or education as a "show" the way that Walt looked at his animation or theme park. Maybe we aren't "entertaining" our constituents with a "story" in the traditional sense, but what's the difference between entertaining and engaging? What's the difference between telling a story and connecting through a narrative? The lexicon might not match the "best practices" or "think outside the box" books we've read, or the discussions we've had with other nonprofit professionals, but I guarantee the bottom line is the same.

Wait a minute—why am I trying to justify this to you? Rather than trying to temper this book to conform to the norms of what our industry expects, I'm here to challenge you! I'm here to get you to not just think outside the box but to toss the box onto a flaming couch to celebrate the end of your senior year at UC Santa Barbara (that is not an admission of guilt). We're here to be creative, to think differently—to imagineer!

And there's a very good reason for that!

Imagineers do what they do so that the child who has lived his entire life in a wheelchair is able to experience flying through space—something that child will likely never be able to do in his lifetime, other than at a theme park. Aside from Imagineers, there are few people who do what they do exclusively to make life better for the people they touch. Nonprofit employees and volunteers are perhaps the only other ones who sincerely follow that exact mission. We are unique and we are special. We are committed to the social good and we are capable of amazing things!

Lest you think this is just fluff to lure you into buying what will inevitably turn into a typical business book, I promise you this—as we learn about things like fundraising, programming, and nonprofit marketing, we will discuss no fewer than 100 genuinely interesting real-life examples from Walt Disney's life, Disney animation, and Disney theme parks that I guarantee you will not find in any other nonprofit business book. I'll also show you the power and value of storytelling, not just by analyzing how great stories are told, but by using this entire book to tell an actual fictional story! Don't act surprised—a few pages ago, I literally told you I was taking a *novel* approach. Like I said, I put myself in my guests' shoes and wrote the book I'd want to read. I like fiction … even in instructional business books! *How's that for thinking differently!?!*

Prepare to explore areas that nonprofits generally don't consider. Prepare to be challenged with concepts that are simultaneously deeper AND higher level than anything you've thought about in your professional career. We're going to start with two dimensions and come out the other end in glorious Imax 3-D with Dolby digital sound and the artificial scent of peanut butter fudge wafting through the air.

So, off we set on a journey to learn a whole heck of a lot about making our nonprofits better the same way Uncle Walt would have.

Nonprofit Imagineers—"We're off to Neverland!"

The Takeaways

- This book is going to be awesome and the author is hilarious and clever.
- You can't just skim—sometimes clever word play is actually foreshadowing.
- This book is not a "how-to" with step-by-step instructions. Although there will be some ideas to implement right away, it's mainly going to cover higher level concepts and reframe how change and creativity can happen in nonprofit environments.
- The fine folks at Walt Disney Imagineering are individuals from more than 100 different disciplines, hired to do more than their job title might indicate, and work collaboratively as a creative powerhouse. We're going to learn some of the guiding principles that make those Imagineers so special and apply them to what we do. In essence, we're going to turn ourselves and our willing co-workers into Nonprofit Imagineers.
- Importantly, "nonprofit imagineering" is a way of thinking creatively and finding new ways to execute those ideas. If at any point you find yourself using Disney's intellectual property in your marketing, programming, or fundraising, you're doing it wrong.
- Just because a lot of people burn their couches to celebrate the end of the school year at UC Santa Barbara that does not mean the author of this book participated.

Next Steps

- Buy copies of this book for everyone on your team. You all need to be on the same page if you're going to be as awesome as possible.
- This book is just the beginning. Head over to thenonprofitimagineers.com where you'll find guiding questions to help your group get the most out of this book, as well as worksheets and examples of the concepts I cover in the book.
- I asked an AI chatbot to write the lyrics for the opening number. Visit thenonprofitimagineers.com to see what it came up with.
- If you have the connections to produce the actual opening number for this book, let me know! I'm sure we'd all love to see that happen. I'm serious. E-mail me at ben@thenonprofitimagineers.com.

CHAPTER 1

Removing Limitations

"We're Off to Neverland!"

If you've ever tried driving to Neverland, you know that nestled in the foothills, just before you begin the winding ascent toward the clouds, you pass through the charming village of Nottatown, where seasoned travelers stop to stretch their legs, fill up with gas, and buy snacks they'd never buy for themselves at home. Who really needs three pounds of gummy worms, except on road trips?

For those of you who just drive through without stopping at the visitor's center, you should know that Nottatown has a rich history dating back more than 300 years. They proudly boast of the fact that they were founded more than a century before their rival city, Anytown, USA.

According to the gentleman in the visitor's center who is seriously fooling no one with that toupe, Nottatown's other great achievement is being the birthplace of the modern pun. For years, Dr. Albert Groaner petitioned Nottatown University to add a Pun course to their catalog, which they finally did in the fall of 1972. His course was so popular that by 1980, students were able to major in puns, earning a BS in Punology. The University regents argued that if they approved the degree, it should fall under the English Department's Bachelor of Arts program, but Dr. Groaner insisted that students should be able to refer to their degree in puns as a BS degree.

Although Nottatown residents commonly refer to puns as "groaners," after the founder of the University's Pun Department, when Charles W. Dad, a former student of Dr. Groaner's, and Anytown native, published his first volume of self-named "Dad Jokes," it fanned the flames of animosity between Nottatown and Anytown residents. More on this later.

During good times and bad, the Nottatown Community Center (NCC) was the heart and soul of their picturesque city. For more than a century, they had been the cultural and social center of their adorable, quaint, and, in case you haven't caught on yet, entirely fictional town. At different times, they have housed a thriving preschool, provided space for religious groups to congregate, hosted temporary art installations, were considered to be "the place" to get married, and hosted a regional comic book convention in 1992, which they continue to include in their brochure to this day for some reason. Additionally, at one point or another, they also served whatever purpose your organization serves in your community. How great is that!?! The organization in the fictional narrative that will be used throughout this book to better understand some of the complicated principles we're learning about is totally relatable to you!

To keep up with the times, the NCC staff has evolved over the years. In checking the "Meet our Team" page on their website, after scrolling past the stock photo of four multiethnic, smartly dressed adults, smiling as they point to a tablet screen, we learn that the NCC currently has "one of each type of employee" on their small staff (again—conveniently, just like you):

- A confident leader, who is knowledgeable, but can sometimes be tough to work with.
- A communications person, who is very good at what he does, but loses too many hours each week fielding tech support questions even though it's not his job.
- A program person, who has potential but is often unmotivated to do her best work.
- A development person, who earns more money than he probably should, but no one really talks about it.
- An office manager, who is very nice and very competent, and generally ends up doing more than his share of work.
- An administrative assistant, who really deserves to be senior staff.
- And several other supporting staff members at varying levels, who definitely don't.

Over time, as the town grew, places of worship were built, preschools popped up, the university opened several art galleries, and young couples found that they preferred to recite their vows in the shabby chic gardens of the Holiday Inn Express over the aging social hall at the Community Center. What was once the beating heart of the city now labors to attract event participants and financial supporters. The Nottatown Community Center is a shell of what it used to be and has become known by local teens as "Not-a Community Center"—a pun that spread surprisingly quickly through the community, considering how disconnected that community is from its once-great "third space."

The Nottatown Community Center is in the midst of an identity crisis, faced with the realization that they either have to reinvent themselves or close their doors.

I was asked by Jonathan, NCC's Executive Director, to lead a series of workshops with his team to help them figure out how to once again become relevant to their community, since the traditional tactics they had been attempting were coming up short. He told me that he loved the idea of looking at the creativity of the Disney Imagineering process for inspiration and felt that his staff would find it more interesting than the other workshop they were considering, which put too much emphasis on the use of posters with sports metaphors as motivational tools.

My first meeting with the NCC team was via video conference. Always wanting to be original and make the most impact, I set up my mobile hotspot and laptop in an outdoor setting that I knew would capture the attention of my new clients.

After we went around the virtual meeting room for introductions, I asked, "Can anyone guess where I am?" I then showed them the beautiful gardens behind me.

I showed them a plaque on a stone wall that read "Walter Elias Disney," and I even gave them a clue by saying, "You're going to *plotz* when you realize where I am." When it was clear that the pun wasn't landing, I explained that I was seated steps away from Walt Disney's burial site. I expected a gasp, or really, any reaction, but got nothing.

That's right—I was videoconferencing with new clients that I had never met in person from a cemetery. (And, no—contrary to any bizarre rumors you might have heard, Walt wasn't frozen … he was cremated and interred in a cemetery in Glendale, California, not far from his Burbank studios.)

Pointing the camera at the plaque, I explained to my clients that where you might expect to read an eloquent and inspiring epitaph honoring a real-life folk hero, all you get is a name. But, in this case, the name alone is plenty.

In its simplicity is its impact, for how do you abridge the life of a giant like Walt Disney on a single grave marker? How do you properly summarize everything he accomplished, and everything he did for the world in just a few characters? (Normally I'd say "no pun intended," but I was told only Anytowners say that … and I'm definitely NOT an Anytowner!) You can't. You shouldn't.

Walt was an illustrator and animator. He pioneered nature films, developed new techniques for the use of sound, color, and story in films, and changed the landscape of animated feature films.

During his lifetime, Walt created more than 600 films, won 32 Oscars, and received nearly 1,000 awards.

As impressive as it is, imagine if that's where his obituary ended.

Imagine if, as a young adult, he had been so focused on his day job of illustrating advertisements that he never learned the craft of animation. Imagine if he had listened to the naysayers and focused only on animation, never leaving his studio to pursue building Disneyland. Imagine if he had been content with Disneyland and never bought land in Florida. Imagine if Walt Disney had gone down in the history books as an advertiser-cartoonist … and nothing more.

Thankfully, Walt had the foresight to not limit himself to just illustration, just filmmaking, or just one park.

Walt's willingness to let himself be serenaded by the siren call of his daydreams is something very few of us have the bravery to do. And in the working world, where supervisors and boards oversee everything we do, it's something we rarely get the chance to do.

***

Just as I was hitting my stride, I noticed the chat bubble pop up on the bottom of the video-conference window, followed by a wave of uneasy commotion among the participants. Perhaps naively, I assumed it was a timely comment about one of Walt Disney's great achievements and how it might connect with the work we were about to get into. It wasn't.

"He kind of reminds me of that annoying guy that was hitting on us at the bowling alley last week, except more effeminate, ha ha ha." I read it aloud matter-of-factly from the chat window. Shoshana turned bright red, realizing she had sent the message to the entire group. I paused as I pondered how to respond. I kind of wanted to ask if they had a picture of this guy. But instead, I made the decision to ignore it and move on.

"Look," I said in a slightly deeper voice, "the bottom line is, during this process, we have the obligation to let ourselves get carried away with creative ideas, just like 'Uncle Walt.' And to do that, there's one important thing we have to do first—stop limiting ourselves!"

What's Your Mission?

I asked the NCC team the simple question that you have probably never bothered to ask about your own organization—"What is your mission statement?"

Odds are, after searching through your website or some old brochures, you'll find that it's several sentences packed with descriptive multisyllabic words that make it sound strategic, profound, and inspiring. Something like, "Our mission is to continue to synergistically empower future-proof paradigms and completely leverage other's prospective collaboration and idea-sharing such that we may continue to intrinsically impact value-added customer service to delight the customer." That mission statement, incidentally, is the product of the "mission statement generator" at joe-ks.com, but it probably shares at least a few words with your own mission statement. What does it tell you when your mission statement can be confused with one from a joke website?

"Good not-for-profits don't gunk up their messages with convoluted rationales and multipart platforms," Nancy Lublin explains in *Zilch: The Power of Zero in Business*. "They focus on a core idea and pound it home. With the best not-for-profits, you can summarize what they do and what they stand for in a few words. That's the test of a great but simple brand."

Aside from sounding formulaic and cliche, the more descriptors used, the more "gunked up" and specific your mission statement becomes, forcing you to think inside your mission statement's box. Mission statements that are too specific prevent dreamers from being able to dream. All of that leads you down a path in which no creative professional can thrive. As Lublin explains, the "core idea" is most important. The rest is just gunk.

The Nottatown Community Center's mission statement was as typical as they get: "The Nottatown Community Center is a nonprofit organization providing a physical space for our community members of all ages to learn together, pray together, and experience art and culture, thereby improving the quality of life for all residents of Nottatown."

The NCC mission statement is by no means bad, but often when it comes to mission statements, vaguery is a virtue. Nordstrom's mission statement, "provide a fabulous customer experience by empowering customers and the employees who serve them," says nothing about selling clothing. There's no mention of cars in Tesla's mission statement—"To accelerate the world's transition to sustainable energy." TED doesn't say anything about publishing short videos on specific subjects in their two-word mission statement—"Spread Ideas." And although Nike alludes to the connection between its products and the human body, they don't mention shoes or jerseys in their mission statement—"Bring inspiration and innovation to every athlete* in the world. [*If you have a body, you are an athlete.]" By being vague, Tesla opens itself up to manufacturing batteries, solar panels, and all sorts of sustainable energy products. Similarly, TED can "spread ideas" through a variety of mediums, and Nike can help "athletes" perform their best by whatever means they choose.

Even Amazon—the second largest company in the world—has just 18 words in their mission statement, "We strive to offer our customers the lowest possible prices, the best available selection, and the utmost convenience." Whether you're a customer of merchandise, streaming videos, web hosting, books about nonprofit creativity, or the hundreds of other services Amazon offers right now and will provide in the future, most will agree that they are delivered to you at a low price, in a convenient way, and with a great selection to choose from. In fact, their mission statement has evolved over time, originally aiming "to be Earth's most customer-centric company, where customers can find and discover anything they might want to buy online, and endeavors to offer its customers the lowest possible prices." Even in 1995, when their main focus was book sales, they understood the importance of not limiting themselves in their mission statement.

Looking at the NCC mission statement, using a term like "physical space," and listing specific types of programs, might put artificial limits on the organization, preventing it from branching out. If they wanted to turn a portion of their property into a softball field and start a new league, would that fit within their mission of learning, praying, and experiencing art and culture together? If they were to organize off-site or online programs, would that fit within their mission, which is very specific about providing physical space?

During good times, when an organization is thriving, having such language is helpful to keep the organization moving in the right direction toward a clear goal. However, when times are lean and creativity is necessary to reinvigorate an organization, or when the world changes and the needs of the community aren't what they once were, those specifics can end up doing more harm than good. Sometimes, it might even be better to consider transitioning from a close-ended mission statement to an open-ended mission question. Rather than telling your community how you will help, ask your community how best you can support it.

It never hurts to analyze your mission statement and decide whether it still works for you. If you feel held back by the language or the restrictions it puts on the types of programs you can run and the types of good that you can do in the world, begin a discussion to update it. To shorten it. To clear out the gunk.

Free yourself of the shackles that a poorly crafted or outdated mission statement can create. "Innovation happens when people are free to think, experiment and speculate." Heed this advice from Matt Ridley in *How Innovation Works.* The greatest factor that helps or inhibits innovation is freedom. Ridding yourself of that nagging, constraining mission statement will enable you to be free!

Since you're probably wondering, here is The Walt Disney Company's current mission statement:

The mission of The Walt Disney Company is to entertain, inform and inspire people around the globe through the power of unparalleled storytelling, reflecting the iconic brands, creative minds and innovative technologies that make ours the world's premier entertainment company.

Entertaining, informing, and inspiring are what Disney is all about, and storytelling is their preferred mode of delivery. It's specific but not too specific. Notice that they say nothing about illustration, animation, film production, or theme parks. Their mission statement doesn't mention travel, locations, or specific technologies. Simply put, if it's entertaining, it's Disney.

It's important to clarify that I'm not saying your mission should be so broad that it stops guiding you. A mission like "To save the world" or "To educate" can lead your organization in too many directions. You might end up doing many things on the surface but accomplishing no real deep-seated change. Your mission should be specific enough to keep your staff inspired but broad enough to allow for creativity.

Have You Considered Your Creative Intent?

If necessary, reworking your mission statement might be a good long-term goal that won't happen overnight. So, what can you do overnight to put your team on the right track and feeling creative? That's where the Disney Imagineering principle of creative intent can be useful.

As Louis Prosperi explains in *The Imagineering Pyramid*, "A project's creative intent defines the experience the designer hopes to create for their audience."

You'll notice that while a mission statement is broad and guides the organization on a macro level, individual creative intents can be applied to specific projects or short-term goals.

The beauty of establishing a creative intent is that it doesn't dictate what to do or how to do it. Creative intent doesn't define the type of decorations for an event or the plot of a book. Rather, it simply explains what you're trying to achieve—the takeaway. It's more about the message that you want people to walk away with than how you actually execute it. Thus, creative intent keeps everyone focused on a common goal, while also allowing each team member to express their own creativity.

Creative intent can be applied to almost anything, but is especially important for longer campaigns or larger programs with many moving parts because it can be very easy to lose sight of the target the campaign is driving toward. Things can quickly become a series of creative but seemingly unrelated pieces rather than one cohesive campaign that delivers the same message.

To better understand creative intent, consider the Peter Pan dark rides found at five different Disney parks. Those of you who have never experienced this attraction will love flying over London and through Neverland aboard your own enchanted pirate ship as you visit sites from Disney's 1955 animated feature.

If you think the theme of this ride is "Peter Pan," you'd be absolutely right. However, "Peter Pan" is not the creative intent. The creative intent is to make you feel like you're soaring through the London and Neverland skies with Peter Pan.

In trying to achieve that creative intent, writers storyboarded scenes, artists designed sets, engineers developed a hanging ride system, and hundreds of other people in a variety of disciplines all understood that their goal was to make the visitors feel like they were flying with Peter Pan. In fact, each of the five versions of the ride at different Disney parks is slightly different, but they are all ultimately guided by the same creative intent, giving the riders the same feeling of flying through Neverland with Peter.

Without the creative intent that specified flying through the air, Shanghai Disneyland's Peter Pan ride, which was designed and built more than 60 years after the original Disneyland California ride opened, might have had ride vehicles that rode on wheels or floated along canals rather than hung from an overhead track, and scenery might have been designed so that you feel like you are inside buildings rather than flying over them. It would still be a Peter Pan–themed ride, but it would be a completely different ride than what the original Imagineers envisioned and intended. By establishing a clear goal from the very beginning, Imagineers were able to create a masterful and memorable experience, and we can do the same!

Importantly, creative intent isn't limited to outward-facing programs and campaigns. Creative intent can be used to establish internal goals and help clarify objectives. For example, rather than arbitrarily aiming to add 1,000 new people to your e-mail database, determine what your intent is for that data and how your team might work together to achieve that goal through a variety of strategies. Are you trying to raise awareness? Raise money? Grow your volunteer pool? You might be able to achieve that intent by connecting with a smaller number of more committed people through social media, word of mouth, or a booth at a farmers' market. Arbitrarily adding 1,000 people to your e-mail database might end up doing none of those. You will also give your entire team the opportunity to be creative in coming up with different ways to reach the shared intent.

***

My friends on the video chat were starting to understand what I was explaining as I made one last point: Creative intent has less to do with how you do something and more to do with the outcome. Ultimately, people care about the end result—about how you make them feel when they attend your event or read your materials—not about the exact methods you use to make them feel that way. They care more about being taught than about how you teach. On the Peter Pan ride, they care about feeling like they are flying—not about the mechanism used to achieve that feeling. Always put yourself in your guests' shoes and make sure that what you're doing achieves the goal of your creative intent.

"OK," Phil said, trying to digest everything I had just put out there. "So, you're saying that if we're hosting something big, like a fair, we should come up with a deeper message or theme, and we should make sure each booth, all the entertainment, all the promotion—everything is done along the lines of that theme so that they all match."

"Sort of," I said. "Remember—creative intent isn't a theme. It's a message or idea that you want people to leave with."

"Oh," Shoshana said, continuing Phil's thought, "like we can host a big fair for Thanksgiving, and the theme can literally be 'Thanksgiving' but the creative intent can be something like 'community building.' And if everyone who has a booth plans their activity with that 'creative intent' in mind," she said, making air quotes with her fingers, "then it's going to be even better than just having a generic Thanksgiving celebration!"

"Yes!" I said. "They can all be Thanksgiving themed, and they can all have activities that focus on community building. By following this model, not only will the multiple booths feel more connected and impactful, but you'll end up with all sorts of creative ideas that one person alone would never have envisioned, because you are empowering everyone to be creative!"

"Except on Thanksgiving we always have our 'Turkey in the Straw' event," Jonathan, NCC's executive director, chimed in with a smile. "I know the board members really look forward to it each year. So, we'll have to find a different time to do something new like that. But I totally get what you're saying."

Oy.

As soon as Jonathan brought up the Turkey in the Straw program, it was like the virtual meeting room was hit by a virtual ice storm. Everyone became silent, sitting back in their chairs with cold stares. Clearly, there was something off in this group dynamic, but I was neither the right person to try to provide group therapy, nor was I in the right position, sitting cross-legged in a cemetery 1,000 miles away, to try to help them through this.

I knew at some point we were going to meet our invisible enemy, "because we've always done it that way." I just didn't think it would happen during our first virtual meeting.

Combatting "We've Always Done It That Way"

We've all heard it before—at work and at home—from a boss, a family member, a friend, and, subconsciously, from ourselves.

To be completely fair, we can't disregard our past. I've worked with many synagogues where 1,000-year-old traditions guided much of what we did. I can't expect the board to throw it away just because it clashes with the user experience I want to create. Nor should I be developing ideas with that expectation.

The key is to develop an environment of creativity that allows for new ideas while embracing traditions. Sometimes "because we've always done it that way" is a beautiful foundation from which to begin building. Sometimes what we've always done can coexist with, and complement, new ideas.

The problem is that innovative ideas often kill outdated ones. They replace things that are ready to be replaced in a concept Joseph Schumpeter calls "Creative Destruction."

I know that sounds scary, but it's the way of the world. The programs that were successful in the 1950s have been replaced time and time again in the decades since. Turkey in the Straw most likely replaced someone else's beloved event, which replaced something else before it.

What's even scarier for those of us pushing for change is that sometimes new ideas end up being epic failures. Sometimes we will replace a tired, stale fundraising campaign with something we believe will be new and exciting, only to find that it receives less participation and raises less money than its predecessor.

But there's good news for those of us trembling at the thought that we are about to embark down a path that will forever change our organizations and lead to their demise! Back when I worked in real estate, my manager used to say that no matter how good a salesman you are, there's no way you're going to convince someone to buy a house they don't want to buy. With so much on the line, there's a sense of relief knowing that no matter how good you think you are at your job, you aren't going to force someone into making the biggest mistake of their life against their will. Similarly, Matt Ridley tells us that "Innovation cannot push new ideas on people unless they want them."

For those of us who don't take big chances on revolutionary, game-changing ideas out of fear that what we're about to do might lead down the road of creative destruction—take solace in the principle that nothing will die unless it has genuinely reached the end of its life. Not only that—if something is ready to die, it's been heading down that path for years, or decades. You and I wouldn't suggest that a program be replaced just because, out of the blue, we decided that today is the day to kill it. We do so because we've been thinking about it for a long time, and today is the day we're finally acknowledging that it isn't working anymore.

In other words, if Turkey in the Straw was still working, it wouldn't find itself on the chopping block (the puns just keep coming … right? I must have some Nottatown blood in my family tree). It's only because it's nearing the end of its natural life that the discussion about replacing it is happening.

However, before you run through the halls quoting Matt Ridley and Joseph Schumpeter as you take a hatchet to some of your octogenarians' favorite monthly programs that you don't connect with, it's important to understand that not all programs are created equally or serve the same purpose. Certain things are not meant for you, and it's OK that you don't personally connect with them. It's for this same reason that Disneyland doesn't just have dark rides or just roller coasters. They have a little bit of everything, so that they can meet the needs and expectations of all their visitors.

From opening day until June of 1981, visitors had to pay to enter the park and then pay again to visit each attraction, for which they were given ticket books with a variety of tickets lettered A through E. In the Summer of 1972, basic attractions, such as walking through *Sleeping Beauty's Castle* or riding on the *Carousel*, required a 10-cent A-ticket. Riding the *Matterhorn Bobsleds* steel track roller coaster, or *Pirates of the Caribbean*—one of the first attractions to utilize a large cast of lifelike audio animatronics—required an 85-cent E-ticket.

Attractions are purposely created at varying levels because there are a variety of audiences. Not everyone wants to ride a roller coaster. Some people will find much more enjoyment watching old cartoons at the *Main Street Cinema* than they would exploring the depths on the *Submarine Voyage*, even though the Cinema required a B-ticket and the Submarines took more valuable E-tickets. If we try to compare the two using the same metrics such as "wow" factor, or turnstile counters, we will likely determine that the *Main Street Cinema* is a failure and should have been removed long ago. But nearly 75 years later, the *Main Street Cinema* still welcomes guests and is undoubtedly beloved and successful in its own beautiful way.

"We've always done it that way" is not a valid reason to continue pursuing an organizational objective that is no longer relevant, or to keep an outdated and unwanted program or campaign—especially if it's the *only* reason to keep it, but we should not be trying to turn everything into E-ticket attractions. "Updating" and "modernizing" for the benefit of the people who need or enjoy something is very different from making something "bigger and better," or replacing it entirely. Be careful as you analyze whether something is a classic that needs to be protected, or is tired and rightfully headed for creative destruction.

Embracing Change

It's scary to do something that is not what we've always done. Sometimes, it's scary just to suggest that we try something new—not only because we might fail but because really big changes can require total philosophical shifts, and it's daunting to think that way.

So, what's our natural inclination when we anticipate resistance to new ideas? What do we do to push the idea through, past each level of supervisor, committee, and board? We work with our counterparts to fine-tune the idea. We smooth the rough edges and temper it to be more palatable to those stakeholders who have aversions to the idea of change. We make it a little bit easier for everyone to understand. We make it fit the mold that things need to fit. And, of course, the more fine-tuning our idea receives, the less creative or innovative it becomes.

In the end, the final product is the same thing we've always done, perhaps with new fonts and brighter colors.

Consistency is comforting. It's easy. We know it works. We know our biggest donors like it that way. It's the reason why they continue to give … right?

Even if deep down we feel that it doesn't work, there will be no ruffled feathers by staying the course, since, at the very least, it's what we've always done.

That's some of the narrow-minded reasoning behind Jonathan's insistence on keeping NCC programs like Turkey in the Straw, eliminating the risk of potentially upsetting a donor that loves it.

Walt Disney would agree, right? Isn't that the reason certain rides, like Disneyland's original *Haunted Mansion*, *It's a Small World* and *Pirates of the Caribbean*, have remained relatively untouched since they were built more than 50 years ago? Isn't that why fans are up in arms the moment they hear that a dated attraction will be renovated or replaced?

The truth is that Walt Disney loved change. From the moment Disneyland opened in July 1955, rather than paying off his debts as quickly as possible, Walt vowed to put a percentage of the revenue toward constantly improving the park. While he was alive, nearly all of the lands and attractions received updates. Some attractions only lasted a few years before being renovated or replaced. If Walt had lived another 20 years, *Pirates of the Caribbean* and the *Haunted Mansion* would certainly have been updated! If Walt were around today, Tomorrowland wouldn't be known as "Nostalgialand" by some critics, and there's no way Fantasyland would still have dark rides closely resembling those from opening day, in which a small cart wiggles its way past flat wooden panels painted to reflect scenes from 80-year-old movies! Come on, people ... where's the fantasy in that?

***

I noticed the chat icon in the video-conference window began to flash again. With a bit of dread, I opened it to see, "I'm trying to teach my dog to dance. It's not going well. He has two left feet."

It clearly wasn't a comment for me, but what was it? In my confusion, I blurted out, "what the hell is that?"

Out of a chuckle on the other end of the computer, I heard Phil explain, "That was Shoshana. We had this staff retreat a couple years ago, and one of the suggestions was that any time it seems like things are getting tense, we share a pun or joke to lighten the mood. There's research that shows that keeping the mood light through jokes and funny comments can keep people focused on the task at hand rather than getting bogged down in personal frustrations."

Clearly, I wasn't the only one to pick up on the tension in the room after Jonathan's comment, and they could probably see my hesitancy to say what I was really thinking. I knew better than to try to give a full lecture about embracing change and getting over "we've always done it that way" during a video conference. That would need to be done in person, one-on-one.

I bit my lip, tapped my fingers nervously out of view of the camera, and then, with a polite smile that I was sure everyone would see right through, continued, "I love the enthusiasm and optimism! We're going to have so much fun figuring out what directions to take the community center in the future—finding out what's working, what needs to be fixed, and what we can really get creative with."

Inwardly, though, my mind was tangled like a big pretzel. We need to get over the fears that prevent us from taking chances and making changes. We need to evaluate whether the mission statement we're looking to for guidance is propelling us forward, or holding us back. We need to figure out how to work creative intent into everything so that we can get our juices flowing and make a real impact on our supporters. And most of all, we need to not fear change!

"Here's what I want you to do for the next time that we meet," I said, while out of the corner of my eye, I noticed a very stern-faced gentleman walking across the cemetery grounds in my direction. "I'm here to push you and your organization to do new, creative things. That's going to require change, and change is scary. Our first in-person meeting is in a couple of weeks. When we talk again, I want each of you to share one concern you have about what we're trying to do here. Let's get all of our concerns on the table from the beginning, so that we're ready to push forward and hit the ground running. OK?" A few heads nodded, which was probably the most I'd get out of this group at this moment. "It was great to meet all of you, and I really look forward to seeing you in person soon!" I smiled at the webcam, waited for a few people to wave goodbye, and left the meeting.

"Can I help you with anything?" Eric, a mortuary employee wearing a black suit with a gold name tag, asked.

"No—I'm just wrapping up a meeting."

"Unfortunately, we can't have you conduct business from the cemetery grounds."

"Sorry about that—I'm leaving now."

Eric stood in a stern yet unthreatening stance. He struck me as the person who gets called in when a grieving widower asks if there are any discounts. "Here's a thought," I said as I picked up my bag and began walking toward my car. "A new marketing campaign—'Our cemetery grounds are so beautiful, they'll make you *plotz*.'" Eric seemed unamused. I was really striking out today with that pun. "Nothing? It's Yiddish wordplay … Plotz … Plots … But if you gotta explain it …" Eric continued to push me toward my car without removing his hands from his pockets. "Over at the Nottatown cemetery that pun would've *killed*. Really? Not even a smile? At the cemetery … It would've *killed*."

The Takeaways

- Nottatown is fictitious, and any similarities to real-life people that you (or I) know who may require nudges to be more creative are purely coincidental.
- Mission statements should be brief and give direction and vision to your organization without getting into specifics. If your organization is struggling, and your mission statement is holding you back from new opportunities, begin the discussion to make changes to it. Consider temporarily changing it to a mission question. If you've never looked at your mission statement, now's a good time to see if it inspires you the way that it should.
- Creative intent is like a mini-mission statement for a specific event or campaign. It's important to keep everyone aligned when multiple people are involved in planning and executing the project, and can help you bring more creativity and a lasting impact to your project. Coming up with a creative intent will also help you add more meaning to your programming.
- Ultimately, creative intent should dictate the outcome for your guests—not the methods used to achieve that outcome.
- "Because we've always done it that way" is not a reason to continue doing something that isn't working.
- Creative destruction (replacing something old with something new) is natural and shouldn't be feared once you recognize that change generally happens when it's time for it to happen, and cannot be forced if it's unwanted.
- Walt Disney loved change and so should you.
- *Plotz* is a Yiddish word, meaning "to faint from enthusiasm." It sounds a lot like *plots*, which are where people are buried at cemeteries. It's one of many puns,

or groaners (or "dad jokes," if you're a lame Anytowner) you'll trudge through while reading this book. Get used to it.

Next Steps

- Can your mission statement use some work? Need a few more examples of creative intent to help you fully understand how to use it at your organization? Head over to thenonprofitimagineers.com for some tips and a helpful worksheet.
- Yiddish words are fun to say. Try to incorporate at least one Yiddish word into conversation today. People will *plotz* when they hear it!

CHAPTER 2

Addressing Concerns

Jonathan has had 27 different employers in his 52 years on Earth.

Among his career highlights were the year he spent as a professional gambler, culminating in a World Series of Poker appearance (he didn't make the money, but has an ESPN screenshot of himself playing at the same table as someone he thinks is famous, but isn't), a partnership with a friend to open a liquor store that was shut down within six months "because of a technicality," district office manager for Ronald Reagan's 1980 campaign for president, and a promotion to general manager at a small rural used car dealership.

A casual, but cleanly dressed man with a playful air of confidence, he generally had a smile on his face and a positive attitude, while simultaneously being oddly unapproachable. He had long salt and pepper curls, wore a polo shirt that probably fit him better a few years ago, and spoke calmly and deliberately with what I believe was a Minnesota inflection when he told me, "This isn't going to work."

I sat at a small iron pedestal table with chipping white paint outside Red, White, and Brew—an adorable coffee shop less than 100 yards from the NCC campus on Nottatown's Main Street, having my first face-to-face with Jonathan. He took large bites from his breakfast burrito as I warmed my hands on my cup of black coffee, making pleasantries and talking about the sites I had to see while I was in town. He told me to take the one-day intensive pun-spinning workshop with the local improv group, Mission Improvable, birthplace of "Did you get a haircut? No, I got *them all* cut." I smiled and nodded, but didn't want him to see how impressed I really was—I use that joke every time I get a haircut!

As the small talk died off, even before I could ease into my first substantive question, he launched into a monologue with a certain matter-of-fact tone that made me think he wasn't just finding the words as he went.

"This isn't going to work. We've tried this before, and each time, the same thing happens." He swallowed his bite of burrito and continued, almost as if he was taking pleasure in what he was telling me. "We try to change something, people get upset, they politicize our efforts to do new things, I get leaned on by a few key board members to back off, and then we're back to square one."

I tried to make a comment about creative destruction to throw him off his game, but without even a short pause, Jonathan continued. "Trust me—it happens every time. When I first started here, we sent out a ton of mailers. Every event, every new class, every holiday celebration had another mailer, and what really drove me crazy was that they were printed on colored paper, and had a form on the bottom for people to RSVP by cutting off the bottom third of the page and mailing it back with a check! Drove me nuts! Black and white copies on green or pink pastel paper, tri-folded, put in an envelope and mailed! Can you believe that? And we're not talking about the '80s—we're talking about a few years ago! I tried to get rid of the mailers and just use e-mail. They said no—'We did a survey a few years ago and it's how people like to get the information.' I tried to print them in color. They said no—'It's too expensive. People are fine with it being black and white.' I tried to switch to postcards, or, at the very least, to combine all the fliers into one envelope to save money, and somehow—god help me—'we' ended up deciding that 'we' should send out a full newsletter each month rather than individual fliers for each event. A full black and white newsletter! And guess who 'gets' to design that!"

Jonathan paused again as he scanned the street with a scowl on his face. I wasn't sure whether he was pausing for dramatic effect or had actually finished his one-man show.

"Did you know that 43 percent of people own a power tool they don't know how to use?" I couldn't tell if this was a pun that I didn't get, or if he was starting on some sort of parable. I followed his focused gaze to see the man across the street walking out of Hammertime Hardware Store with a belt sander under one arm and his son under the other. "Do you think he really knows what he's doing," he said, first looking at the man across the street, then whipping his head back toward me, "or is he going to do more harm than good?"

Was that a real question? Was I supposed to pretend I didn't pick up on his oh-so-clever double meaning? Why was he pausing again for so long? Was I really supposed to answer? I didn't want to interrupt his flow, but—"Trust me," Jonathan finally continued as he looked down at his burrito and then back at me. "This isn't going to work. It's just the way this place is. Maxine, a very generous board member—you'll meet her—is paying for you to be here, so I'm happy to have you give it the 'ol college try. To try to 'win one for the Gipper' as we used to say at the Reagan office. But I've worked at enough places to know when things aren't going to work, and I'm sorry to say, this place ain't changing anytime soon. I honestly think you're setting yourself up for failure. I wouldn't blame you for packing up and heading home today."

He stared at me again, clearly intending that last line to be an order rather than a ponderance.

Well, this was news to me. I was under the impression that it was Jonathan's idea for me to do this workshop, but suddenly he was telling me to back off.

There were three things Jonathan failed to understand about me, though: His theatrics didn't fool me; I too played the Jackbox party game with the trivia question about how many people own power tools they don't know how to use; and failure is what I do best!

Concern 1: We're Going to Fail

Yes—of course we're going to fail! Everyone who tries to do great things fails. Especially our greatest role models!

After returning from Europe following World War I, Walt Disney worked for a Kansas City company illustrating advertisements. Within the first year, he was fired. Fail!

He then started up his own company—Laugh-O-Gram Studio, where he and a good friend, Ub Iwerks, created a series of animated shorts based on fairy tales and Aesop's Fables. Two years later, Laugh-o-Gram Studio went bankrupt. Fail!

Following the bankruptcy, in the mid-1920s, Walt moved to Los Angeles and started a new studio with his brother, Roy. They created a character that became quite popular—Oswald the Lucky Rabbit.

Unfortunately, due to some bad deals Walt had signed, his distributor owned the rights to Oswald and cut the Disney brothers out of the deal by hiring away most of their animators and continuing to produce the cartoons without Walt and Roy. Fail!

Fortunately, Walt came up with a new character—Mickey Mouse—and as his team was finishing the last of the Oswald cartoons that he was contractually obligated to create, they secretly worked at night on two short films featuring Mickey. Walt spent his life savings to produce *Plane Crazy* and *The Galloping Gauchos*, which hit the theaters just before 1930 … and both of them flopped. Fail!

Over the course of many years, Walt pushed more and more for realism in his films. He delayed the production of the movie *Bambi* so long, trying to perfect the animation, that by the time he was finally able to release it, it was met with negative reviews, saying that the light-hearted animation he was known for was gone, in favor of an attempt to be too realistic. Fail!

Everyone fails. Over and over again. Even Walt Disney. But there's a reason we don't look at Uncle Walt as a failure.

The key is failing the right way—quickly and often—and never giving up. Failures aren't a bad thing—they help us determine what doesn't work, so that we can focus on what does. As Thomas Edison said, "I have not failed. I have just found 10,000 ways that do not work."

We learn by being wrong. Every trajectory toward innovation and success is dotted with failure after failure along the way. The problem is, if we spend months, or years, nursing a hunch, and it doesn't pan out the way we had hoped, those are months (or years) we'll never get back. As Jim Collins explained in *Great By Choice*, we should fire inexpensive "bullets" to figure out the right trajectory before we fire expensive "cannonballs." If we regularly try out small, new concepts that bring us closer to our ultimate goal, and one (or many) of those tests don't work as expected, we can adjust and try something new. It doesn't kill our dream—it just makes the path a little different than originally expected. Once we know that something small works, then we can go big.

***

Of course, rather than wasting my time trying to convince him of that, I just smiled and nodded as Jonathan finished his breakfast burrito, allowed him to pay the bill, and made up an excuse so that I wouldn't need to walk back to the NCC with him.

Not long after my breakfast with Jonathan, I found myself seated within the multicolored, bare-walled meeting room of the NCC. It was here that I finally met JJ, Vanessa, Phil, Hector, and Shoshana.

Shoshana was always the artistic one in her family. She dressed up as Bob Ross for Halloween in first grade, then again in second and third grades, even though each year her friends teased her for not having leg warmers on her Richard Simmons costume.

In high school, not a semester or summer break went by when she wasn't enrolled in an art class at school or at a local art studio. She loved charcoal and oil pastels, both of which were quickly banished by her parents, but her absolute favorite nonstaining medium was chalk.

At a young age, Shoshana entered and won prizes at "chalk walk" events, where artists were given sections of sidewalk, street or parking lots to make large murals on the ground as on lookers watched and took selfies. The year that she won the grand prize, her mural depicted Bob Ross looking at himself in a mirror as he painted a portrait of Richard Simmons. The hipster college crowd got her.

Now in her second year as program director at the NCC—a job she took as she continues to hope that her art career takes off, Shoshana has started to enjoy planning events and working closely with volunteers to figure out what the NCC can do better for the community.

On this day, Shoshana, with her 5'2" petite frame, ironically large glasses and short, straight, artificially darkened hair, sat across from me in the conference room, surrounded by her co-worker wondering what the heck I was doing.

I took a deep breath in. And let it out. Looked around the room. Took another deeper breath in, and out. Gave a sly grin at the confused faces around the table. Took one more deep breath, then, in one exhale, "We're going to fail, it's too difficult to change, false positives and false negatives are going to mess with us, it's impossible to make big changes, we're going to upset people—especially our big donors, everything we do today is going to eventually be outdated, we don't always play well with other nonprofits, yet we also don't have a beneficially competitive marketplace, and the board will never approve any of this, so why bother?"

The expressions on their faces were priceless. JJ and Phil looked at Jonathan to see if he knew what I was talking about (he didn't, nor did he seem interested in finding out), Shoshana and Hector squinted a bit, aware of what the list meant, as they tried to play it back in their heads and digest at least some of it, and Vanessa, who was trying to take notes, simply gave up somewhere around "false negatives."

"Did I leave any out?" No response. "Back on the video conference, I asked you to think about your concerns before we start this creative process together. Did I leave any out?" Their unconvincing nods were exactly what I expected. "Or did I make it worse? Bet you hadn't thought about all of those things that seem to stand in our way of making real change." More unconvincing nods.

"Not a problem. Let's go through them one by one, and see why they really aren't as bad as you think."

Concern 2: Change Is Difficult

No kidding. Going with the flow is always easier than challenging the status quo! If you plan on never growing as an individual or an organization, then by all means, do what's easy.

I can't tell you how many programs I've seen run year after year since they please members, and, of course, since it's easier to recycle a program than to write a new one. It's not necessarily a bad thing. People enjoy those programs. They keep coming back each year, right?

So, "is there really a reason to spend the money, even if you have the lines?" This is a common question among theme park operators—if you're attracting a crowd, filling your queues, without spending money on developing new attractions, or improving what you own, is it worth additional investment?

In our nonprofit world, we need to ask ourselves the same question—is it worth investing time, and possibly money, in developing new programs and campaigns, if our old ones are still reaching levels of success that we deem to be acceptable?

Compounding this problem is the tendency when things are good, to stay the course rather than potentially cause problems by attempting change. Why mess with a good thing? But when things are bad, we operate in a state of triage and don't have the resources to commit to innovation.

To be fair, even Imagineers struggle with change. Every Magic Kingdom has a castle. *Peter Pan's Flight* is in five different theme parks. Countless attractions appear in multiple parks and have been around for decades without significant changes. And people are not just content with it—they love the consistency! If Imagineers get to do what's easier, why can't we?

Well, it's not quite that black and white. While it's true that every Magic Kingdom has a castle, each castle is different. They are different sizes, different shapes, have different themes, and each hold different attractions inside. There are three distinct styles among the five, and Disneyland Paris's version of Sleeping Beauty's Castle goes so far as to shape its surrounding trees as boxes.

Even though certain concepts are mimicked, Imagineers will never do the exact same thing twice. What's the fun in that? Why would devout Disneyphiles travel around the world visiting every Disney Park if each was a carbon copy of the last? Imagineers give us something new with each iteration. They start with what they know works, and improve from there, incorporating new technology and new ideas that came to mind based on what they learned in the previous iteration. You should too!

You might not hear complaints about stale programming, but why would your constituents continue to attend programs and read your materials year after year if each one is a carbon copy of the last? If you're going to recycle a program, always review what worked, what didn't, and adjust your plan to add new elements the next time around.

Laziness or fear cannot be a reason not to try! During lean times, when all you can accomplish is something easy, make incremental improvements, and when you have the time and resources to do something more challenging, develop something new and exciting! The bottom line is, keep moving forward.

Concern 3: False Positives and False Negatives Are Going to Mess With Us

You should have seen the press coverage of Disneyland the morning after opening day. Writers blasted Walt Disney, saying his theme park would be closed within a year. The asphalt in the streets wasn't set; due to a plumbers' strike, the drinking fountains didn't work; half the attractions broke down; the Mark Twain River Boat temporarily started taking on water; and they had no idea how to control the massive crowd that swelled due to thousands of bootlegged tickets and ladders propped up on the outer fences to smuggle in guests.

And you should have seen the reviews following the release of *Fantasia*, a groundbreaking feature-length film that paired vivid animation with rich classical music. One woman said it nearly caused her a nervous breakdown. In fact, *Fantasia's* release went so poorly, and lost so much money, Walt nearly gave up on experimenting all together—realizing that another failed experiment might lead his studio to financial ruin.

Those reviews are classic false negatives. They gave the impression that something was a failure, even though it was destined to succeed.

False negatives, and their equally frustrating cousin the false positive (where something appears to work at first, but ends up a failure), are a part of experimenting and growing. Before Pixar was an award-winning animation studio, they were a hardware and software company. In fact, Pixar's RenderMan software was the industry standard, and at one time, it was the only thing making Pixar money. Where some might have assumed that Pixar should have leaned into the RenderMan business and stopped pursuing things like animation that were losing the company money, when Steve Jobs took over control of Pixar and analyzed the business, he soon realized that even though RenderMan was the only piece of the company operating in the black, it was a distraction that would ultimately doom the company. The market for the software was small—a user base of industry professionals that hovered around 1,000 users, each of whom was paying around $3,000 per year to license the software.

There's a strange but appropriate saying—"Don't make tuba oil." You might produce the best oil for lubricating tubas, but so few people play the tuba, even in the best of times, you'll only sell a few quarts per year. Pixar management knew that because the market for their software was so limited, the time and effort to sell and support RenderMan would never produce the income the company needed to grow. They had to focus on things that could help them thrive. They had to drop the software and focus on animation.

False positives and false negatives come in all shapes and sizes, and there's nothing we can do to avoid them, but we can temper them by taking small steps rather than huge leaps toward our goal, and constantly re-evaluating the big picture and what we're doing.

It's not always possible, but if you can base your next move on previous examples of proven success, you're more likely to be successful.

Although Disneyland might have seemed like a huge leap of faith into a groundbreaking, brand new concept, it actually wasn't. Walt Disney based most of his ideas on tried and true foundations. He and his team of designers spent years visiting other theme parks, studying crowd movement, ride queue design, and ride capacity. Even though the rides themselves were different from anything anyone had ever seen, the underlying principles that the park was built on were seeded in lessons learned from amusement park successes. Additionally, the rides he created were mainly based on his own popular intellectual property that he knew everyone loved. Although the idea of heavily theming the lands and rides was new, Disneyland was actually a well-researched, iterative step in a new direction (though, admittedly, a very large step from anything that came before it).

You too should start with the basics that you know will work and find creative new ways to build on them. By doing so, even if the initial reaction is negative, you can sleep soundly knowing that you are still making forward progress, and that with a few small tweaks, it should turn out better than it seems.

Also remember that even if your idea isn't an instant success, that doesn't mean it's a bad idea. It just might be a false negative! Keep at it!

Concern 4: It's Impossible to Make Big Changes, So Why Try?

Well, I think you're being overly pessimistic, but I get what you're saying. Sometimes, you feel like you're trying to move a cruise ship with a paddle, right?

Let me first say, maybe that's a good thing! Making huge changes, while exciting and potentially great, can also go very wrong. We talked about false negatives.... Sometimes, there's nothing "false" about the negative. Sometimes, it's just a bad idea. Forcing a large-scale, drastic change could cause significant damage! Your inability to enact drastic change is a natural safety net and might be your saving grace.

Having said that, big change or innovation hardly ever happens all at once. There are very few "aha" moments that send shockwaves through civilization. Edison didn't just suddenly come up with the light bulb one day. He started with a concept that other inventors had also been working on, then experimented unsuccessfully a thousand different times, and finally, after finding the right combination of materials … AND spending years convincing people that electricity was safe … AND convincing those same people that they "needed" light bulbs rather than oil lamps … AND (most people don't realize this) coming along at just the right time when electricity was starting to become available to consumers in their homes, was the lightbulb considered an innovation. Had any one of those chain links failed—had he given up after his 500th failure, or had his final success come 20 years earlier, before electricity was available in homes, someone else would be considered the innovator of the light bulb.

The light bulb became an innovation thanks to a combination of research, inventions, incremental progress, and thousands of failures by hundreds of people, over the course of many decades. That means, there are an unknown number of people who spent years of their lives working on an assortment of light bulb-related experiments, without which Edison would not have been crowned the innovator that he was. There was no "aha" moment when Edison suddenly innovated the lightbulb out of thin air. He just happened to be the one holding the baton at the right time in history.

Let's hope those hundreds of people that contributed along the way didn't feel like failures just because they didn't single-handedly make one big mind-blowing, world-changing discovery. They were equally, or possibly, even more responsible for the light bulb than Edison was!

The truth is, you most likely aren't going to be able to quickly and drastically change an organization, or go down in the history books as the face of the innovation that changed your industry for the better, but that doesn't mean, in the long run, you won't be able to accomplish a lot! Over time, the small changes you make today and every day in the future will amass. Over time, when the progress you make compounds with progress made by others, together you will be able to change the direction of the cruise ship with just a paddle!

The Innovator's Dilemma

You're probably pointing a finger at one person in your organization, blaming them for the stagnation you feel. Maybe it's your boss or a board member who determines which of your revolutionary, brilliant, groundbreaking ideas you get to pursue, and which to shoot down next. It's *their* fault you can't make the big changes you wish you could.

You might be surprised to learn, they're probably doing the right thing by holding you back!

In a sense, our organizations' inability to make large, sudden changes shares the same foundation as Clayton Christensen's "Innovator's Dilemma." Now, stay with me here—I'm about to get real serious for a few minutes.

The innovator's dilemma boils down to the problem that established organizations face when confronted with something new, whether it be an opportunity or a threat (Christensen calls this "disruptive technology"). Experienced managers will evaluate a new opportunity based on the return on investment, and if that return isn't worth the investment, a well-educated, well-trained, experienced manager will make the correct *business* decision by sticking with the "product" that is making the most money for the company, given the current market base. In other words, when presented with a forward-thinking, innovative idea, they'll make a good business decision by staying the course and not pivoting to quickly adopt the disruptive technology, because at that moment in time, it will actually hurt their current business.

Cornerstone Church of Nottatown was a prime example of this. They were a church that catered primarily to a middle-aged and older population who valued traditional services and fellowship opportunities. They held services and programs that appealed to that particular demographic, and had a strong, committed congregation that contributed plenty of funding to keep the church stable.

Not finding what they needed at Cornerstone Church, a small group of young singles, couples, and families joined together to form an independent group that gathered on a regular basis to volunteer, raise money and awareness for local charities, and socialize with other like-minded Christians, without the pressure to affiliate with an established church or feel required to attend weekly religious services. More than anything, they valued authentic, immersive, hands-on experiences that produced tangible results for their community.

Knowing that the 30-year-old church did not have the staff, space, and financial resources to develop the types of programs this particular millennial population was interested in, without sacrificing what they were providing to their existing members, the church leadership agreed to set aside the potentially "disruptive technology" that the new group represented, and to continue focusing on the religious services and programs their existing membership base valued. This was the correct business decision at the time—it met their needs and ensured steady income from membership dues and donations. The new group of younger families was small, appealed to a different demographic, didn't require dues in order to be a member, offered programs that didn't directly conflict with Cornerstone's, and was not considered a threat to the church.

Over time, the independent group grew. They became Compass Ministry, registered as a nonprofit, slowly hired a small staff, and formed an agreement with the Nottatown Community Center to use their social hall for social action events, and an unused classroom for storage of their charity collection items. Cornerstone still did not see this group as a threat—simply as an alternative that catered to a very different crowd, with specific interests, on the other side of town. They saw no negative impact on their membership or finances at that time.

Eventually, though, Cornerstone's membership began to shrink as their members moved away, and Compass' community grew and began paying dues, which enabled them to add nontraditional worship experiences to their growing lineup of options. By the time Cornerstone's leadership decided to try to engage with the younger crowd, whose interests were different from the traditional programs and services they were providing, it was too late. The "disruptive technology" had become the new normal, and Cornerstone, which had previously been considered mainstream, was slowly becoming outdated.

The innovator's dilemma was front and center in this example— had Cornerstone shifted too soon, and committed too many resources to appeal to the younger audience, they might have alienated their core market, sacrificing the income that they provided without replacing it with sufficient income from the younger audience. They might have put themselves out of business by transitioning too quickly in an effort to be forward-thinking and innovative. However, by the time they tried to make the switch, it was too late, and they had already been overtaken by the disruptive technology.

We hear stories like these all the time in the business world. Blockbuster, with their video rental storefronts, first failed to realize how disruptive Netflix would be in mailing rental DVDs directly to customers' homes, and then again didn't prepare for the disruption that streaming video would pose. Kodak stayed the course, providing film to their professional and consumer customers at a time when digital photos were low resolution and poor quality. They did not expect other companies like Nikon and Canon to create digital cameras that could surpass the photo quality of film as quickly as they did, nor did they expect cell phones to eventually take better pictures than most of their point-and-shoot models. They also failed to realize that society as a whole would choose to share photos digitally rather than print 4 × 6s as they previously had. By the time Kodak tried to adapt to new technologies, it was too late. Ironically, both Blockbuster and Kodak made sound business decisions at the time, and remained strong businesses for years after first recognizing the existence of the disruptive technology, but by doing so, were unprepared for the eventual implications of their choices.

Of course, for each innovation that changes the world, there are countless inventions that fail to meet their potential. Knowing that high-definition video was the future of television, and that DVDs couldn't play high-resolution recordings, Sony invested an immense amount of money in Blu-ray disk technology in order to be prepared for the disruption that such technology might someday create. Unfortunately for Sony, within years of that $100 million+ investment, streaming video surpassed Blu-ray use. Although high definition certainly disrupted standard definition video, Blu-ray was not the correct answer. Most consider this investment in Blu-ray to be an epic failure. Today, the continued push to produce videos on Blu-ray is simply an effort to make back some of their investment, even with the knowledge that eventually, disk technology will be obsolete.

This possibility of failure by committing too many resources to disruptive technology is what makes the innovator's dilemma so challenging and is part of the reason why you might feel resistance when recommending that your stable, decades-old organization try something drastically different, especially if it means sacrificing something that is currently working. Our drive for innovation is a balancing act, in which risk must be weighed against reward, and mitigating that risk often means limiting creativity.

A Quick Economics Lesson

How many stockholders does a publicly traded fortune 500 company have? Don't bother crunching the numbers in your head—it's a trick question. It can't be answered. Why? Because while there certainly are a large number of individual stockholders, a much larger number of shares are held by mutual funds, which each have thousands of investors. On top of that, mutual funds are often held by pension funds, which also have thousands of investors. So, it's literally impossible to identify every owner of a publicly traded company.

With that many voting shareholders, they will never agree on anything other than that they want the company that they are investing in to show profitable quarters for as long as they hold the stock. No one wants to hold a stock that they think will lose money.

Because of this, large companies focus on the short-term return they can give to their investors. The average stockholder (most likely a mutual or pension fund) will only own that stock for a few months, and the average executive at one of these large companies will only hold their position for a few years.

Investing in innovation and disruptive technology produces little or no return in the immediate future, which means today's stockholders and executives will not be able to reap the rewards of that investment. Under that model, why would anyone want to own stock today in a company that chooses to sacrifice short-term profits for long-term gains? Why would a corporate leader want to run a company at a deficit year after year if he won't be around to see the investment pay off a decade later?

Small start-ups, on the other hand, can sit with all of their investors around a table and decide how to spend their money. If they choose, they can prioritize long-term innovative goals, which might not produce profits for years, rather than attempt to turn an immediate profit.

If you followed all of that, you understand why large companies rarely put a significant amount of capital into future innovation, and why almost all of the successful disruptors are start-ups. I promise, I'll get to why this is important for nonprofits in a minute....

That doesn't mean large companies don't innovate! They just have to get creative about how they do it.

The most common process for innovation within large, established companies is through acquisitions. Under the leadership of Jack Welch, General Electric grew leaps and bounds, and became known as an innovative powerhouse thanks to dozens of acquisitions, including RCA and NBC.

When a start-up shows promise, a larger company often buys the start-up and continues to build upon its success. Shortly after being founded in 2010, Instagram began posing a threat to Facebook. It was a disruptive technology that could eventually siphon off Facebook's core user base, similar to the way Facebook overtook Myspace in 2008, and Myspace overtook Friendster, one of the original social networks, before that. Rather than establishing a new division within the company to target Instagram's user base, and commit time, manpower, and a lot of money to building something from scratch that might not succeed, Facebook simply bought Instagram in 2012. Disney did the same thing in 2006 by acquiring Pixar when it was clear that Pixar's movies were significantly better performing than any recent Disney animation at the time.

Large companies also approach disruptive technology and innovation by setting up "skunkworks" operations. These are small start-ups, generally treated as outside entities, that basically remove the larger company from the equation. In the smaller start-up environment, a few decision makers can create progress without board scrutiny or the pressure to succeed that the larger company might be burdened with. If the skunkworks fails, or the disruptive technology they were chasing ends up not being disruptive at all, there is no major harm to the larger corporation.

If, however, the skunkworks product becomes the wave of the future, the corporation is ready to reabsorb the start-up and meet that need head-on.

Believe it or not, Walt Disney Imagineering started as a skunkworks! Walt's brother, Roy, who was the business head of their animation and production company, thought Walt's vision for a theme park was absurd and destined to fail. He refused to sacrifice the studio's profits, manpower, and good name for the venture, forcing Walt to create a skunkworks operation. WED Enterprises was officially founded in 1952 (first as Walt Disney Inc., and then changing its name when studio stockholders worried that people might confuse this skunkworks project for the established production company) and was mostly self-funded by Walt Disney himself. Once the theme park concept progressed to the point where outside investors were interested, Roy agreed to provide additional funding and use their production company to help secure loans. As you probably know, the theme park business did pretty well, and WED Enterprises was acquired by the Disney Productions family in 1965, eventually changing its name to Walt Disney Imagineering.

How does all of this relate to us? After all, nonprofits don't get bought and sold, and they don't "acquire" other nonprofits in the same way large corporations acquire smaller companies. They don't have short-term stockholders to appease and quarterly earnings reports that will impact stock prices.

All of this is true, but there's plenty for us to learn from the ways that successful companies function. If there's a smaller nonprofit doing great things, consider partnering or merging with them, and incorporating what they do successfully with what you do successfully. If another organization has staff with expertise in a particular field that you would like to branch into, this is a perfect opportunity for partnership. Imagine if Cornerstone Church had offered the new group of young families pastoral guidance and free space to use, rather than forcing them to meet in their homes and at the NCC. Even without providing funding or dedicated staff, and keeping their organizations as two separate entities at first, how might that relationship have turned out differently for both groups in the long run?

If you begin to see a new organization as "disruptive technology" that could negatively impact you in the future, use a partnership or incubator model to your advantage. By joining forces, you can provide the stability and reputation that larger, established organizations often have, and they can provide the momentum to make change happen. As an added perk, since investing in innovation is always a risk, by keeping your organizations separate, you mitigate risk to yourself.

If you have a great, forward-thinking idea, but think that you will not be able to get the approval that you need because the risk might not be worth the reward (aka the innovator's dilemma) consider creating a skunkworks. Many times, an established organization will not want to try something new for fear that it will use too many resources, reflect poorly on them, or upset their longest standing supporters. In a skunkworks environment, the parent organization might provide some support, such as office space to work from or limited funding, but will treat it like an outside organization. It's going to be difficult for your manager to turn down your request to work on a project that might revolutionize your organization in the future and will only cost a few hours of your time each week. You will enjoy the freedom to think differently and do things the parent organization might not endorse, and eventually, once you prove your idea works, you'll be able to incorporate it back into your larger organization and enjoy even more success. If your idea ends up falling flat, there will be no harm to the organization.

We Never Try to Make Money

"If you want to know the real secret of Walt Disney's success," said Ward Kimball, "it's that he never tried to make money."

At nonprofits, we're just like Walt Disney (the person—not the multinational corporation). We don't try to innovate in order to patent our inventions and exploit them for profit. We're in it for the purest of reasons!

Donors are not stockholders. They care deeply about what we do, but they don't write us a check today in order to see 7 percent growth in their portfolio over the next two quarters. There are no expectations associated with donations—no dividends to be paid—other than that our organizations use that money prudently in achieving our objectives for social good.

Nonprofits don't enforce intellectual property constraints on their employees. They don't restrict us from sharing ideas or offering suggestions to other professionals that will help them succeed. Nonprofit employees are encouraged to find new creative ideas and collaborate with others. Nonprofit employees ask questions and share ideas on discussion boards because we all want one another to succeed. We all want to make the world a better place.

It might not always seem like it, but if there's any environment capable of making big changes in the long term, the nonprofit sector is it! Approach a donor and say "We'd like to use a portion of your donation to try something exciting and new. It might fail, but it also might end up changing the world." You really think they'll say no? If anything, they might be so excited that they'll contribute even more to your organization!

Concern 5: We're Going to Upset People— Especially Our Big Donors

It's going to happen. There's no way around it. There will always be someone upset by big changes. But the sooner we rip off that Band-Aid, the sooner we can begin to heal. The longer we go without changing at all, the longer we're going to be making black and white copies on pastel paper.

The thing we need to keep in mind, and remind people of, is that we're not changing just for the sake of changing. We didn't wake up this morning after a very vivid dream and decide, "we should stop teaching math and start teaching banana juggling!" We're not suggesting some arbitrary shift just because we feel like it.

The goal of change is to make things better. The change we are suggesting is the next step in the evolution of our organizations, and it has come about because of signals we have seen that indicate change is needed.

In his article *Innovation*, Timothy Sandefur points out that:

The discomfort that innovation generates has led many people to condemn it outright or to try to regulate it. Reasons for opposing innovation range from the practical concern that unforeseen consequences of untried innovations might cause disaster—as when a new drug causes unpredicted side effects—to immediate self-interest of those who benefit from the status quo—as when film studios sought to stifle the development of the home video recorder, which, they thought, threatened their profits.

Whether for fear of the unknown or any other reason, by preparing those people with the greatest concerns, explaining that failure is a part of moving forward, and that the change you recommend is based on experience and data, they will understand that this is a necessary next step. We're not trying to make things different—we're trying to make things better.

That doesn't mean we will please everyone. There will still be some nay sayers and "we've always done it that way" holdouts, but with the right approach, and enough empirical data to back our recommendation, we will slowly but surely win the support we need.

Concern 6: Everything We Do Today Is Going to Be Outdated, So Why Bother?

Yes. That's the way it is with everything. The hottest toys of last year's holiday season are in the donation bin this year. The greatest, most technologically advanced rides from 1960 Disneyland have either been replaced or heavily updated by today's Imagineers. You will absolutely put your heart and soul into a program or campaign that will run its course and be old news very soon (or, hopefully, recycled by a colleague at a different organization).

But isn't that the whole point?

Our successes and failures can't be thought of as the end goal. Rather, they are plots on the map, leading in a certain direction. No matter how great your event or campaign goes, it is a stepping stone to the next great thing. No matter how terrible your failure is, it too is just a stepping stone.

The key is to think of this not as replacing one program with a completely new one—it's to take the most successful features from one and use them as a basis for the next. That doesn't mean each new program should simply be an iteration of the last. It shouldn't be the same program, evolving little by little each year. Rather, start with something fresh and incorporate into it the principles that made previous events successful.

If people loved learning from a scholar in residence, don't just host more scholars in residence. Rather, include more outside scholars in new and innovative future programs. If people loved that your biggest fundraising event of the year was something other than a traditional "gala," build on it next year by hosting another creative event.

The reason Walt Disney loved Disneyland more than movies as a medium to express his creativity was because Disneyland could always be a work in progress. As soon as a film was delivered to the theater, it was done. He could not edit or improve it—it was complete and untouchable.

Disneyland, on the other hand, could be improved every day, forever. Walt Disney famously said, "Disneyland will never be completed. It will continue to grow as long as there is imagination left in the world. It is something that will never be finished. Something that I can keep developing and adding to."

The fact that everything you work so hard on today will eventually change is, in many ways, a source of comfort and inspiration. Yes, your next event might be amazing, and yes, as amazing as it was, it will inevitably just be a distant memory, but it is a stepping stone and will lead to even greater things in the future. What you will do 10 years from now could never happen without tomorrow's success or failure.

Concern 7: Nonprofits Lack the Capitalistic Force That Drives Change and Innovation, So What Are the Odds We'll Actually Change?

It's ironic—whereas businesses are always competing with each other, enabling capitalism and Darwinism to weed out the weakest, the nonprofit industry is different. On the exterior, we all try to get along. We generally won't see one charity openly criticizing another charity or going head to head against them to steal business. In fact, it's generally the exact opposite: Nonprofits exist to solve problems in the world, and many of our nonprofits either work to solve the same problem, complementing each other with similar goals, or solve small subsets of larger problems. If our goal is to solve a problem, why would we work against other organizations working to solve that problem too?

Without the competition to drive some out of business, however, there's no incentive or requirement to invest in ourselves the way traditional businesses do. After all, most nonprofits don't sell a product in order to stay in business—they solicit donations to cover their operating costs. If someone agrees with our mission, and they feel like we're achieving that mission, they are likely to continue contributing to us, whether we innovate or not. Mediocrity is perfectly acceptable.

But not feeling the pressure to innovate is actually a good thing. Venture capitalists look at investments based on their exit strategy. That is, at what point will they be able to sell or merge the company they're investing in, in order to reap the financial profits of their investment. They tend not to invest in new ideas that have never been tried and tested before, because they are not sure when, or if, that investment will pay off. Sometimes that means new ideas that will benefit the greater good, but don't have a clear path to profitability, will never receive an investment. A low-cost, portable medical device for use in rural African villages, for example, may improve humanity for decades to come, but will never turn a profit and, therefore, will never receive for-profit funding.

This is where nonprofits burst through the door, cape flapping in the breeze, ready to save the day! Without the capitalistic drive to generate profits, we can focus on those innovative projects that are otherwise overlooked. Ultimately, we end up with *more* freedom to try new things. The lack of capitalistic pressure can end up enabling *more* innovation to happen, as long as we keep pushing for it!

Concern 8: There's Still the Issue of Board Approval

First, don't assume your board is going to hate the idea of change. Once you explain everything you've learned so far—that you'll take it slow, make incremental improvements based on past successes, and use a broader creative intent to guide your vision, they might be open to trying new ideas.

Sometimes, however, building on the past is not what you want to do. Some ideas are totally new, and if there is a requirement to build on the past, you will eventually hit a glass ceiling. How do you approach this sort of change with a board that's already resistant to new ideas? Perhaps you can share the story of AlphaGo.

AlphaGo was a computer created by DeepMind, a team of scientists and engineers interested in advancing the field of artificial intelligence and machine learning. AlphaGo was created for the sole purpose of determining whether a computer could beat the world's best human Go players.

Go, originally developed more than 4,000 years ago, is considered to be the oldest board game still played today. Two players compete in this game of strategy by placing white or black stones on a gameboard grid, in an attempt to surround their opponent's pieces.

When the team at DeepMind created AlphaGo, they first trained the computer by loading its database with the moves made during thousands of games played by humans. With that knowledge as a base, and artificial intelligence under the hood, the computer played against humans at varying skill levels to further develop its strategy.

Eventually, the system was ready for the 2016 headline match against Mr. Lee Sedol, the world's greatest Go player. Since the computer was trained using the same strategies that all great Go players follow, the crowd of more than 200 million spectators around the world assumed that they could anticipate each of the computer's moves. Surprisingly, in one of the games during this best-of-five match, AlphaGo made a move no one saw coming. To the onlookers, the move went against all common best practices, and the spectators instantly assumed it had made a mistake that would cost it the match.

Much to everyone's surprise, AlphaGo ended up winning that game, and the series! The move that should have led to its demise, turned out not just to lead to victory but to earn AlphaGo a *9 dan* professional ranking—the highest possible certification.

After seeing what the computer's artificial intelligence accomplished, the programmers had an idea. What if, rather than preloading a computer with the data of human matches, they simply loaded it with the game rules, and let the computer learn on its own from day one. That idea led to the creation of the next generation of artificial intelligence, which they named AlphaGo Zero.

Since AlphaGo Zero did not have 4,000 years of human "institutional memory" to base its play on, it ended up creating brand new strategy. In just three days of self-play, it had accrued enough knowledge to beat the original AlphaGo. Within 40 days, it had become the greatest Go player ever. Not only did it beat the world's best human and machine players, but it also scored higher scores than humans believed was possible. It surpassed the 4,000-year-old theoretical limit!

Why is this story important? The original AlphaGo showed us that trying something new, while building on past experience, can enable us to reach new levels. The artificially intelligent computer beat the human by making an unexpected move, while using past human strategy as a starting point. This was great news, until AlphaGo Zero stepped in and showed that human-based strategy was actually flawed and limiting. Starting from scratch ultimately shattered that glass ceiling and took the game to new heights.

Your board might gloat that you're doing amazing work, trying new things, and taking the organization to places they've never been. You, on the other hand, might know that deep down there's a theoretical limit to what you can accomplish, simply because everything you do is based on the past. You know that even though your organization is better than it's been, it might never be as great as it could be.

You might ask, "what if, rather than thinking like the 60-year old organization that we are, we could act as if our organization was established today." Would this brand new organization choose the same marketing strategy? Would it print color fliers instead of black and white? Or would it not print fliers at all? Would it aim to reach the same demographics? Would its mission be exactly the same as it is?

Are you really doing your best, or are you doing the best you can, knowing that you must base your decisions on the evolutionary path set in motion decades ago? The best you can, knowing that in some ways, what someone did 50 years ago impacts what you can do today.

If we refuse to set aside institutional memory, and try something new from time to time, we will never realize that even greater things might be out there. Sometimes we need to try moves that everyone warns us won't work in order to figure out what will.

***

I looked around the room at a thoroughly exhausted group of nonprofit professionals. It was a lot of information to absorb in one sitting, made even more daunting by the fact that many of the solutions to our long list of concerns weren't necessarily solutions, but rather information that could be used to inform their decisions and help convince board members and others in positions of power that change is good.

We agreed to break for lunch and continue refreshed and ready to meet the next set of challenges bright and early the next morning. The NCC crew had their usual work to get back to, and I had lunch plans with the man, the myth, the legend—Dr. Groaner! His exact response to my invitation was "Sure—there's lots we can *taco* 'bout." Well, this is either going to be a lot of fun ... or it'll be the *wurst*.

The Takeaways

- Failure is a part of creating change. Expect it. Don't get deterred by it. And do it the right way—quickly and often through small iterations toward a big goal, rather than trying for one big leap.
- Even though it can be difficult, attempt to change or improve everything with each iteration. When you're busy, make small, quick changes. When things are slower, take advantage of that time to plan something totally new.
- Don't let false positives and false negatives throw you off track. By taking small steps, you can temper their effects.
- There's a reason it's nearly impossible for you to make huge, dramatic changes at your organization ... and as frustrating as it may seem, it's for your own good.
- The innovator's dilemma and basic management principles tell us why large companies need to put revenue and stability before investing in long-term innovation and explain why our managers aren't always wrong for sticking with what works.
- As nonprofits, the fact that we don't have investors to please means we are able to invest in projects that don't pay off immediately, which might work to our advantage.

- Innovation is often the result of a capitalistic drive to make money. Since nonprofits don't function under the same model as normal businesses, it's up to us to create the drive for innovation.
- If your board (or anyone else) is requiring that you preserve the past rather than move forward, remind them that sometimes, even if it seems like we've reached the highest peak, we need to take a few steps down the other side of the hill to reach an even higher summit.
- Even though there are all sorts of challenges that make it difficult to be innovative, we just need to keep pushing forward!

Next Steps

- The eight concerns that you just read are obviously not a comprehensive list. Share your concerns at thenonprofitimagineers.com, so that we can either help figure out how to address them, or at the very least, share in each others' misery.

CHAPTER 3

The Truth About "Innovation"

Phil wasn't able to focus on organic chemistry. Across the room was the most stunning person he had ever seen. It didn't take long for him to start sitting closer and closer to her. Through a combination of eavesdropping and social media detective work, he learned that she was a mechanical engineering major, loved *South Park*, and was a member of three Disney fan groups on Facebook.

Phil spent weeks shopping for the perfect *South Park* T-shirt that made him look thick rather than plump, ran it through the wash a few times to make it look well worn, and eventually built up the nerve to ask Wendy out.

They went on a series of activity dates, as shy, self-identifying geeks tend to do. They took a wine-tasting class with friends, went on a hike with the same group of friends, and, of course, went to see the *South Park* movie, also with friends.

As their relationship blossomed, Phil thought it would be fun to do something special for Wendy, so he secretly took an online engineering course and, for Valentine's Day, built a working scale model of the *Tea Cups* from Disneyland. The cups spun, music played, and there was even a turnstile at the entrance that counted each time you moved a figurine from the line into one of the cups.

That *Tea Cups* model was the first thing they unwrapped when they moved to their new home in Nottatown the summer after graduation. Wendy had been recruited for an amazing job with a local engineering firm, and Phil, after searching for some time, settled for a job at the NCC.

"I'm really sorry," Phil said as he slouched next to me on a weathered wooden bench in the NCC courtyard, fidgeting with his thumbs, looking everywhere but at me.

"You're sorry about what?" I asked, drawing a blank as to what he could possibly be upset about after only meeting me 24 hours earlier.

After a long pause, he looked up at me. "I'm sorry. I really tried. But, I just don't get it."

"You don't get what?"

"I don't really get what you're doing here. I mean, I know that you're supposed to be using Disney to get us to be more creative, which is really cool, and Wendy is quite jealous, but I don't get what all of this innovation stuff has to do with what I do? I mean, I'm the development director. I ask people for money and put on fundraisers. What am I supposed to be innovating? What am I supposed to be changing? And what was all that stuff yesterday about capitalism and institutional shareholders and pissing people off? Why do you want me to make campaigns that might piss off board members? And back on that video call—why were you in a cemetery?"

I smiled at Phil. It was a question that I had never really thought about before. *Why innovate?* In my head, it just made sense. To me, if we aren't doing something new and exciting—if we aren't moving forward—then we were falling backward. That applies just as much to my personal life and lifelong career trajectory as it does to the daily tasks I perform at work. Doing the same thing is boring to me. But doing things that are genuinely new and different might scare or upset people (myself included). So, if someone isn't either scared that I'm about to fail, or upset by the changes I'm making, then I'm probably not pushing hard enough.

I would have thought that the desire for forward motion is a basic human trait, but clearly, that's not the case. Some people are simply content. And that's OK too.

"That's a great question," I said.

I began to respond a few different ways in my head and finally settled on "Do you feel like you've moved forward in the past year? Do you feel like you're in a better place professionally now than a year ago? Actually— better or worse, do you feel like you're in a *different* place now?" Phil sat back on his generously proportioned frame and cupped his hands behind his head as he thought.

"Our years tend to be cyclical," I continued. "We run the same campaigns and programs each year, at roughly the same times. Compared to this time last year, do you feel like you just went in a circle? Or are you in a different place? Is the organization in a different place?"

Phil sheepishly nodded affirmatively, but I could tell he wasn't really connecting to what I was asking.

"Are you doing the exact same thing this year as you did last year? Have you made efforts to improve anything? Has the staff improved anything? Are you aiming for more complicated challenges?"

He nodded again, starting to understand.

"If you went to the gym every day for a year, and at the end of that year, you were still using the same 10-pound dumbbells for arm curls as you started with a year earlier, would you consider that a successful year?"

"Not really," Phil replied, lifting his arms in a curling motion. "I'd want to be lifting more after a year."

"Right, and the thing is, you probably aren't lifting weights at the gym in preparation for a weightlifting contest. You're doing it ... I don't know ... so that on a random Friday afternoon, you can impress Wendy with how many grocery bags you can carry at once." Phil smiled at the thought. "It's the same thing here—we aren't necessarily challenging ourselves to think creatively in order to change everything right away. We're training our minds to be able to think creatively so that we are prepared for opportunities that arise in what we already do."

"Just like your biceps, creativity is a muscle," I continued. "We can either do the exact same thing all the time, and be 'good enough,' or we can push ourselves and our organization to do more. The thing is, if we just do 'good enough,' no one will complain, just like no one will complain that you're going to the gym without showing any real progress—it's still a good thing. At work, no one will tell you that you need to do more than what you were hired to do. It's up to us to make that happen for ourselves. Our favorite athletes got to where they are because they constantly pushed themselves. They're at the top of their game because they started with the 10-pound weight and slowly pushed for more and more."

His eyes began to brighten. He was getting it now.

"And I know that you're asking about 'innovation,'" I continued, "But it's not really about 'innovation.' It's about progress. It's about pushing ourselves every day to be more creative. It's about doing new, exciting things. It's about effecting change. That's what I'm here to discuss with you guys. And that's why we've spent so much time on it. Before we get to the real Disney stuff, you need to understand how this all works."

I shifted my body and faced Phil head-on. "But not everyone enjoys change. So, as you try to make progress and make each year different from the last, you're going to face challenges. You're going to fail. You're going to be met with pessimism and resistance from people who are too lazy to push themselves, or people who simply like things the way they are. You're going to lose momentum. You're going to have to rely on people who aren't feeling the same way you do."

"Yeah, no kidding," Phil said, trailing off at the end. I paused—it seemed like he wanted to say more, but he just sat there, looking at the dead leaves hypnotically dancing circles across the walkway in the breeze.

"But you don't want to look back, 40 years from now," I eventually continued, "and retire from the exact same job, in the exact same place as you sit right now, do you? Even if you're still the development director here, you want to be able to show that each year this place got better and better. That *you* got better and better. Right?"

"Yeah!" Phil replied with a smile, his posture vastly improved since the start of the conversation. "You're right. We can do better. And we shouldn't let 'certain people' knock us down."

I paused again, raising my eyebrows slightly, giving Phil the "it sounds like you want to offer more details … I'm listening" gesture, but he just continued to stare off into the distance. Finally, he turned back to me, and with a sincere look in his eyes, asked, "So, why did you do that other meeting from a cemetery? Was that some sort of metaphor for innovation?"

I took a deep breath as I decided how I wanted to respond. Clearly, I would not be holding any more meetings in cemeteries. But what really frustrated me was how he used the term "innovation."

Innovation Isn't What You Think It Is

People misuse the word "innovation." They love to claim that everything is an "innovation." The synagogue holding services outside rather than inside, after seeing other synagogues do the same thing, boasts their innovation. The launch of a new website sounds like an exciting innovation, until you realize they purchased the same $49 template as thousands of others. The cup holder in your new car that fits an even-more-obnoxiously large drink is the car-maker's latest brilliant innovation and, of course, is worthy of a three-week marketing campaign with an ad buy exceeding your nonprofit's annual budget. Wow! Our world is brimming with innovations left and right!

"Innovation" is everyone's favorite descriptor, even though it's literally never true. Yes—literally.

New, creative, original, cutting-edge, and clever are NOT synonyms for an innovation. An invention is not the same as an innovation.

At its core, innovation isn't something you do—it's something that happens. It's a phenomenon. A result. At times, it's even a by-product.

"Innovation is novelty with impact," Luis Perez-Breva explains in his book *Innovating—A Doer's Manifesto*. It's "a seemingly small change that will change the community that receives it in a profound and lasting way."

Many things are novel, but they rarely have profound and lasting impact. And many things that people claim are huge, game-changing innovations, are not particularly game-changing, nor do they last beyond the life span of their marketing campaign. Innovation is the mass adoption of a change. It is very rare that something happens that forever changes an entire population.

Since impact can only be measured after the fact, innovations can only be determined in retrospect. Reread that last line. Nothing that we do today for the first time is an innovation until we look back at it decades from now and see that it was the catalyst for significant change. Everyone who calls their new product an "innovation" is wrong ... or, at least, is a decade or more from being able to prove themselves right.

Take, for example, the technique that Samuel Nicolson developed in the mid-19th century of paving streets with wood blocks soaked in creosote, a substance similar to tar. At a time when most roads were dirt or cobblestone, wood blocks prevented dust and mud, were easier to fabricate than cobblestones, and were far more abundant. Nicolson Pavement also reduced the loud clomping sounds of horse-drawn carriages and was quickly installed on many streets around the world. Nicolson surely thought his wood block pavement was an innovation that would revolutionize how streets were built, until the public realized that wood blocks were slippery when wet, rotted quickly, and on hot days, not surprisingly, smelled like horse urine mixed with tar.

Although Nicolson's idea was creative and novel, his technique did not have a lasting impact. As you know, we no longer pave our streets with wood blocks, nor are modern paving techniques in any way built on the wood block technology. Today, just one wood block street remains in the United States and takes millions of dollars to maintain.

Innovation Doesn't Happen Nearly as Often as We Think, and It Rarely Is as Glamorous as You Would Expect

Do you recognize the name Theodore H. Maiman? Probably not—his innovation wasn't particularly sexy or high-profile, but he changed the world. Maiman developed the first working example of light amplification by stimulated emission of radiation, or LASER. In 1960, when he first discovered the technology in a continuation of the efforts of other scientists who were unsuccessful in their experimentation, he didn't change the world at all. This innovation (though it wasn't called that at the time) was simply a discovery that had no practical application. Like most scientific endeavors, it wasn't done with capitalistic benefit in mind—it was simply to advance science. However, looking back, we now know that optical disk drives, laser printers, barcode scanners, and laser surgery, among thousands of other things we interact with every day, all became possible because of it. You're able to check out at the supermarket in seconds because a guy that you never heard of, in 1960, made a seemingly useless discovery. His invention was novel at the time, and we now know, had a wide-reaching and lasting impact.

The Internet and GPS were both developed by the military for very specific, small-scale purposes, without the intent for them to be world-changing innovations. At the time, they enabled our soldiers around the globe to communicate and navigate. Now that pretty much everything we do all day, from exercising to reading books is either guided by GPS, or downloaded over the Internet, there's no denying that both of these ended up being innovations.

Of course, not all innovations are accidental or developed without innovative intent. There are occasionally exciting, high-profile, purposeful innovations. For example, the standardization of shipping containers made it possible for the world trade to grow from a very small, expensive operation to what it is today. Air-conditioning made entire regions of the world livable and enabled population booms in the southern United States and tropical climates everywhere. Both of these were commercial ventures intended to be innovations, and decades later, proved to be exactly that.

Similarly, at a time when cell phones were trending smaller and lighter, Apple's large and heavy original iPhone was created to change the way we use the devices. Unlike most failed products that are created with the hope that they will become an innovation, Steve Jobs succeeded, as we now know it changed the design of every phone sold since then.

At the time that they were introduced, the first cartoons with sound, first color cartoons, first feature-length cartoon, and first cartoon characters to show human emotion and plot development were just Walt Disney's attempts to push the boundaries of what he had previously done with his craft. He didn't experiment with those techniques to call them innovations. There were no "aha" moments of great discovery involved—rather, they were more along the lines of "Hey—for the next cartoon, what if we try doing it this way instead…." At the time, they might have seemed evolutionary. It wasn't until years later, when it became clear that his practices sent all future animation down new paths, that they could be called innovations.

Innovation Happens Through "The Adjacent Possible"

Did you know that there's an animatronic robot developed by Disney Imagineers that's capable of performing acrobatics? Unlike standard animatronics that we see bolted to the floor on theme park attractions, "stuntronics" (stunt-animatronics) are able to be launched through the air, perform elegant flips, and land perfectly almost every time!

You're probably not that surprised, right? After all, artificially intelligent robots are everywhere these days. Self-driving cars are on the streets, drones light up the sky in sophisticated formation like next-generation fireworks, and with a simple voice command, vacuum cleaners can navigate to the crumbs under the kitchen table before the dog even knows they were dropped.

But go back to the 1950s and tell Walt Disney the same thing and he'll ask you to share your crazy sci-fi ideas with the "world of tomorrow" creative team. Why? Because back then, when Imagineers were experimenting with ground-breaking, first-of-its-kind technology that would allow a character to open and close its mouth in sync with a soundtrack, there was no way they could have created anything close to what we have today. They were thrilled just to figure out how to make a noisy, hissing actuator (the small internal mechanisms that open and close in order to give motion to the figure) open and close at just the right time, while fitting within the small frame of an *It's a Small World* figure, Abraham Lincoln mannequin head, or *Tiki Room* bird.

What allows us to have these incredible animatronics today, and what allows all innovation to happen, is a concept known as the Adjacent Possible.

Steven Johnson, in *Where Good Ideas Come From*, explains:

> You begin in a room with four doors, each leading to a new room that you haven't visited yet. Those four rooms are the adjacent possible. But once you open one of those doors and stroll into that room, three new doors appear, each leading to a brand-new room that you couldn't have reached from your original starting point. Keep opening new doors and eventually you'll have built a palace.

While traveling through Europe with his family, Walt Disney saw a small mechanical bird figurine that could move its body and chirp when levers were pulled. He brought it back to his Imagineers and said, "build this!"

From that toy, think of all the different iterations and prototypes that it took to develop the very first Disney audio-animatronic figure. Then, imagine how many more years of development and Imagineering it took—experimenting with different actuators, internal skeletal structures, and "skin" materials—to create some of the animatronic figures that today we consider to be outdated and basic. Each step—each little bit of progress—was another adjacent possible door being opened. Imagineers could not have made a character smile—an action that involves dozens of tiny actuators working perfectly in unison, mimicking real facial muscles, without first figuring out how to make a single actuator move on command. It took 70 years of Imagineering, and thousands of new adjacent rooms, through door after door, to enable the "stuntronic" robots to fly through the air. The doors were opened not just by Imagineers, but by physicists perfecting gyroscope technology, computer programmers working on artificial intelligence, and countless others in a variety of fields that had nothing to do with Disney Imagineering.

Had Walt Disney demanded that his animatronic birds fly through the air in the original *Enchanted Tiki Room* attraction, or that the first *It's a Small World* children walk around and interact with the guests on their boats, he would have set his Imagineers up for failure. The technology simply didn't exist in the 1960s. Today, however, Imagineers, scientists, and programmers have unlocked enough adjacent possible rooms to almost be able to accomplish that exact feat.

The theory of the adjacent possible isn't limited to scientific breakthroughs. By constantly pushing for small changes, and having our eyes set on the right goals, nonprofits can utilize the concept as well.

Today, nearly every synagogue provides an online option for participating in religious services. In 1990, had I suggested that you join us on our livestream, you wouldn't have understood what I was talking about. You probably would have thought it had something to do with a large number of fish in a river. It took a series of adjacent possibles, including the development of basic online video players such as YouTube in the late 1990s, high-speed Internet being available in homes and businesses in the early 2000s, the development of streaming hardware, the cost of that technology to become affordable to larger synagogues, the leadership of synagogues approving the use of the technology during services (which is something that religious Jewish organizations would not normally use on the sabbath), and ultimately, the COVID-19 pandemic.

Strange as it may seem to include a pandemic as a door to an adjacent possible, but being forced to either adopt a new technology or eliminate an essential service, turned out to be a catalyst for livestreaming technology to be installed in synagogues and churches everywhere. It forced organizations to walk through a door to an adjacent room that they probably weren't ready to visit, and in doing so, has led to even more progress in the field, including new companies that can remotely operate cameras, giving small organizations the ability to produce high-quality, multicamera broadcasts at an affordable price. Such companies did not exist until all of those adjacent possible rooms were opened, in part because the pandemic changed the way we attend religious services.

In our nonprofit environments, if we focus on big, groundbreaking, revolutionary "innovations" that are too far ahead of their time, without unlocking the adjacent possibles first, we're setting ourselves up for disappointment. In 2010, we might have seen the potential for streaming online services, holding virtual board meetings, or allowing children who are at home to connect and interact with their live classroom at school, but pushing to make it happen immediately would have ended in failure. Those capabilities were still a few adjacent rooms away. The world had to unlock those doors for us. But by keeping our eyes on the long-term goal, when the time came to walk through those doors, we were ready.

Dreaming big is wonderful, but you must face the reality that your vision might be a 5- or 10-year plan. It might be something you set in motion today and hope that your successors achieve after you've moved on to bigger, better things.

It can be frustrating to see a target that cannot be hit. In these situations, in order to stay motivated knowing that the revolutionary change is too far away to reach, consider the difference between "innovation" and "Innovation." Did you catch that? Many scholars have argued that whereas "big 'I'" Innovations are the game changing, disruptive innovations that come along rarely and can only be measured in hindsight, "little 'i'" innovations are the incremental advancements that happen all the time. To me, this is the difference between something being an Innovation, and something that is innovative.

It's estimated that the largest electronics companies replace more than 75 percent of their products with newer versions every five years. If we look at cell phone manufacturers, that number is probably significantly higher. Each of those evolutionary updates—adding second, third, and fourth cameras, better screens, and faster processors—are innovative.

They are small but necessary iterations. And, of course, every now and then the "little 'i's" open enough adjacent possibles to reach that "big 'I'" that was once too far away to reach.

Walt Disney once said, "We keep moving forward, opening new doors, and doing new things, because we're curious and curiosity keeps leading us down new paths."

Keep pushing through. Open new doors. Stay curious. The future world will thank us for it.

Innovation Is Built on Tradition

Fans of the television series *Silicon Valley* might remember the file-sharing platform that they built, which was brilliant and could have been a world-changing Innovation, but failed miserably when it was launched. The problem they discovered was that it was so far ahead of its time, the general public could not understand how to use it. Their platform was able to compress and store files on the cloud so efficiently that there was no need to slowly upload and download the files each time that the user wanted to access them. To the programmers, this made perfect sense, but to the consumer, who, over decades of Internet use had become accustomed to uploading and downloading files, the platform did not make sense, and seemed broken.

The programmers failed to remember that innovation must be built on tradition. Inventions that are "ahead of their time" are fun to dream about but generally fail. Essentially, they skip too many adjacent possible rooms, and the world is not ready for them yet.

When my parents were younger, they had a video camera that recorded images onto a roll of film. After the camera's film was developed, they could watch recordings on a reel-to-reel projector. Around the time I was born, they upgraded to a VHS camcorder to film my first steps and a VCR to watch recordings. When my son was born, we recorded videos with digital video cameras and watched DVDs. Today, we record HD video on our phones and watch streams on our TVs, phones, and tablets.

The technology changed over those 40+ years, but a surprising amount also stayed the same. Everyone knows that you hit the red circle to record. The little arrow facing to the right plays the video. The square stops it. You could put an iPad in the hands of an octogenarian who has never held a tablet, open the media player, ask him to play a video, and he would know exactly what to press, because today's technology is based on that of the past. The media controls we use today have been in use since the 1960s.

Innovation is a balancing act between retaining and building upon the most important pieces of the past and pushing forward to the future. It's a tightrope walk along that line between what's safe and what's challenging. In his book *Wonderland: How Play Made the Modern World*, Steven Johnson tells us, "Most effective learning takes place at the outer edge of a student's competence. Make a game too hard and no one will buy it. Make it too easy and no one will buy it. Make a game where the challenge evolves alongside your skills, and you'll have a shot at success."

The reason the iPad controls are intuitive is because Steve Jobs didn't mandate that his designers create a new set of media control symbols to go with his touchscreen technology—he took what worked for the previous 50 years and mixed it in with an array of swipes and taps that we could comfortably learn. He pushed us far enough past our comfort zone to excite us but not so far that it frustrated us. It's likely that a few hundred years from now, we will control videos in an entirely different way, but the path there will be through small steps that the world is ready to take.

In our nonprofit world, just as in designing new technology, creating new games or, really, all progress, we must recognize that innovation is nothing more than a series of small steps in a certain direction. If we disregard what came before, people will be lost. If we attempt to leap too far forward, people will be lost. We need to push only as far as people will comfortably accept. But we have to keep pushing that line a little farther with each iteration.

At elementary schools, for example, technology has enabled students to learn using iPads, Smart Boards, and in virtual environments in ways that were simply impossible 10 years ago. The reason these technologies have been so successful is because they complement and supplement traditional pencil and paper learning. Children still have books, though sometimes those books are digital. Teachers still stand in front of the class and write examples on the board, though chalk boards have been replaced by Smart Boards. Teams still compete against each other in basketball and volleyball matches, though parents who might not be able to attend in person are now able to watch on livestreams or get real-time updates from fellow parents through messaging apps.

Before you assume that "innovation" is always going to be a grand leap into what's never been done before, you need to realize that everything successful is based on what came before it. People are much more likely to adopt a change that still feels familiar. They are less likely to stick with a change that requires a long and steep learning curve. If your goal is the mass adoption of your novel idea, tradition might just be one of your closest allies.

Innovation Solves Problems

Even if you don't realize a problem exists, innovation will solve it. In fact, there are many examples of inventions that inadvertently solved problems and resulted in them becoming innovations!

In the example of the laser, Dr. Maiman wasn't challenged by a clerk to find a quicker way to check out at the grocery store, nor was he trying to correct peoples' vision. He was trying to help prove a theory proposed by a couple of other scientists, who were having trouble finding success on their own. But as it turned out, once Dr. Maiman unlocked the door to the laser's adjacent possible, an assortment of unexpected paths were awaiting on the other side. And it was only because those problems needed solving that the laser became an innovation.

In another example, back in 1952, Don Stookey was working for Corning Glass Works when he accidentally put a piece of special glass in a furnace set for 900°C rather than 600°C. He expected that he had destroyed the sample (and probably his furnace too) but, instead, found a milky white plate with characteristics of glass that bounced rather than shattered when he accidentally dropped it. Corning began experimenting with this new substance that they called Chemcor and found that it was a brilliant invention with no uses and no one to buy it … so they stopped producing it.

Fast forward to 2006, when Steve Jobs approached Corning with a request for ultrastrong, ultrathin glass for his latest project. Rather than committing years to developing a new product, Corning dusted off the old, previously useless product and said something slightly more eloquent than "how 'bout this?" Thank goodness for Don Stookey's mistake 54 years earlier, or the iPhone, with its thin, durable touchscreen, might be a completely different device, or taken years longer to bring to market! In one fail swoop, Steve Jobs solved his problem, and Stookey's glass, 50 years after it was first discovered, became an innovation.

Problem-solving is one of the best ways to innovate and is at the heart of the creative process, as we'll discuss in Chapter 4. Sometimes, we'll brainstorm for solutions to problems that we know exist. Other times, in our efforts to move our organizations forward, we'll discover that our innovative drive inadvertently solves problems we didn't realize existed! There will even be times when Innovation ends up being a byproduct of something completely unrelated. The only way we'll know this is in hindsight. That could mean that in a beautiful turn of events, decades after your brilliant idea seemingly flopped, you might be recognized as the most forward-thinking, innovative mind in your organization's history, who solved problems ahead of your time! And it's all because you kept pushing forward and trying new things. How's that for a false negative!

As we make our way through this book and put its lessons to use in the real world, if we set out trying to innovate just to be able to claim an Innovation as our own, we're setting ourselves up for failure. Our goal here is not to Innovate—it's to ask the right questions, find problems that need to be solved, learn from our failures, and come out the other end with something amazing. Our goal is to be creative, imaginative, original, cutting edge, and clever. To invent—yes. To Innovate—not so much.

To do this, our duty is to challenge the status quo! We need to push the envelope and not just try to meet the needs of our audience, but to make them see the potential in new ideas, new adjacent possibles, and entirely new directions. Sometimes, the paths will be finely groomed and ready for us to take our organizations down, but other times we will need to bravely blaze a trail toward a destination that is completely unknown, even to us.

Henry Ford famously said of his Innovation, "If I had asked people what they wanted, they would have said faster horses."

***

"Listen," I said to Phil, after what must have been a very long pause, "Don't get too caught up on that word—innovation. *Progress* is what we're really after, and by making progress—by doing things differently today than we did last month or last year—innovation will naturally happen."

The two of us began walking toward the back door of the building as Jonathan flamboyantly shoved open the double doors and marched toward us.

"So, you're never going to explain the cemetery thing, are you?" Phil said quietly, half kidding. I gave him a half smile as Jonathan approached.

"We'll see you inside in a minute," Jonathan said to Phil, and then waited for Phil to disappear through the double glass doors. I could see Phil look back as if he knew something wasn't right.

Jonathan looked over his shoulder to make sure we were alone. "Listen," he said, "Can I be honest? We've met with you a few times. Everyone's saying that they aren't getting as much out of this as we were hoping. Everyone's just feeling exhausted more than anything else. Physically and emotionally drained. They're not happy."

"Everybody?" I asked. "I hate to hear that. Can you give me more details? Who specifically? Maybe I can talk to them and figure out how to connect better."

"No one specifically. It's something I'm hearing from everyone," he answered, without breaking eye contact.

"OK," I said, knowing full well that "everyone" really meant one person—Jonathan himself. "What sorts of things aren't 'they' happy with? You know, this whole thing is a process. It's going to take time to lay the foundation."

Out of the corner of my eye I saw Phil's head peek out from the shadows of the lobby, watching intently through the tinted wall of windows, with his phone in his hand.

"Look, I feel like you came here to do a specific job—to teach us about Disney Imagineering and how we can take their methods and apply them to what we do. But you just keep giving lecture after lecture about why everything is a problem, and that we can't make the 'right kind of change,' and that our mission statement is wrong, and why we can't be creative—but we actually can … or something along those lines…." Jonathan stopped waving his hands for a moment and paused, most likely for dramatic effect during another rant that was supposed to sound like stream of consciousness, but again came off as rehearsed. "I've taken the temperature of the rest of the group, and we don't think this is working. We think we want to cut our losses and not put more time into this."

His rant reminded me of a story I had heard about Walt Disney. In early 1955, with less than six months to go before Disneyland was scheduled to open, Walt walked through the razed orange groves of his soon-to-be Anaheim theme park, looking across the expanse of rough dirt roads and concrete foundations with a combination of fear and outrage percolating within. "I've spent millions of dollars and have nothing to show for it!" He cried.

Not a single building or attraction had been completed—most were just underground pipes and conduit, or mounds of dirt. Even a number of trees that were marked to be saved with colored ribbon had been accidentally removed by a colorblind bulldozer operator. It was true—he had already exceeded his original budget just to clear and grade the land, install the plumbing and electric infrastructure, and begin planning and building new attractions that were nowhere to be seen. But in his frustration, Walt forgot that the only way to build the happiest place on earth was with a solid foundation that no one would ever see or truly appreciate.

"I hear you," I said to Jonathan. "But we need to lay the groundwork. We need a foundation. We need to manage expectations and understand what our goals are and how we are going to overcome challenges that will stand in the way of progress. Otherwise—" In my pocket my phone buzzed, throwing off my rhythm. I paused for a moment to regroup. "Look, we're going to get to the fun stuff soon enough. Stick with me just a little longer. It'll be worth it."

Jonathan looked me in the eye, gave a sympathetic smile, condescendingly put his hand on my shoulder, and then, without hesitation or an ounce of uncertainty, said "Nah—we're gonna go a different way. But thanks for your time. Don't worry—we'll pay you your full fee."

As Jonathan put his hands in his pockets and strolled away, pretending the line in the concrete was a tightrope, I pulled my phone out of my pocket, a storm building inside. I could have talked him into giving this another day or two had this damn device not completely derailed my train of thought. I tapped the text message alert at the top of the screen. What could possibly have been so important that Phil texted me in the middle of such a tense moment—especially when he knew I was in the middle of a serious conversation? "Eucalyptus—the plant named after what it would say if you pruned it."

I'm still not on board with this whole "puns to diffuse tense situations" thing. Especially tree puns! It's not like they'll ever get to the *root* of the problem.

The Takeaways

- Innovation (with a capital "I") is ***novelty with impact***. It is not the same thing as invention or creativity. It must be something new that is adopted by the masses and can only be measured in hindsight.
- Innovation generally isn't an "aha" moment, but rather a series of smaller innovative (with a lowercase "i") steps that eventually reach a tipping point and lead to the bigger change.
- Setting a goal for big changes is great, but it usually will take a series of small progressive steps—adjacent possibles—to reach the end goal.
- Successful innovation builds on the past. Changing too much at once can be challenging for users to understand and can cause a good idea to fail. If your innovative idea doesn't have any connections to what exists today, it probably means that you are ahead of your time and need to unlock a few more adjacent possibles to get there.
- Most Innovations solve problems. If you feel like you're stuck in a rut and want to make changes, figure out what problems exist and come up with creative solutions. Take small steps to solve those problems,

and when you look back upon it years in the future, you might realize that your change was actually an Innovation.

- Problems aren't just things you feel your organization can do better. Problems are also what your organization exists to solve! What problems exist in the world that you are there to address? Are you actually addressing them?

Next Steps

- Head over to <u>thenonprofitimagineers.com</u> for more innovation inspiration. Let's figure out what problems exist at our organizations that we can help solve together!

Intermission

That's right—this instructional business book for nonprofit professionals not only has an opening music number.... It also has an intermission.

Drop the curtain. Raise the house lights. Go stretch your legs and get yourself a cocktail. You've earned it.

A Musical Interlude

It's a good thing you didn't take too long in the restroom, because something's happening! It's a musical interlude during the intermission! This book just keeps delivering!

Up on the stage four men just appeared in white shirts, red bowties, and straw boater hats. Before you pull out your phone to Google "straw boater hat," I'll save you the distraction—It's what you'll see on the heads of a barbershop quartet.

Yes—this book opened with an incredible, well-choreographed song and dance reminiscent of a big budget flash mob, and now, the second act is preceded by a snappy monolog by a quite-endearing and, just between us, overly confident heavy-set fella who's cracking dad jokes (his word—not mine) as a lead-in to a barbershop musical number! How fun!

Unfortunately, it's right around now that you remember that there's a reason for everything in this book. The quartet isn't just there for your listening pleasure, and it's certainly not progressing the story line. That must mean there's a lesson to be learned! Music lovers, prepare to geek out.

A barbershop quartet comprises four parts: the lead, who sings the melody line; the tenor, who sings the higher notes that harmonize above the lead; the bass, who sings the rich lower notes; and the baritone, who is given the task of singing what the professional barbershop community refer to as the "garbage notes." Yes, seriously.

The lead, tenor, and bass all follow relatively predictable melodies and the three of them usually form a triad, which is a very traditional chord that you'll hear in everything from classical music to The Beatles to the soundtrack of your favorite Disney film.

What makes barbershop music distinctive is the addition of that extra note that changes normal (music geeks might say "tonic") chords into "seventh" chords. It's that well-placed seventh chord that makes barbershop exhilarating and exciting! The baritone's job is to dance around the lead (with his voice—not physically), by singing an incoherent melody line that rises and falls at random intervals, and when heard on its own will seem like, well, garbage. To the untrained ear, and even to many well-trained ears, it's barely music on its own. But add it to the trio, and you experience something wonderful. Something unheard of in any other types of music.

You might even notice a "phantom 5th note" from the four singers! When sung at just the right tones, the notes can produce a phenomenon (science nerds, feel free to geek out as well), that rings at a frequency strengthened by the blended sounds of the four performers. It's OK if you didn't follow that—the takeaway is that there's a scientific reason why barbershop is so cool.

That baritone is really something … right? You thought the heavy-set fella with the witty dad jokes at the beginning was the star of the show, but it's actually all about the baritone.

That poor guy is totally misunderstood on his own. In a real world setting, he would appear to be out of his mind, fluttering around in a random sequence while his friends follow along in the footprints of those who sang before them. But in just the right setting, with the proper support of those around him, and as a support to those around him, the baritone completely transforms the mundane into something magical. The baritone is even able to make 1+1+1+1=5.

You've probably figured out where I'm going with this, but just in case, I'll come right out and say it: Be a baritone! Don't worry that others want to follow the rules and join the triad. Don't worry that they might not understand what you're trying to accomplish. Don't worry that what you're doing is unlike what everyone else is doing and might not be understood or appreciated by the masses. Arthur Schopenhauer once said that "talent hits a target no one else can hit; Genius hits a target no one else can see," You have genius inside of you!

But remember—without the rest of the quartet, the baritone is just noise.

Now that you're charged up for the 2nd act … On with the show!

CHAPTER 4

Find New Ideas Through Blue Sky Dreaming

JJ loved video games. As a kid, you'd often find him feeding quarters into arcade games or playing Nintendo with pizza grease-covered fingers at friends' houses. In high school, his computer science teacher encouraged him to look into digital media courses, which ultimately led him to major in Game Design with a minor in Game Theory in college.

Born and raised in Nottatown, he used to spend afternoons at the NCC when his parents worked late. He loved that place and turned down job offers in Silicon Valley to take the job of NCC Communications Director—his way of giving back.

If asked what his greatest achievement at the NCC was, he wouldn't tell you about the total brand refresh that he implemented when he started working at the NCC. He wouldn't tell you about the virtual car race campaign he created that people continue to talk about years later. No—he'll tell you his greatest achievement was getting rid of Jonathan.

In an *Ocean's Eleven*-style caper, JJ was able to rally a number of unhappy co-workers to voice their honest concerns to an assortment of board members in a variety of ways, bombarding them in a precisely choreographed campaign that, to the board, seemed entirely organic. With Jonathan on the ropes, he then encouraged fellow employees to stop covering for Jonathan as tasks slipped through the cracks and frustrations grew. Although the plan was slowly but surely working, the final nail in the coffin was a stroke of luck, when JJ happened to drive by the NCC one Friday night and noticed a full parking lot.

The fifth Friday of the month was supposed to be a night off for the entire staff. While they had recurring programs and events regularly scheduled during the first four Fridays of the month, nothing was ever scheduled on the rarely occurring fifth Friday.

As it turns out, Jonathan quietly took advantage of the empty build-ing to host an off-the-books illegal casino in the NCC social hall. What started off as a small card game among friends, eventually ballooned into a complete casino setup with professional dealers and chips with Jonathan's face printed on them. Forensic research turned up evidence that this casino had been in business for more than five years and that Jonathan often used cash donations to the NCC as "house" money to cover losses.

Once this was brought to the board's attention, Jonathan quickly offered his resignation (and then was arrested and charged). Shortly there-after, I received a call from the board of directors asking if I would come back and resume our workshop. Apparently, most of the team enjoyed learning what I was teaching and wanted to get to the good stuff. I gladly obliged.

***

"Amaze me. Surprise me," I said, looking around the room at my soon-to-be Nonprofit Imagineers. Just as they did at each of our previous meetings, they stared back at me in confusion.

I explained that, in a nutshell, those were Michael Eisner's instruc-tions to Disney Imagineers, tasking them with turning Disneyland in Anaheim, CA from a stand-alone theme park into a multiday destination. The then-CEO of the Walt Disney Company didn't tell them to build a second theme park or a water park. He didn't tell them to incorporate a hotel or theater. He didn't even say where it would be built! His mission was specific enough to guide them but vague enough to let their creativity run wild—Build something that will make people want to stay for more than one day.

And with that, Disney Imagineers did what Disney Imagineers do: blue sky.

Blue sky is the process through which some of Disney's greatest ideas are born. Sequester a small group of employees from an assortment of disciplines and ask them to come up with something new and exciting. It doesn't matter what it might cost, how much land it might need, how long it might take to build, or if it's even technologically possible in today's world—the goal is to be creative.

That is exactly what we were about to do at the Nottatown Community Center! I had assembled a small group whose job titles were communications director, program director, development director, and administrative support staff, and whose backgrounds included an assortment of hobbies and past jobs from charcoal drawing to video games to military service, threw them together in a room, and challenged them to dream.

It is under these exact circumstances, which have been used by Disney and similar companies for decades, that creativity is truly able to flourish.

Blue Sky Is Pseudo-Serendipitous

If you were to plot all of the greatest Innovations (capital "I") throughout history on a map, you'll find that most of them occur in urban areas. The larger the city—the more Innovation. Why? Because that's where ideas can mingle.

The medieval pubs, in fact, were often the innovative centers of most small villages, since that's where the worlds of the scholars, soldiers, merchants, and blacksmiths collided. They were the sites of the impromptu, serendipitous blue sky meetings of the olden days.

As author Steven Johnson notes in *Where Good Ideas Come From*, most innovation isn't the result of sudden breakthrough—it comes from slow hunches, nurtured over time, eventually met with opportunity. A scholar who has been pondering a slow hunch for decades might stop for a drink in a pub and start up a conversation with a blacksmith that he'd never met, and through casual conversation, realize that a basic step in the blacksmithing process is the missing link that his scholarly pursuit had been chasing for years! A trivial, everyday task performed by one man might be exactly what another man needed in order to transform a slow hunch into an Innovation. The fact that the two of them were in the same pub at the same time, discussing a topic that led to an Innovation, is quite serendipitous. It's also far less likely to happen to a rural farmer who spends most evenings isolated on his farm than to residents of densely populated villages.

Similarly, if you put an animator, architect, landscaper, and mechanic in a room together to throw around ideas, you're much more likely to end up with a creative, groundbreaking result than if you put five animators in a room together, or if you asked them to submit their ideas separately, without ever meeting. Of course, in the blue sky process, the meeting of these minds is engineered. These people were put in a room together on purpose—not by chance as it would have in a medieval pub, so it's not truly serendipitous ... just pseudo-serendipitous (sounds like something Mary Poppins would sing about ... right?).

As they said in *Imagineering: A Behind the Dreams Look at Making the Magic Real*:

> Working together, we are a creative melting pot, but working as individual Imagineers, we approach every idea with specific regard to our own fields of expertise. Someone with a talent for theatrical lighting looks at an idea differently than someone who produces special effects. Someone who is well versed in practical building design and construction does not view it in exactly the same way as does the composer of the music that will be heard inside. One imagineer may know what needs to happen while another must know how to make it happen.

Ahhh ... pseudo-serendipity. What a marvelous thing.

Every facilitator has his favorite brainstorming method. One might ask participants to warm up by coming up with the worst possible ideas for their organization, while another might have participants write down 10 ideas on note cards before entering the group session.

Knowing the value of connecting unrelated ideas to form new and innovative concepts, I chose a different approach with the NCC staff. My laptop was connected to a projector, and on it I had opened a fresh Google Doc entitled "things we love." JJ, Phil, Shoshana, Hector, and Vanessa sat around the table, and rather than asking them to brainstorm program, fundraising, or marketing ideas, I wanted to get our minds loosened up by simply asking them what sorts of things they enjoyed. Blue sky thinking doesn't come naturally to everyone, and in many ways, it's a muscle that must be trained and exercised. My goal was to show them how easy it could be to take basic things that we like and turn them into brilliant programs and campaigns.

The first suggestions were pretty broad—"sports," "my family," and "our community." As they began to warm up and understand that there really was no limit to the things they could love, we ended up with a fascinating, scatterbrained, five-page document that included:

- How Starbucks gives me a free drink after several visits
- A new board game that I'm playing with a few friends that's kind of addictive
- My Peloton bike
- Using the word "effervescent" to describe anything other than lemon-lime soda
- Soft and thick toilet paper
- Everything Disney
- Chalk art
- Giant, bright murals to take selfies in front of
- *The Book of Mormon* Broadway Musical
- The very satisfying ending to *The Sandlot* movie
- Public pianos that anyone can sit down and play
- Holding business meetings in cemeteries (I knew it was a joke, but I put it up there anyway, because you never know where a good idea will come from)

"I love it!" I said. "It's amazing how many little things there are that we love, including some really wild and oddly specific things, like 'pens that write well on glossy paper.'"

"Oh—can you add 'Sharpies that aren't dried out?'" Shoshana interrupted.

"Absolutely," I said, adding it to the Google Doc. "And when we look at these, it's fascinating to see how some of these ideas evolved, right? You can see the path from something really basic, like 'fresh art supplies,' and then five steps later, a really specific thing, like a non-dried out Sharpie. It's weird how satisfying it feels when you test a marker and it's not dried out, but we never would have gotten there without this process of one person's suggestion feeding another's. There's no connection between loving your family and loving sharpies.... Yet, we found a path to it. That's the power of brainstorming as a team!"

"I think it's safe to say that we already picked that up just by doing the exercise. Is everything that we do here going to turn into an over-explained, really basic lesson?" Hector asked, looking at Vanessa for support, but getting none.

I thought for a moment and then simply replied, "Trust the process, Hector."

Blue Sky Is Whatever You Want It to Be

A friend of mine held a blue sky meeting, after which his boss called him into his office and said, "That was an interesting meeting, but I think you need to do a better job keeping us on track next time. It didn't feel like you reached the goal." My friend responded, "If that's what you think, then maybe you don't understand what the goal was."

The beauty of being creative is that there are no rules dictating the creative process or the goal! A blue sky session can happen in a parking lot as you head home for the day. It can happen with the security guard or your son's teacher. Ask 10 people the same question and you'll get 11 responses, each of them valuable in their own way.

"You just let your imagination go," Marty Sklar, Imagineering legend, once explained. "The only people who aren't popular are the people who keep their mouth shut.... The 'blue sky' is the loosest of structures. But it's not unstructured. It's with the hope and intent that we're going to get somewhere."

In one blue sky meeting, someone might write ideas on Post-its and stick them to a wall. In another, someone might take notes on a computer or chalkboard. Others might enjoy writing ideas on pieces of paper, crumpling them up, throwing them into the middle of the room, and then having a different person pick up the idea and continue with it in a potentially new direction.

Sometimes, we'll come out of blue sky sessions with actionable items. Other times, we'll have nuggets of ideas that will generate conversation for weeks to come. We don't always need to worry about forming complete thoughts, especially since ideas should continue to evolve over time. Thanks to the flexibility of blue sky sessions, a concept might start as a piece of an attraction and, after months of discussions, end up as an entire land or theme park. Seeing where an idea ultimately ends up is half of the fun. The important thing is that you get people talking and that the conversation doesn't end just because you've reached the top of the hour.

Blue Sky Is Best Done With a Group

Every author and motivational speaker will share with you their secret sauce for blue sky pseudo-serendipity success, and they all have one thing in common—they can't be done in solitude.

Jeff Degraff will tell you about his *Innovation Code*—that there are four types of creative people who drive innovation:

- the Artist, who is imaginative, thinks radically and outside the box, and is interested in "wow" factor and experimentation;
- the Engineer, who will look mainly at improving functionality in pre-existing concepts, and uses discipline and observation to seek steady growth;
- the Athlete, for whom competition is the driving force to innovation, and for whom the goal is extremely important;
- and the Sage, who values ethics, reflection, and is most creative when collaborating.

Degraff points out that all four archetypes are necessary to maintain "constructive conflict." A start-up might have originally built momentum through the vision of an Artist and energy of an Athlete, but if it's going to survive long-term, and especially thrive, will need the input of all four actors. You might fancy yourself the Artist and puff your chest at being the most creative in the bunch, but if unchecked by the Sage or Engineer, you'll quickly burn out or fail.

Seated around the table in the Nottatown Community Center's conference room were examples of all four! In fact, in getting to know the staff better, I discovered that many of my new friends had a little bit of multiple traits. As we spoke about creativity, and continued with our blue sky meeting, it was clear that JJ and Shoshana got along well in their role of "artist" as they threw idea after idea out, while Hector, part "engineer" and part "sage," tended to be more grounded in his suggestions—something that others found frustrating. Their diverging opinions kept the conversation interesting, since, as Winston Churchill said, "If two people agree on everything, one of them is superfluous."

Walt Disney also had a recipe for creativity in the blue sky process, but rather than separating them into personality types that worked together at all times, he separated his roles into separate stages of creative development, giving all participants the opportunity to act in each of the roles.

In Walt's method, it started with *The Dreamer*. When we hear the term "blue sky"—this is what we think of. In the dreamer's world, there are no budgets or zoning restrictions. Dreamers can swim without getting wet, fly without an airplane, and step on Legos without hurting their feet. To The Dreamer, there are no limits—just fantasy.

Once the most fantastic of ideas are on the table, enter *The Realist*. This stage is not about shooting ideas down—it's about figuring out how to bring the best ideas to life. It is about identifying what's possible with existing technology and what new technology would be required. Of course that also means weeding out those ideas that the world isn't quite ready for. No idea is thrown out—they get sent off to a special file cabinet, hopefully to see the light of another day when their time has come.

Following The Realist comes *The Spoiler*. Not every ideas is perfect, and even brilliant ideas sometimes come along at imperfect times. This is where those ideas are analyzed not just for whether they *could* happen, but whether they *should*. The Spoiler is the ultimate critic, and was often where Walt himself entered the Imagineering process. It is said that only the ideas that made it past all three of these creative souls were good enough for the man himself.

Working in this multistage environment allows us to see that criticizing an idea doesn't mean the idea is dead. It might feel like your heart was just ripped from your chest and put through a cross-cut paper shredder, but in many cases, after your Dreamer-level creative idea has been cleaned up by the Realist and then further refined by the Spoiler, we'll end up with something even stronger and more resilient than originally imagined. It's difficult to see the flaws in our own work, which is why it's crucial to work through ideas in multiple stages with peers to fine-tune our vision.

Unfortunately, the way our organizations and meetings are structured, it's likely we encounter Dreamers, Realists, and Spoilers, all at the same time. Odds are, in your staff meetings, an idea can be presented, picked apart, and shot down within the 10-minute slot you were allotted in the meeting agenda, all before being given a fair chance. This can be incredibly destructive because in creative environments, we often measure our self-worth by whether our ideas are accepted or rejected and will prefer to keep clever ideas to ourselves rather than risk the humiliation of presenting an idea that is not met with praise or acceptance.

That's why it's critical that the stages be compartmentalized. The Dreamers need their time to dream without fear that each clever idea will be instantly prodded. Even the most cynical among us will appreciate the liberating feeling of not having to bear the burden of constantly explaining why everyone else is always wrong.

When all of this is taken into consideration, and the blue sky process is given a chance to work, the end result can be an amazing thing. As you brainstorm and let your mind wander to impossible places, you will end up in a completely different destination than you originally planned! The idea that you imagine as The Dreamer, develop with The Realist, and push past The Spoiler will be unlike anything your organization has ever done, and because you did it as a team, it will have the full support of everyone in the room—even those normally cynical and frustrating people who usually poo-poo creative ideas. By making them part of the process, they'll feel ownership and root for the idea to succeed just as much as you.

The blue sky process needs to be a collaborative experience within a protected environment. When Michael Eisner asked his Imagineers to come up with a plan to transform Disneyland into a multiday resort, he gave his team the time and protection it needed. What they came back with was nothing short of brilliant!

In the Disneyland parking lot and the unused land adjacent to Disneyland, his team proposed building "WestCOT Center"—a park similar to EPCOT Center at Disney World, featuring a 300-foot gold sphere, nearly double the height of that at EPCOT in Florida. The project would also add 4,600 hotel rooms spread over several new hotels, a shopping district, state-of-the-art transportation system connecting the resort to three new parking garages, acres of public space, and the Disneyland Bowl—a 5,000-seat amphitheater.

This plan came out of years of blue sky meetings with The Dreamers, discussions with The Realists and compromising with The Spoilers, and even after all of that, it would have been the most revolutionary and advanced theme park resort ever built at the time.

Unfortunately, as down-to-earth as Disney Imagineers and Michael Eisner might have thought it was, WestCOT still proved to be too ambitious. A combination of factors, including opposition from local residents, costly necessary infrastructure improvements to surrounding roads and freeways, the poor performance of Euro Disney in Paris, and the overall price tag of the project, led to downsizing of the scope of the project, and its eventual cancellation.

What we ended up with instead was what most Disney fans would describe as the worst Disney theme park ever built. After WestCOT was canceled, Michael Eisner and 30 of his budget-minded executives converged for a three-day summit that resulted in the idea for *Disney's California Adventure*—a $1.4 billion dollar theme park, hotel, and shopping district, which was to be built in California and, for some reason, themed after California. Unlike the $3.1 billion dollar original concept created by Imagineers, this heavily scaled-down option created by executives would use numerous off-the-shelf rides that you might find at amusement parks around the country. Saving money was the name of the game and that led to dismal reviews by early visitors.

What went so horribly wrong? The original charge by Eisner was for Imagineers to do what the Disney Company is known for—to create something new and inspired that would transform Disneyland into a multiday destination. By the time WestCOT was canceled, the goal was simply to build something … anything … as long as it gave a second gate to the Anaheim resort. It was less about the blue sky creativity that makes Disney stand out, and more about executives coming together to figure out what could be done to accomplish a minimal goal within a budget. They had disregarded their mission and creative intent and went in the face of Disney Imagineering principles. Rather than solving a problem, they created one.

Blue Sky Solves Problems

After reviewing guest feedback at EPCOT Center in Florida's Disney World, Imagineers found they had a problem. While adults loved exploring the World Showcase—a series of exhibits, attractions, and restaurants themed after different locations around the world, children felt differently. The architecture and cultural nuances of each pavilion didn't appeal to children the same way they engaged adults, leaving children bored. Imagineers had to come up with a solution to this problem and had to do so in a way that would fit within the overall creative intent of the existing theme park. They couldn't simply add Disney characters where they didn't belong, nor did they want to sacrifice the authenticity of each themed zone.

In blue skying the problem, they determined that sending children on a mission with a series of objectives that took them throughout the park would give them a sense of adventure and excitement as the adults in their group appreciated the park on a different level.

What they came up with was *Kim Possible World Showcase Adventure*. As Disney fan site disney.fandom.com describes it, "Guests use customized cellphones in the form of Kimmunicators to receive clues and directions of where to go in the World Showcase at EPCOT to help Kim Possible and Ron Stoppable on their various missions in the different pavilions."

As families reach different markers hidden around the theme park, they use their Kimmunicator to activate interactive features. Nonplayers would not notice these features, which appear to be basic set decoration, or are entirely out of sight, but once activated by the young adventurers, audio animatronics enable a shelf full of mugs to begin singing, or a small boat to emerge from behind a building and drop an explosive in a moat.

The Kim Possible Adventure was such a big hit that it has since been rethemed for newer audiences twice! The first reimagining brought us *Disney Phineas and Ferb Agent P's World Showcase Adventure* in 2012, and in 2020, it was refurbished to become *DuckTales World Showcase Adventure*.

The reason this concept was such a success was because it solved a clear and prominent problem. Had children been as excited with the EPCOT attractions as they are at other Disney theme parks, they would not have given the Kim Possible Adventure the attention it received, and it likely would have failed.

Whether it was "why isn't there a clean place where adults and children can go on attractions together?" (the problem Walt experienced with his grandchildren that led to the original building of Disneyland), "How can we prevent people from littering as they walk around the park?" (the problem that led to trash cans at all Disney parks being placed no more than 30 feet apart), or "How do we fix Disney's California Adventure?" (the problem Imagineers had to solve during the years following DCA's opening), the best blue sky results come from a clear problem.

***

With our creative juices flowing, and the understanding that we had to work together in a positive environment free from criticism (at least for the first step of the process), it was time for my NCC cohort to figure out what our focus should be.

"By now we know that creativity and innovation happen most when there's a problem to solve. It's fun to do new things, but ideas are more likely to have an impact when they solve a problem. So," I said, looking around the room, "what's your problem?"

I opened a new Google Doc and titled it "Problems we face." I scanned the room, awaiting a response. Hands slowly began to rise.

By the time this brainstorm session was over, our list included:

- Not enough money to do what we really want to do
- Not enough money raised from fundraising
- Too few people at events
- Teens call us "'not-a' community center"
- Building in need of updating
- All our Sharpies are dried out
- Too many other things to do in the community—too much competition. Children don't want to come here anymore
- Weird smell in room 11

"Now we're getting somewhere!" I said, "We have two lists—a list of problems, and a list of solutions." I could see the puzzled looks on their faces. The list of problems was clear. But to what list of solutions what I referring?

Blue Sky Asks "What If ..."

"Many times, I'd be drawing up designs for an attraction, and Walt would come in to check on my progress," Imagineer Bob Gurr explained. "He'd see a drawing I had hanging on the wall, and he'd tap his finger on it and say, 'Hey, Bobby, this is starting to look good! But what if—?' And he would give me an insight into a totally new approach. I'd think, 'That's a great insight! Why didn't I think of that?'"

In the blue sky approach, asking new questions and reframing existing ones is critical to reaching new adjacent possibles. This will not come naturally to most people. Although we are all curious as children, over the course of our upbringing, society tells us that it's not always appropriate to ask questions or challenge the status quo. Tired parents sometimes scold their children for asking too many questions. Elementary school children make fun of each other for asking "dumb" questions. In looking at the most successful executives in large companies, they don't reach higher status by questioning their superiors—they reach it by agreeing with them and doing what they're told. Those who challenge their bosses tend not to be kept around for very long.

Fortunately, in the protected blue sky environment, questions are not just acceptable—they are encouraged! Questions serve as gateways to identifying problems and solutions that we never knew existed. "What if we brainstormed for Questions?" Hal Gregersen asks in his book, *Questions Are the Answer: A Breakthrough Approach to Your Most Vexing Problems at Work and in Life.*

Some of the great Disney Innovations happen through question asking. *Indiana Jones Adventure* at Disneyland, an attraction that makes guests feel as if they are venturing through an ancient temple, over rugged terrain, and across a crumbling rope bridge, came about because someone asked "what if we mounted a motion simulator to a ride vehicle?" The half-mile interactive queue for that same attraction came about because Imagineers reframed the traditional amusement park question of "how can we keep this line as short as possible" to "what if we can make this line *feel* shorter?" Newer fireworks shows filled with projections and special effects were the result of someone asking "what if our fireworks show didn't just happen in the sky?"

***

"We know what the problems are—we have them on this list," I said, opening up the two Google Docs that we had been working on. "And we know what sorts of things we love. Rather than trying to solve our problems with traditional inside-the-box nonprofit thinking, which is so ubiquitous, we could slap our logo on someone else's campaign and call it a day … how about if we borrow from the list of totally random things we love, to solve some of our problems in totally random ways, by doing things we love!"

The group scanned the two lists again, attempting to draw lines between the problems and the "solutions."

Shoshana's eyes lit up! "Oh my god!" She said, "When I was younger, I went to an orthodontist who had this one wall that was just a giant chalkboard, and each month, they'd have an artist come and change the art. Like, at the beginning of the summer it would be characters in swimsuits and there'd be fireworks, and in October it would be witches and stuff."

I could see the wheels turning as her enthusiasm grew.

"So," she said pointing to the left side of the screen, "if our problem is that we need to do some updating to our building, rather than doing a normal paint job or replacing the tile or something, we can make one wall a huge chalkboard! One of the things I love is to draw chalk murals," she said pointing to the right side of the screen, "so maybe I can do different designs every month or two! It would be effervescent!"

There it was! Aside from misusing "effervescent," she got it! "Yes!" I said. "Perfect! To put that another way, Shoshana is asking 'what if we could put *anything* on our walls?' or 'what if we could change what we put on the walls anytime we wanted to?'" I saw Phil's eyes widen as the possibilities poured in.

"Let's keep going with this! Phil—you're the development director. What if the walls were available for anything you'd like to put there, and could be changed at any time? How would you use that space to bring in more donations?"

Phil turned bright red. Phil was not the type of person who appreciated being put on the spot. He started to touch his forehead and smile nervously. I felt horrible. I quickly grabbed my phone and held one finger in the air. The room was silent as they watched in anticipation as I completed my mysterious task, put my phone down, and waited. Finally, everyone's phones buzzed with the text message, "Parallel lines have so much in common—it's sad they'll never meet." It took them a moment, but they got it, and more importantly, for the first time, I had successfully defused a tense moment with a pun.

Feeling a sense of acceptance in the group, I continued, "How about this, what if people could sponsor Shoshana's murals? What if their business logos could be worked into the art? Would that generate some revenue?"

"Yeah!" Phil responded with a relieved smile. "And what if it wasn't just in the lobby? What if we could do chalk all over the outside of the building? People would be more likely to pay big money if their logo could be seen by everyone on Main Street."

"And what if we didn't just have Shoshana drawing—no offense Shoshana—but what if we had art school students or visiting artists?" JJ asked. "That might get even more people excited and end up spreading the word organically! Maybe we could even get the newspaper to write about it if it was a well-known artist."

"We can't paint the outside of our building," Hector interrupted. "It's art deco. It's been this color forever. It would totally ruin it."

"Hector, be a Dreamer—not a Spoiler," I said. "No rules. No limits right now."

"Yeah, Hector—don't be a Jonathan," Shoshana said with a devilish grin.

"What if we did workshops where Shoshana, or the 'artist in residence,' taught children how to do chalk art?" Vanessa chimed in.

"What if it wasn't just for kids! Adults would probably like it too," Hector said looking around the room for acknowledgment from the staff that he wasn't being a Jonathan.

"Yes! Yes! Yes!" I celebrated. "This is what I'm talking about! And this is just *one* tiny piece of *one* possible solution to just *one* of the problems! We might never do any of this, but how fun is it to think this way! Let's circle back around to this later and try another one." I scanned the "problems" and "things we love" Google Docs for inspiration. "How about this … What if we used 'addictive games' to solve the problem of … the 'public not coming on campus much anymore?'"

The crew pondered this for a moment.

Phil finally raised his hand half way and said, "People love arcades. What if we installed an arcade and people could come play for free? Or we had a monthly pass for $20, or we could make them pay for certain games at certain times as a fundraiser!"

"What if we made that part of some sort of a childcare service for working parents?" Hector asked. "They can play video games and we can do other programming for the kids, and charge hourly, like a babysitter would charge."

"What if, when a parent comes for a chalk art workshop in the evening," Vanessa said, with a wink in Shoshana's direction, "they can drop their kid off in the arcade!"

"You know," JJ calmly said, inadvertently tempering the group's raging enthusiasm, "there's actually a lot more to 'addictive games' than a joystick and screen. There's this whole world of game design behind what makes them addictive. It's what I studied in college. Like, there are some games where you have to log in every day to receive a free bonus. Or how most games start you off on a very basic level that's easy to beat—just to teach you how to play, and then as they get harder and harder, you become more and more addicted to playing."

"So, I think JJ is saying that we should look at more than just arcade games?" Phil said, sensing the fragility in JJ's voice.

"Right—like, it doesn't need to be a literal 'game' like that at all," JJ said, making air quotes with his fingers. "Not a literal board game or arcade game. Like, what if we had something that rewarded people for coming on campus once a week or once a day. It kind of makes *us* the game."

"A day streak!" Hector yelled.

"Yeah," JJ bubbled, his smile widening as he sensed growing enthusiasm for his concept. "So, people come by every so often—daily, weekly, whatever—to keep their streak alive. And the longer their streak, the better the reward they get."

"And maybe there's a leaderboard, like with video games, where you can see how many days your friends have," Vanessa said. "Or you can get points, and see how many points they have. And then participating in stuff here, or sending their kids to our daycare once a week, becomes a game to them."

The group became quiet as they thought of the different simple activities or tasks people could be asked to perform in order to keep their streak alive. Vanessa finally continued her thought. "And, eventually, without us having to desperately pull people on campus for programs, they start looking for opportunities to come here. They eagerly look at our newsletter to see what programs they are most interested in. They're literally addicted to coming here to get their points!"

Bingo! Vanessa got there even before I did. This was awesome! We were totally jiving! "At the risk of interrupting our momentum, can I just point out to anyone who was wondering why we spent so much time before today talking about creativity and innovation and blue sky theory—this is why! We had to understand that innovation and creativity is a process. We had to know that there are challenges standing in our way, but there are tools to overcome those challenges. And we had to acknowledge that there are no bad ideas in the brainstorming phase."

I knew that this group was open to learning, but also very quick to jump down my throat when I tried to turn things into lessons, so I proceeded with caution.

"Once we had that basis to build on, we freed ourselves to put a bunch of people with different experiences and different knowledge in a room together, create a list of random problems and a list of random things we like, and let one suggestion evolve into another one. We never would have thought about painting the walls with chalkboard paint if it wasn't for Shoshana's artistic background, and we wouldn't have gone in the direction of getting people 'addicted to us' without JJ."

They were still listening intently, so I decided to push my luck. "We started with some basic ideas that would be totally doable immediately, like buying an arcade game or painting a single wall, and ended up with a very lofty concept of getting people addicted to us! It's not necessarily something we can do right now, but it's an intent that we can aim for. And what's more—if we end up implementing any one of these ideas, it will not only be one of the most creative things this organization has ever done, but it will lead us down a completely new path that will lead to even more creative things in the future! And will inspire other community centers to do the same! How amazing does this feel!"

"It feels effervescent!" Shoshana said with a big smile.

With the classic *Seinfeld* television episode in the back of my mind, in which George always wants to leave on a high note, I decided that was as good a place as any to end our morning session. Their lunchtime homework would be to continue the discussion in the break room, at each others' desks or over group chat, and come back after lunch to take it one step further.

Blue Sky Can Lead to Brilliant Stories

They say that every Pixar movie can be summarized in six sentences: Once upon a time there was ____. Every day, ____. One day, ____. Because of that, ____. Because of that, _____. Until finally, _____. This minimal storyline is called the Pixar Pitch. It's the elevator pitch that you might use if you had 30 seconds to explain what you're working on to someone much more important than you, or more likely, to friends with very short attention spans.

In his book *To Sell Is Human*, Daniel Pink gives the following example of the Pixar Pitch to summarize the Pixar movie *Finding Nemo*:

> Once upon a time, there was a widowed fish named Marlin who was extremely protective of his only son, Nemo. Every day, Marlin warned Nemo of the ocean's dangers and implored him not to swim far away. One day in an act of defiance, Nemo ignores his father's warnings and swims into the open water. Because of that, he is captured by a diver and ends up as a pet in the fish tank of a dentist in Sydney. Because of that, Marlin sets off on a journey to recover Nemo, enlisting the help of other sea creatures along the way. Until finally Marlin and Nemo find each other, reunite, and learn that love depends on trust.

The beauty of the Pixar Pitch is that not only does it give clear beginning and end points, it allows us to fill in the story with details for the plot or the lessons learned that are only limited by our imagination. It's incredibly simple, yet extremely powerful at the same time.

***

Just two hours had passed since our last session and I could sense the enthusiasm as soon as we all reassembled in the meeting room. Shoshana passed around her phone, showing pictures of some of her chalk art, explaining how much she would love to do something like it at the NCC, even if it was in a hallway, or another out-of-the-way spot.

Once her visual field trip concluded, I lassoed the group's attention for the continuation of our earlier blue sky conversation.

I opened a third Google Doc. This document, which was now projected on the screen, contained the six story elements ready to be filled in. "We're going to write our own Pixar Pitches using the problems and solutions we brainstormed this morning. The first line or two set the stage and begin to explain the problem, and then the last line shares the resolution. Feel free to pick and choose those from the lists as a starting point and then come up with a creative way to fill in the middle. Who wants to try it out?"

"I have one!" Shoshanah volunteered. "Once upon a time there was an organization struggling because of its terrible boss. Every day the boss had onion breath from eating his stupid breakfast burrito. One day the boss got fired and was no longer able to tell everyone to 'win one for the Gipper' every two seconds. Does anyone even know what a gipper is? Because of that, the staff rejoiced and were happy—some might even say, 'effervescent.' Until finally, they all won the lottery and lived happily ever after. The end."

"Wow! Jonathan really did a number on you guys," I said, in a little bit of disbelief at the sense of camaraderie her story evoked. "OK—who else? Maybe a real one now."

"I'll try," Phil said. "So, using the problem of people not really coming here, and the solution of the video games—Once upon a time there was a community center that people stopped going to. Every day the staff would try new things, but people still didn't come. Until one day, they filled one of the unused classrooms with an assortment of arcade games and invited everyone to use them for free. Because of that, people started hanging out at the community center. Because of that, they saw fliers for other events they were interested in, and attended those. Until finally, the community center was saved, and all the staff won the lottery and lived happily ever after. I thought Shoshana's ending was a good one."

"Excellent," I said as I finished typing it into the Google Doc. "I see this as a totally realistic series of events that we could start implementing in a few weeks and achieve in a few months or a year. It gives us a mission and creative intent that guide our decisions, so that even if we got more creative with the steps, we know what the end goal is—for more people to organically attend events."

The group seemed to zone out a little bit more with each keyword I dropped in.

"Let's say we keep the first two lines and last line the same, does anyone want to try pushing the middle points to something even more extreme and imaginative? Remember—we're still 'Dreamers' here."

After a long pause, JJ offered to give it a try. "OK—so, once upon a time there was a community center that people stopped going to. Every day the staff tried new things but it didn't work. Until one day, they put arcade games in a bunch of places that teens hang out, like the coffee place with the logo that looks just like Starbucks, but isn't Starbucks, and the yogurt place around the corner, and they put signs on them that said 'visit the NCC for free tokens.' Because of that, teens stopped by each day to pick up a free token, and then headed to the yogurt place a block away to play the game, which the yogurt place loved and offered free yogurt to all NCC employees anytime we want. Because of that, when teens came for tokens and saw the new climbing wall and trampoline park we built in the courtyard," JJ said, raising his eyebrows suggestively, "they stopped coming just for tokens and then leaving, and they just came to hang out. Until finally, just like the last scene of *The Lion King*, color returned to the land, the NCC was saved, and we won the lottery."

"Nice. I'll let your run-on sentences slide this time. And love *The Lion King* reference. Anyone want to go next? Same first and last sentences, but different middles?"

"Once there was a community center that people stopped going to," Vanessa began. "Everyday the staff tried new things that didn't work. Until one day, they realized that the world wasn't the same place as it was 50 years ago, and there wasn't the same need for a classic 'community center,'" she said, making air quotes. "Because of that, they re-evaluated and updated their mission to something that could serve the community in a better way, and even changed their name to something fresh and more difficult to make fun of because it didn't include 'not-a' in it. Because of that, and all of their new alternative programming that was now relevant to more people, they became an important and indispensable hub in the community. Until finally, the 'community center' was saved, and we all won the lottery and lived happily ever after."

The room fell silent. No one was quite sure what to make of Vanessa's statement. Vanessa was much keener than I had been giving her credit for. Maybe she was even as bright as me…. Maybe.

She had a very astute understanding of what was possible in this blue sky dreamer environment. She figured out that not only are there no bad ideas, but the more outrageous, improbable, and challenging the ideas are, the more celebrated they might become. Outrageous, of course, doesn't always mean dropping trampoline parks and new buildings into the dream. She took advantage of it to give a very pointed and deliberate commentary on what she felt the organization had become, and what might be necessary to fix it. This was something she had clearly been thinking about for a while, and finally felt comfortable enough, in this protected environment, to say it. And best of all, she kept the group's attention by presenting it as a story with a happy ending.

"You really think we should totally change the name and mission statement?" JJ asked. "That seems drastic."

Not wanting to let JJ's comment ruin the Dreamer spirit, I quickly asked, "Just for fun, what would the new name and mission be?"

"Actually, I agree that the term 'community center' is sort of outdated—just like Vanessa said," Phil said. "Some people love it—mostly older people, from what I've seen. But I feel like, in our community especially, there might be a stigma. I think it's still something that's needed—communities still need community centers, but maybe it would be more like 'the center of the community.'"

"It's the same, but different. I like that," Shoshana said. "Center. Middle. Heart. Hub. Core," she read after Googling "center synonyms" on her phone.

"Like we're the hub of the wheel," Phil said, "and all the spokes to the different businesses, schools, churches, organizations, people—they all connect through us. Like the idea of having the arcade games in a bunch of stores, but we are the only place to get the tokens. Those are on the outside of the wheel and they all connect to us in the middle."

Shoshana perked up. "So, it's not like people need to come to us to do things at our building—it's more like we go out to them. It doesn't all happen in the middle of the wheel—things happen everywhere but are connected through us," she continued, speaking her stream of consciousness. "Like, we facilitate community-building. Community connections. We aren't just another organization in the community—we are *the* center of the community."

"That's it! We can be 'The Hub!'" Vanessa said, looking around the room, not sure if she was on to something or just throwing out another phrase for the blue sky thought train. Everyone looked at Vanessa, wondering what she was talking about. "Like, if we were going to have a new name and mission, that could be our new name," Vanessa continued with caution. "'The Hub!'"

I scanned the room, gauging the reactions from each of the participants as they absorbed the information. I thought it was an interesting idea. It showed promise. The others seemed to warm to the idea as they unpacked it, though it was clear some of them were not quite sure about it.

"Once upon a time there was a community center that people stopped going to," Vanessa began to recite as if she was telling a story to her niece. "Every day the staff tried new things that didn't work. One day, a guy who was video chatting from a cemetery," she said, winking at me, "explained how they should rethink their mission, rebrand, and establish new creative intent to meet the needs of their community, while continuing to build on the past. Because of that, they expanded their reach beyond their walls and became a valuable resource not just for community members, but for the organizations that never used to feel connected to one another. Because of that, they became indispensable, and no longer had to struggle to connect with the community. Until finally, the community center—or, actually, the 'center of the community'—was saved, and we won the lottery and lived happily ever after."

Wow. Vanessa was definitely smarter than me. How the hell did she spontaneously find all the right words?

"That's a nice story," Shoshana said softly, looking over at Vanessa.

JJ put down his pen and excused himself from the room, but not in an "I'll be back in a second" sort of way. I looked over at Phil to see if he knew what was going on. He clearly had no idea what was happening. I decided to go after him.

I caught up with JJ at the end of the hall. "Everything OK?" I asked as he looked back at me in silence and collected his thoughts.

"Yeah …" he said trailing off, pausing again to put together the right words. He finally looked up at me. "I don't think you get this place. Maybe Jonathan was right…. We're not just some random community center in some big city. This place is different. And you're coming in here and you're going to destroy it in the name of progress without ever really getting it."

"OK," I gently answered. "Tell me what I don't get."

"You know, I grew up here. I used to ride my bike inside this hall. I used to sneak up on the roof and fly paper airplanes off it with my friends," JJ stared out the window at the courtyard as if he was watching one of his airplanes descend from the third floor. "You see this scar?" He said, pointing to his right elbow with a smile. "One of the counselors found us up there and my friend and I ran so fast and I tripped on an air conditioning pipe and cut my arm wide open. Eight stitches."

He paused again and looked around the hall.

"You talk about painting the walls with chalk and turning it into a video arcade, which is all fun to laugh about, but you can't come in here and make it sound like this place is some has-been that we don't need anymore. You can't just show up with your mini projector and Google Docs and decide that the NCC—which has been around since my grandparents were kids by the way—shouldn't exist anymore. That we should make it into a sideshow novelty for people to gawk at and earn points. Not everything can be Disney-fied."

"Fair enough," I said, opening the door to the courtyard and gesturing to JJ to come on a walk. "Back when you were a kid, what did they use those rooms for?" I asked, pointing across the courtyard at a set of dark windows on the first floor.

"I think the church used them for Sunday school and some other stuff, before they built their own building over on Park Street."

"Do you guys still do things with the church?" I asked, the disintegrating autumn leaves satisfyingly crunching under our feet as we slowly made our way through the chilly courtyard.

"Yeah—On Christmas we hand out food with them. We've been doing it forever—since before I was born. Somewhere in this place there's a picture of my mom doing it when she was a kid!"

"That's awesome!" I said as I meandered us through the double doors at the end of the courtyard, back into the lobby. "Did you go to preschool here back when there was a preschool?"

"Indeed I did," he said with a certain pride. "In fact, the room that we're meeting in, was one of my classrooms. I think when I was in pre-k. That's why the walls are all different colors."

"I hope my portable projector and Google Docs do it justice," I said with a wink.

"Well," he said with a smirk, "it's no cemetery, but you seem to have figured out how to make it work."

"When did the preschool move out?" I asked.

"It didn't really move out. When Amazon opened their distribution center with their own daycare, we lost a bunch of teachers to them, and a bunch of children, and between that and the church, our preschool just sort of fizzled out over the next few years." I looked at JJ and saw the pain in his eyes. He was looking at a building that once stood a mile tall, bursting at the seams with laughter, energy, and friends. He was finally coming to terms with the fact that it was now just an empty shell.

"Hey!" He said, with a crack of energy, "Did you know the outside of this building is what the school on *The Simpsons* was modeled after?"

"Seriously?"

"Yeah, at least that's the rumor." JJ paused and looked around. "I haven't watched that show in years. I used to know every episode by heart." He paused again, staring at the holes in a bulletin board where fliers used to hang. "If we do that chalkboard wall idea, we can have you write 'I will not destroy community centers' 50 times just like Bart." He gave me a smile, but I could see there was some truth and pain in his words.

"You know I'm not here to destroy this place, right?" I asked, looking at JJ as he studied the bulletin board. "I'm not here to take away anything from the past. But places like this change. The church came and went. The preschool came and went. I bet, when you were a kid, they couldn't fit all the fliers on this bulletin board, and now it's practically empty. Things are just different now. It's not that this place has failed—it's that what used to work doesn't work anymore. People don't value the things they used to. They don't connect the way they used to. They channel their energy elsewhere, and put their financial support behind the organizations where they're most active. It's natural evolution."

"I know," JJ reluctantly admitted.

"Remember how I said that creative destruction doesn't happen unless it's time for it to happen?" JJ didn't respond. "Not sure if you noticed, but those ideas to rebrand came from you guys—not from me.

The 'problem' of people not coming here anymore was one that you guys suggested. And the enthusiasm when Vanessa brought it up—that was all you guys. I haven't done anything but push you to be Dreamers. Clearly, the need for change is already there." JJ stood still, nodding slightly, but still not looking me in the eye. "But the thing you need to remember is that we aren't throwing away the past and starting fresh—the idea is that now rather than doing one event with the church each year, you'll do 10 with them, and you'll get other organizations involved too! Everything that's working will still work under whatever new model you guys choose. We're not tearing it down. We're building on top of a foundation created by the successes of the past 50-plus years. And even though you won't have your preschool back, you can find other ways to fill those colorful rooms with kids. You can have an Amazon Prime Day family celebration or something."

JJ smiled. "I bet Prime Day is the bane of every Amazon employee's existence."

"I'll tell you what—how about if we go back in there, and you can be 'The Spoiler' and try to convince everyone that The Hub won't work."

"Nah," JJ said as we started back toward the conference room. "It's not a bad idea. I'm not gonna be a 'Jonathan.'"

The Takeaways

- Creativity and Innovation happen most when people from different backgrounds and strengths talk and allow their ideas to mingle.
- Blue sky meetings require that people with different areas of expertise come together and dream.
- In blue sky meetings, people must be able to dream without fear of their ideas being ridiculed. Ideas should be discussed and fine-tuned, but not until after a round where everyone has the chance to be a "Dreamer."
- The blue sky process, just like all innovation, works best when it solves a problem.

- Asking "What if ..." is a good way to take ideas to the next stage and encourage creativity.
- The Pixar Pitch is a fun way to explain a problem and solution in a concise story.

Next Steps

- There are infinite ways to brainstorm. We barely scratched the surface. Visit thenonprofitimagineers.com for more ideas, including thoughts on brainstorming on your own.

CHAPTER 5

Connecting With a Story

From middle school through her senior year of college, Vanessa was a straight-B student. She is actually quite bright, but also quite lazy.

She's able to play nearly anything on piano and guitar, not because of her combined two years of piano and guitar lessons, both of which she protested early on, but because she inherited the gift of a musical ear from her father.

She grows her expansive knowledge base not by studying great works, but by listening to mostly nonfiction audiobooks on her runs, and by watching mostly Discovery, History, and the Learning Channels. When she's not watching substantive television and absorbing information, the pendulum swings 180 degrees, to foolish programs like *Family Guy* and *National Lampoon's Vegas Vacation*. "You're a smart girl," her girlfriend says. "Why do you watch that garbage?"

Her friends find her to be one of the most irritating people they know, not because she's a narcissist (the exact opposite, in fact), and not because she's a "mean girl," but because it seems like she actually knows the answer to everything, is incredibly humble, and always offers advice that is genuinely helpful. And she never puts on any weight. She's the kind of person you selfishly love to hate for no other reason than because she's the best person you know.

During our time together, I had grown to enjoy Vanessa's contributions to our discussions and was excited when I received a strange package in the mail with her name on the return label. Wrapped extra carefully in two layers of bubble wrap was a small cardboard box—the kind you'd find inexpensive earrings or a bracelet in. I opened the box to find some sort of powder, as fine as flour, with an iridescent quality like translucent glitter. When I sprinkled it in the air, none of it seemed to hit the floor.

Accompanying the box was a handwritten note, "All you need is faith, trust and a little pixie dust. We're ready."

More than three months had passed since the breakthrough session in which the NCC staff realized they might need to rethink their entire mission statement and creative intent. They needed time to mull it over, discuss it with their board, and reach out to community members and local businesses and organizations to figure out how they might best meet the needs of the community. They conducted online surveys and made a big deal about their potential makeover, knowing that the more people who took ownership and became excited about the upcoming changes, the more successful it would ultimately be.

I received e-mails from time to time, asking for input on different ideas, but overall, I stayed as hands-off as possible, letting them use the tools we had discussed, and the business savvy of their board and stakeholders, to make their own decisions. They knew a change this big would require a lot of baby steps and that it wouldn't be easy. But they also knew that if they unlocked enough adjacent possible doors through conversation and research and that if they based what came next on proven successes from the past, they could convince the people that needed convincing and could enact the change they hoped for.

I wasn't worried about forcing change on the NCC if it wasn't ready for it, but I also knew that the decision to change had to be one that they came to on their own, with internal momentum and enthusiasm driving the decision, rather than my outside energy pulling them in the direction I thought they should go.

After our final meeting a few months back, I told them to send for me if all the stakeholders, including the board and community, felt that moving forward was the right thing to do. Even in my wildest imagination I had never expected that their proximity to Neverland, and the fact that they were an entirely fictional community, meant I could travel like Peter Pan! I scooped a small handful of the dust, sprinkled it over my head, thought of the happiest things, and off I went!

Kidding! I drove. But it would be a great story if it was true! Right?

Stories Are Central to Great Campaigns

There's a reason why we love Mickey Mouse, and it has nothing to do with his big ears, white gloves, or falsetto voice. We love him because of his story.

In a time when animation studios wrote cartoons that were nothing more than a series of gags strung together, Walt Disney realized that to make the audience care about his characters, the cartoons needed fully formed stories. Just as in plays, television series, and movies, in the early 1930s, Disney cartoons gave the audience the opportunity to really get to know Mickey and his cohort. The characters were given emotions we could empathize with and care about and they were placed in story lines that we could relate to on a human level. Pluto wasn't just a dog that got stuck in fly paper; he was a living, breathing creature whose frustration became our frustration. The animated stories, filled with real characters, are what we connect to and continue thinking about on a subconscious level, long after the gag has ended.

Similarly, the campaigns and events that stick with us are the ones that tell a story that we connect with. Next time you're watching TV, pay attention to the commercials. In a span of 30 seconds, you'll meet characters, learn about their struggles, and find out that a certain product helped them succeed. Tired working adults, just like us, find energy in any number of drinks or snacks. Construction foremen who need to transport heavy loads on the job site, and parents who need to transport a half-dozen dirty children after soccer practice, find just the right car to meet their needs. Families in different rooms, different states, or different countries overcome the distance through crystal-clear audio and high-definition video chat, thanks to 5G coverage.

Of course, stories are central at Disney theme parks as well. Once upon a time, a group of miners on a scouting expedition discovered a vein of gold in a remote mountain in Southwestern United States. The mining in this scenic hillside was prosperous, and a boomtown quickly arose, complete with a railroad to transport the gold ore. However, unbeknownst to the inhabitants of this small town, the location of their mine and buildings was sacred to Native Americans, and it quickly became clear that their presence had brought a curse upon them! The town was soon abandoned, but the mine trains can still be seen racing through the mine shafts and around the canyons, without a soul on board.

Cute story, right? I never realized this is the story Imagineers wrote in the late 1970s as they began designing a new roller coaster for Frontierland in Disneyland in Anaheim and The Magic Kingdom in Disney World. I've been a Disneyland regular for decades and simply thought *Big Thunder Mountain Railroad* was a roller coaster through mountains designed to resemble the southwest. But the story, even if it isn't fully told to the audience, helps make the experience significantly more powerful and immersive because it gave the Imagineers something to grasp onto—a creative intent—as they designed the queue, roller coaster trains, and scenery. The story made this roller coaster special. To this day, the story helps us form a connection.

Nonprofits have known the value of stories for quite some time. Stories help nonprofits demonstrate their impact in a memorable way. They can translate broad statistics and demographics that are often difficult to grasp into grandparents, neighbors, and children. On a scientific level, stories have even been known to cause "neural coupling," which is a phenomenon where the person listening to the story literally synchronizes brain wave patterns with the person telling the story, thus forming a close emotional connection to the information being shared.

Stories come in all shapes and sizes, from humanizing "behind the scenes" stories that show the real people hard at work at your organization, to dramatic vignettes that show how your program has changed lives. You've seen the commercials about the starving child in Africa who you can feed for just 29-cents per day. You've seen the commercials about the individual lives Children's Hospital saves and the importance of your contribution. You might even have watched the Jerry Lewis Labor Day Telethon back in the 1980s and 1990s, and can still picture the vignettes that played between each of the entertainment acts, showing stories of patients struggling with Muscular Dystrophy. You remember them because they told a story that you connected with.

As nonprofit professionals, our job is all about forming connections. We want our audience to attend our events. We want them to donate to our organizations. We want them to go to our schools. We want them to feel so committed and connected to our causes that they can't help but gloat about what we do to their friends and family! We want them to tell our stories.

Great stories share common elements that you are probably already familiar with, such as story structure, central characters, and a hero's journey. When it comes to narrative storytelling, which we see in marketing campaigns like those mentioned above, these basics are critical.

Stories, however, are not limited to marketing campaigns and they aren't always a basic narrative. Stories can be told during individual events, over the course of fundraising campaigns, or can even slowly progress over the course of an entire year. It's easy to envision how a story can be used in marketing your organization, but understanding how story elements find their way into a 12 month annual campaign is a bit more challenging to grasp.

If it's not too "meta" for you, let's continue to use one story to unpack another:

***

At last, I was back in the room with JJ, Phil, Shoshana, Hector, and Vanessa. Unlike the first time we workshopped, where our initial meetings were filled with skepticism about whether change was possible at an organization with as much history as the NCC, and concern about what the process might entail, this time the room was filled with excitement for the future.

"From what I hear, you've come a long way since the last time we met! I love your new name—'The Hub,' and I love that I can basically recite your mission statement from memory—'to connect the community of Nottatown.'"

"Yes and no," Hector responded, "It's more like 'The Hub at the NCC' or 'The Hub—a project of the NCC.' We aren't formally changing our name—we're doing a skunkworks."

"Yeah," JJ said, continuing Hector's thought. "Everyone's on board, more or less, but the way that the board approved it, any big changes are going to be worked in over time. We are still going to be the organization we've always been, as we transition to something bigger and better. If the skunkworks works out—boy, that's a mouthful—then we might be able to change things for real."

"Great!" I said. "That takes all the pressure off and allows us to be creative without needing to worry as much about the board approving everything. Obviously, we can't disregard what's come before, but we will have some good freedom under this model. And because it's experimental and not totally replacing the entire organization, if we fail, we fail. We can just learn from it and try again."

"Oy! OK! We get it!" Shoshana interrupted. "Enough with the teachable moments. Can we just get on to how we're going to actually do this?"

"Trust the process, Shoshana. But sure!" I said abruptly. "Let's jump right in. Shoshana, what's the story we're going to tell?"

Shoshana thought for a moment but was clearly caught off guard by my pointed question and unremitting eye contact. I let her wriggle for an extra beat before I followed up. "People connect through stories, so, Shoshana, what's the most effective story to tell to help people connect with The Hub? What will the chapters be? What will the challenge be? What will the preshow be?"

"Umm," Shoshana said with a humbled smirk on her face. She knew I was just playing around with her, but also realized there's more to it than just jumping right in.

Vanessa raised her hand and somewhat timidly, with a completely straight face, suggested, "Ducks have feathers to cover the butt quacks." One by one the group began to laugh uncontrollably, like actors on a set that had been struck by a fit of laughter.

"That's a good one," I said, as the table began to calm down. "I like that one. OK," I re-focused, "before we talk about what goes into a good story, I want to make sure you understand why this is so important."

The group settled in with straight, lets-get-this-over-with faces, preparing for another lesson.

"You're going to attend plenty of great events with elaborate themes. You're going to donate to plenty of organizations running very successful fundraisers. You're going to go to plenty of programs that you thoroughly enjoy. But the difference between what everyone else does, and what we are trying to do here, is that we are creating something bigger. We aren't just talking about one-off events or programs or fundraisers. What we're doing is going to impact our community members much more deeply, because every single thing we do will be part of the story, within a theme, with an eye on our creative intent, and to further our mission. Honestly, have you ever considered all of those things at once?"

Mostly blank stares, with a few nods.

"With a view from a thousand feet up, our goal is to see the Candyland-style map that illustrates how an event fits into a campaign, and how the campaign fits within our mission, and the journey it takes our members on. We must make sure that every piece of collateral, and every point of contact gives our guests exactly what they want and need. And, often without anyone realizing just how many dominoes we've precisely set up, we execute the chain reaction that might continue for months or years in the future. The chain reaction with a single goal that is always in the back of the Nonprofit Imagineer's mind—to make our supporters fall in love with our organization over and over and over again."

Their eyes perked up at "Candyland," and again at "dominoes." I made a mental note to use more childhood games in my imagery.

"You might have heard me say something like that before, but I think it probably means something very different now that you understand just how deep all of these things connect, and how much impact they can have."

I paused to let it sink in (and for you to reread and highlight those last few paragraphs, in case you didn't do so in the preshow chapter, because they explain why we've taken such deep dives into some of these areas).

"OK, now, let's talk about good storytelling."

Stories Have Themes

Take a mental field trip to the last beach boardwalk or local carnival you visited. Walk around. Take in the smells of fried foods, the sounds of the rides whirring, carnies calling out for you to knock over milk bottles and win a stuffed animal, and the thousands of blinking lights that line the midway.

Destinations like these are a lot of fun—they provide amusement while you're there and indigestion when you get home, but there's a reason why they don't impact you on a deeper, lasting level. There's a reason why parents don't save up for years and plan big family vacations centered around visiting the Santa Monica Pier or a Six Flags amusement park the same way they plan years in advance for their "trip to Disney." That reason is the theme…. Or, lack thereof.

Anyone who's taken a fifth grade writing class will tell you that a theme provides underlying meaning and guides the entire piece. Whether it's a five-paragraph essay, or 10-page term paper, every fact, figure, and quote should build on, and support, the theme.

While an **amusement** park, like a boardwalk or carnival, is a series of unrelated amusements, just as early cartoons were simply a series of unrelated gags, a **theme** park represents something deeper. It's about an immersive experience that begins when you walk through the front gate and stays with you long after you head home. Each land, ride, scene, and prop supports the theme and tells a piece of the story.

Walt Disney was the first to bring themes into cartoons, and when he pondered building a park for parents and children to enjoy together, he knew that stories, supported by themes, would play a pivotal role.

***

"We're here to figure out what this next year or two will look like. We want to make sure whatever this campaign is that launches The Hub, it draws people in and really connects with them." I looked around the room, being sure to make eye contact with each person sitting around the table. "The best way to do that is through story, and the best stories have killer themes. Any thoughts on what the theme for The Hub's inaugural year might be?"

"Could the theme be the actual events? Like 'a year of exciting new events?'" Hector asked.

"That's one possibility," I said. "But the events themselves aren't really a theme. Calling events the theme is like calling 'Big Thunder Mountain Railroad' the theme of Frontierland. It's one of the story elements—a prop that enhances the story—just like the shops, shooting arcade, and even the types of plants. The theme of Frontierland is something along the lines of 'a western town.' The theme is what ties all the story elements together. With that in mind, what are some other possible themes that would tie all the events and other pieces together?"

"How about, 'celebrating 100 years,'" JJ suggested.

"Wait—Is this the NCC's hundredth anniversary year?" I asked.

"I don't think so," JJ said.

"No! It's like 50 or 60," Shoshana speculated in Vanessa's direction. "Maybe 62 or something?" Vanessa shrugged.

"What are you talking about? It's like 125," Hector said with waning certainty. "It's 'pre-war.' That's what Jonathan always said."

"Depends on which war you're talking about," JJ said. "Franco-Prussian?"

"You think this place predates Prussia?" Vanessa asked incredulously.

"It's not as far back as you think it was," Shoshana said, her smile growing as she saw my frustration with the tangent we were on. "The Ottoman Empire was still around in, like, the 1920s."

"Doesn't matter!" I yelled, throwing my hands in the air. "Why would you make 'celebrating 100' the theme if it's not our hundredth year?"

"I just think it would be a good theme in general. We're Dreamers, right? No bad ideas?" JJ smiled.

"Fair enough," I hesitantly agreed. "In general, an anniversary is a good theme, because you can have different events that celebrate the past and the future. But let's talk about this particular year at the NCC."

"If our new mission is to be 'the hub'—the center that connects the community," Phil offered, "then the theme can be something like that— something like 'building community connections through The Hub.'"

"I think that's a great theme *and* creative intent!" I said. "I want to make sure you all understand why—because everything that we do can fall under the main theme of 'building community connections.' That can include advertising campaigns, events, fundraising, even something like forming an adult basketball league can be done within the theme of 'building community connections.'"

"So, each of the events can be different ways to build community connections," Vanessa said, "whether they're at our building, or things we help organize at other places."

"Right!" I said, "And by establishing our story's theme up front, we can plan each piece of the story to organically fit within that theme from the very beginning."

Stories Should Feel Organic

We've talked about the importance of having a broad mission statement, so as not to limit your creativity. The same is true for a theme. If it's too specific, there won't be room to include the elements of your story that might excite you and your supporters the most. If it's too specific, your attempt to include those ideas will feel out of place and inorganic.

When it comes to designing attractions, a key part of the Disney Imagineering process is making the attraction itself feel like it is a natural piece of the theme. It should feel like it has always been a part of the story—not added later on a whim. Whereas many amusement parks might build a roller coaster, and then add ornamental elements to make it feel themed, Disney Imagineers do the opposite. At Disneyland, Imagineers put painstaking work into ensuring that *Big Thunder Mountain Railroad* was built to look like the mountain was there first and the roller coaster was added into it. The roller coaster drops into the valleys and climbs toward the peaks of the "million-year-old" mountain. If you remove the roller coaster track from the mountain, the space would continue to feel like a mining town set at the base of a large southwestern mountain range. Compare that to the *Incredicoaster* in Disney's California Adventure, where the steel coaster, originally built to resemble a standard boardwalk thrill ride, was later given theming elements based on the Pixar movie *The Incredibles.* By adding the theme and story elements years after it was first constructed, Imagineers were limited in what they could do, and simply added a few characters in different spots along the track, making the story feel labored and out of place.

To develop immersive and impactful campaigns in the nonprofit world, we must start with the theme, and design our events to fit into the story, rather than the other way around. If the story feels like it was added on to the campaign as an afterthought, or if pieces of your campaign completely ignore the theme and story, your community will notice, and it won't be as impactful.

But what do you do if you find that the story elements you're most excited about don't fit within the theme? Perhaps you need to change your story … Or your entire theme.

Take, for example, Bear Country—a small land in California's Disneyland that is no longer in existence but once hosted a whopping three attractions. Disney Imagineers had no choice but to change the very focused name when they decided to add *Splash Mountain* in 1989, since the new attraction didn't fit the old theme and story being told. By changing the name to Critter Country, it also opened the door for additional shops, eateries, and attractions to be added later on.

Imagineers could have tried to design *Splash Mountain* to fit within the existing "bear" theme, but they made the better decision of expanding the land's theme.

While we're on the topic of poorly chosen themes, let's roll our eyes again at Disney's California Adventure. When it opened, all the rides and lands celebrated everything that California has to offer. Imagineers quickly realized that the requirement that all rides and lands fit within the theme of "California," while also feeling like a Disney theme park, was difficult, if not impossible. They also learned that the executives were misguided in the original theory that people who traveled to California wanting to see attractions like the Golden Gate Bridge and Hollywood would not feel the need to leave a Disney theme park if they could see small replicas of them along the route toward the e-ticket attractions. As such, they began the process of de-theming the entire park. The large "California" letters that welcomed guests in the entry plaza from the day the park first opened were removed in 2011, as was a replica of the Golden Gate Bridge that the monorail once crossed, which now looks more like a 1920s freeway overpass.

Although the park is officially named Disney's California Adventure (for now), unofficially, it is known as DCA, subtly shedding a certain trigger word the way Kentucky Fried Chicken began marketing itself as KFC, which many assume was done in hopes that you will forget their chicken is fried in oil. By taking the "California" out of Disney's California Adventure, it gave Imagineers the opportunity to put in Pixar Pier, Carsland, and the Avengers Campus—all of which only loosely connect to the golden state, if at all.

DCA's current theme is … well … who knows. But most Disney enthusiasts will tell you the mishmash of ultra-themed lands, even without an overarching park theme, is a vast improvement over the original park as it was on opening day.

The cool thing about this approach is that each land tells its own story, just as lands in other Disney parks do, while still being interconnected, just like chapters in a book.

Stories Have Chapters

In traditional books, chapters serve a few purposes. Among other things, chapters help add structure, they break up the full story into manageable chunks that the reader can digest more easily, and they provide clear separations between smaller anecdotes or events within the overall story. Great writers weave individual stories together to form a complete narrative—each chapter complementing the others, building a compelling, and memorable tale.

In the theme park world, multiple attractions, restaurants, and shops are all included in a chapter, or, what we more commonly refer to as a "land." *Space Mountain, The Autopia, Star Tours,* and *Buzz Lightyear Astro Blasters* are four different attractions in Disneyland's Tomorrowland, each with their own stories, but all fitting within the chapter of "Tomorrowland." By visiting these attractions, as well as by observing the scenery, browsing the souvenir shops, and noshing from a Star Wars themed popcorn bucket, the futuristic chapter of your Disneyland story takes shape.

Picture yourself walking through Disneyland or one of the international Magic Kingdom Parks. As you move from one land to another, such as Tomorrowland to Fantasyland, there is a distinct separation. The music, architecture, and even the flooring changes. Imagineers have set you up to subconsciously leave behind the story of Tomorrowland and begin the story of Fantasyland. They've given you an array of indicators telling your mind to take a breath and regroup in preparation for the next adventure. In other words, they've ended one chapter of your complete "Day at Disney" story and started another.

When it comes to a nonprofit's story, the idea of chapters is most effectively used behind the scenes, in a figurative manner, to separate your goals for the year into manageable segments and ensure you are making progress as time passes. Whether your year is divided into months, seasons, or semesters, you want to be sure that everything you have planned within a given chapter is well thought out, on-theme, and that you accomplish everything you planned for each of these chapters before moving on to the next. Doing so will help you achieve your internal goals while also guiding your patrons, step by step, through your complete story.

Importantly, while chapters should smoothly flow from one into the next, they should also be distinct. There's a reason why we don't see any Disney princesses on the *Jungle Cruise,* or Buzz Lightyear wandering into Toontown. The creative intent of a Disney attraction or land needs to remain focused, so that it is clear and impactful. The same is true of your nonprofit events or campaigns. Your Christmas celebration shouldn't bleed into a Valentine's Day event any more than Passover matzo should be served at Hanukkah (despite the many grocery store displays that indicate the contrary). Even though you might have extra promo items that were handed out to celebrate Summer, that doesn't mean they should still be distributed in the Fall. Photos from a program in May shouldn't be posted to your school's social media pages the following September, since they are parts of two different stories—one for each school year.

Just like an author, you must create a plan, or outline, ahead of time, and complete each piece of the constituent's journey before moving on to the next. It can be confusing and sometimes counterproductive if pieces of different chapters overlap. Don't ask people to donate toward your GivingTuesday campaign in January. GivingTuesday was a single day of global generosity that every nonprofit celebrated at the end of November. It should remain there.

Similarly, some organizations purposefully raise money toward their annual campaign for only the first few months of the year, and then focus on relationship building the rest of the year, without the burden of the transactional relationship weighing them down the entire year. If there isn't a clear and deliberate separation between these two chapters of the advancement year, donors can easily feel nickel and dimed all year long, ruining what could have been a positive experience.

But what do you do if you've reached the end of a chapter but don't feel like you've accomplished your goals or moved your story forward? Much like a tour guide taking visitors through the Magic Kingdom, you have the ability to adjust your plan based on how your guests respond to your story. Need more time to take it all in? Extend the chapter a bit. Feeling a lack of interest? Move on a little quicker to the next thing. At your organization, over the course of your chapter, you must constantly re-evaluate whether you've accomplished your goals and moved your community members far enough forward to be prepared for the next piece of the story, or whether your next event or message needs to be adjusted. Remember—over the course of the year, your goal is to tell a complete story—to take your constituents on an emotional journey. It requires planning, leadership, perseverance, and above all, flexibility. If you feel like one event or fundraiser missed the mark, you might need to adjust the next one accordingly. (That doesn't mean turning

GivingTuesday into a three-month campaign! It means being agile and developing a quick, meaningful and fun mini-campaign to bridge the gap between your progress and your goal, or simply accepting your shortfall and aiming higher in the next chapter.)

It won't be easy, but when done right, you will effectively transform your organization from several random magazine articles into one cohesive, beautiful, impactful novel. You will no longer hold dozens of unrelated campaigns and programs throughout the year—you will develop a collection of interrelated, synergistic tiles that fit together to form one stunning picture. Where once you were a run of the mill carnival, now you are a Disneyland.

**

"I'm so confused," Hector said, with nods of agreement from everyone in the room.

"Yeah. There's a lot to unpack. Let's go piece by piece," I said, trying to figure out where to start. "OK. So, big picture—if our theme for the year is 'building community connections,' what is a story that we can tell to help people connect to it?"

"*An American Tail* was a good movie about community. Though I don't think it was Disney. If that matters …" Shoshana said.

"Were you even alive when that movie came out?" Hector chuckled.

"I don't think so," Shoshana answered. "Does it matter?"

"There are no cats in America!" JJ sang joyfully.

"Tell us about *An American Tail*, Shoshana. What was the story there?" I asked, wanting to encourage her creative approach and not be a Jonathan.

"Well," Shoshana said, thinking for a moment, "Fievel Mouskowitz is a mouse that immigrated to America to get away from the evil cats that ruled his town in Europe, but I think his family was killed on the trip over, and he has to assimilate on his own and build a new community for himself in New York. Something along those lines."

"I don't really remember it well, but that sounds more or less right," Phil said.

"OK, so our theme is 'building community connections,' and just for fun, our story for the year is based on *An American Tail*," I said.

"We obviously won't tell the exact story of *An American Tail*.... So, how can we transform it into a sequence of events that our community can experience?"

"Are we really doing this?" Hector asked in disbelief. "We're planning out the coming year based on *An American Tail*?"

"Hey, *Jonathan*—live a little!" JJ said, mocking Hector. "Trust the process!" He continued, mocking me.

"Maybe it can be something about the way that—um, what's the mouse's name?" Vanessa asked, cutting herself off.

"Fievel," Shoshana said.

"Right—The way that Fievel has no one when he comes to America— his family is gone, he has no friends ... but over time, he found his community in America. Or, at least, that's what I'm assuming. I've never seen the movie," Vanessa continued. "But there are some people here at the NCC who know everyone and have been here forever, and others who don't have a lot of friends, and they might feel the same way Fievel did. So, maybe we have a few different types of characters in our story— those who invite people in and those that get 'adopted,' like the immigrants did."

"I like that," Hector said with a smile. "I bet my parents felt the same way when they immigrated."

"That's a great beginning!" I said. "How might you separate it into different distinct 'chapters?'"

"I can see this being three different acts, or 'chapters,'" Phil said, using his fingers to make overly dramatic air quotes in my direction. "The first part would be before Fievel arrives in America, the second part is while he's assimilating and making friends, and the third part would be after he feels connected. I don't know where the evil cats come into play, though."

"OK," I said, "So, how would that translate to what we're doing here? Let's assume no evil cats in our version."

The group thought deeply, trying to find some way to connect the stories.

"Past, present, and future?" Vanessa asked.

"Explain please," Shoshana said with a smile.

"Well, again—I never saw that movie, so this won't literally be the same story line, but it can be something about telling the story of our past, which would be like the character's time before he immigrated, then celebrating all the people that are involved today, which is like the time he spent as he built his community in America." Vanessa paused as she continued to connect the dots in her head. "And who knows what the future will be, but we can set things up to prepare us for a bright future. Like, the third 'chapter' can have a group brainstorm with the community to figure out what to do next year!"

"I think you're onto something!" I said, like a proud father. "Past, present, and future is a great way to talk about community and make everyone feel connected. It's one complete story split into three chapters, and the events for each chapter can help tell that portion of the story. The three chapters will flow nicely, since they are connected, but they will also be separated. And the 'characters' that you mentioned earlier can play a role in further connecting the community at those events."

"But, what I don't get is how we're going to 'tell a story' that lasts a year and is 'about' community building," JJ said with critical intonation. "How do we use events and fundraisers to actually tell the story?"

"Good question," I said. "Let's keep talking about great stories."

Stories Have Challenges, Guides, and Heroes

There's a point where many nonprofit marketing novices get in trouble, and it's almost always the same spot. They set up their website and promotional materials touting their rich history, gorgeous campus, and the work that they do for the community, without realizing that most people will instantly tune it all out since none of that matters to *them*. Simple rule of thumb—if someone cannot personally relate to your material, they won't particularly care about it.

The story you should be telling isn't *your organization's* story—it's *theirs*! Your guest's! You don't want them to *hear* a story, you want them to *live* the story.

As visitors enter Disneyland, they walk under a railroad bridge containing a plaque. It doesn't say, "Welcome to Disneyland, est. 1955, home to more than 50 attractions, dozens of restaurants and a stellar cast." It says, "Here you leave today and enter the world of yesterday, tomorrow, and fantasy." It's all about *you*, and your journey for the day!

Ironically, this concept wasn't fully understood or implemented when Disneyland first opened. Many of the original Fantasyland dark rides were essentially book reports—retelling stories from Disney movies for the guests as they sat in a small cart that moved along a track from one life-size diorama to the next. They were fun, but they weren't what kids were talking about the next day on the school yard.

Compare those classic Fantasyland dark rides to modern attractions like *Indiana Jones Adventure* or *Star Wars Rise of the Resistance*, in which the guest is the star of a brand new, ever-changing story. Rather than being "book report" attractions, very little of the stories from the original movies are told. These attractions are set in the same world as the original story but do not simply take the rider through the sequence of events from the films (i.e., someone else's story). Instead, this newer generation of attractions interacts with guests, sometimes changing the ride sequence based on how the guest responds to it. The guest becomes the hero of the adventure with a clear challenge to overcome and various elements within the attraction that guide them in the right direction.

Similarly, those who have ridden *Buzz Lightyear Astro Blasters* will recall that as you enter the ride queue, the attraction doesn't prepare you to view Buzz Lightyear's story—it puts *you* in the story! Life size animatronics in the queue speak directly to the rider, preparing you for the battle you're about to wage. It's not Buzz's quest—it's your quest to battle the evil Zurg and save the universe.

All of these attractions share common elements—a hero (the guest), a challenge or quest, and a guide that helps the hero on their quest.

The best way to create a dynamic and interesting campaign that will bond you and your supporter together is by incorporating all these pieces. Set up a challenge, such as filling empty bookshelves in your library, set yourself up as the guide who will give students and their parents a simple way to meet that challenge head on, such as through a monetary donation to buy books, or an Amazon wish list, and let them be the heroes that fill your shelves!

***

"Whoa, whoa, whoa!" Phil interrupted. "Wait. You're wrong! The stories of the starving children in Africa from those commercials aren't about the donor, they're about the children half-way around the world. And, as you said, those are some of the most effective solicitations."

"True," I said, thrilled that someone was still paying attention. "They're talking about a child and showing pictures of his dire condition, but the story they're actually selling is yours! *You* can literally change a starving child's life for a few cents a day. The commercials don't say '*our* organization can help feed children,' they say '*your* donation can help feed children.' They set up the challenge—children are starving. They show you that they are the guide who will help you make a difference, and most importantly, they make you the hero."

"OK," Hector said. "That's lovely, but let's be honest.… We plan pot-luck dinners and needlepoint classes. How are we going to turn that into a plotline with a challenge and a hero, and fit it all into this *American Tail* story and theme that we're talking about?"

Stories Are Not Always That Kind of Story …

Before you have a nervous breakdown trying to find the story, challenge, hero, and guide in your publicity about the new hot lunch schedule, I will admit that not everything you do will have a story—at least not in a traditional sense. We tend to think of a story as linear, taking us from point A to point B, with a few points of interest along the way. We see the story the way early Imagineers did when they designed the original dark rides—taking a viewer room by room, scene by scene, from start to finish.

Perhaps your story needs to be more like that of the *Haunted Mansion, Pirates of the Caribbean* or *It's a Small World*—none of which have a true and obvious linear story. Rather, each of these has a central theme and immerses the visitor in that world. Your goal in such a situation might simply be that the viewer leaves with a full understanding of the information or lesson you're trying to impart. Or perhaps your goal is to take them from point A, where they have no connection to your cause, to point B, where they are more likely to get involved or donate.

Sometimes, the story isn't something you tell, but rather, something that is experienced. Sometimes the story is *their* path—their journey through the information you present to them. Think back to the attractions mentioned above—as guests climb out of their boat after riding *Pirates of the Caribbean,* a dark ride that uses a large cast of audio-animatronic figures to depict different fully immersive story-book-style scenes from pirates' lives, they feel as if they've experienced the life of a pirate themselves. Similarly, guests step out of their *Haunted Mansion* Doom Buggy having temporarily played the role of the 1,000th happy haunt as they witnessed friendly ghosts in their natural habitats such as a decrepit mansion, graveyard, and eerily quiet street. And guests depart *It's a Small World* with a warm feeling of unity and friendship, and possibly a headache from the repeating soundtrack, after hearing animatronic children from various regions of the world singing the same song in a variety of languages. (As Walt used to say, "people don't go out of the park whistling the architecture." But I digress....)

With something like a needlepoint class or next week's hot lunch menu, you don't need to tell a linear story, but rather, you have the opportunity to give your participant or school parent a glimpse into how their participation can impact their life. Consider the difference between "Fried Chicken Strips" and "Be a superhero and order your child crispy, breaded chicken strips and tangy ranch dipping sauce, loaded with much-needed protein to give them energy to learn a new Thanksgiving song or win at dodgeball." Even with something as simple as hot lunch, you can sell them on the experience. Make them picture their child enjoying the delicious, healthy meal that will help them do better in class, and make them a hero by ordering it for their child. The rest of the story writes itself.

***

"So, for our *American Tail*-inspired story, and really, everything we do, you're saying that this story isn't literally 'once upon a time you immigrated to Nottatown,'" Vanessa said defiantly. "Even though *An American Tail* is a linear story, and even though you want us to base our year on that linear story, you don't want us to tell a linear story. I feel like you buried the lead there. It's sort of an important concept."

I looked over at Vanessa, not sure how to respond to her unhelpful comment. "Trust the process, Vanessa," I said with a snooty grin. Vanessa rolled her eyes at me.

"I have a question," Shoshana interrupted, trying to diffuse the tension. "Why do police use drug-sniffing dogs? Sober dogs would be much more effective." The group chuckled.

"OK, so you're basically saying that over the course of the entire year, we aren't literally trying to tell a sequential story," Phil summarized. "We're trying to take our community members on a journey—*their* own journey—from one place to another, where they are the heroes going on the journey and we are the guides. In this case, the journey starts with them learning about our past, and ends with them having a sense of excitement for the future, and ultimately, feeling like they've been a part of our community's journey over the years."

"Yes!" I said. "In a nutshell, yes. They don't necessarily have to feel like they went on a sequential journey. Like I said, the journey could be going from a place where they didn't know anything about our past, to a place where now they know about our past."

"Didn't I literally just say that?" Phil interrupted. "I think I should get the credit for the over-explained teachable moment."

"Sure," I said with a smirk. "Someone give Phil one credit." JJ threw a breath mint at Phil. "But let's not get too caught up on the exact details. There's more to storytelling, and I want to lay it all out there, so that you won't complain that I was withholding critical information," I said, smiling directly at Vanessa.

Stories Can Start ... Before the Beginning

If you're under the impression that an event's story begins when your audience walks through the entryway, you're missing out on an important and valuable story element—the preshow.

The *Big Thunder Mountain Railroad* experience doesn't begin when you take your seat in the mine train—the story begins as soon as you step into the queue. Actually—it starts as soon as you see the spires of the southwestern desertscape reaching skyward in the distance, beckoning you toward the ride. Actually—it starts when you look at your park map while finishing the last crumbs from your Star Wars popcorn bucket and decide to ride *Big Thunder Mountain Railroad* next. Actually—it starts when you walk through the tunnel leading from the turnstiles to Main Street, and see movie-style posters on the sides of the tunnel advertising all of the great attractions you are about to experience. Actually—well, we could keep jumping further and further backward, but I think you catch my drift.

Stories often begin long before they actually begin. Imagineers call this a preshow, and it is an opportunity to set the stage and start introducing story elements long before the guest loads a ride vehicle.

***

"Let's put the big year-long *American Tail* discussion on hold for a minute," I said. "Someone tell me about an event you held recently that you really loved."

JJ immediately raised his index finger. "We had a backyard barbeque last summer that was fun."

"Perfect," I said as I stood up to pace, mimicking great lawyers in mediocre made-for-tv dramas. "When did the event begin?"

"Around 3:30, I think." JJ looked around the room for confirmation but saw only perfectly still heads. Everyone sensed it was a trick question; they just weren't sure what the real answer was.

"That might have been the time on the invitation, but when did it *really* begin for your guests?"

"4PM?" JJ said, very unsure how to answer.

"No—go back in time."

"2PM?"

"Farther back."

"When they got dressed that morning? I don't know. When?" JJ said, frustrated by the feeling he was on trial.

"I'd say, it actually started back when they first found out about the event. You see, the 'show' might have begun at 3:30 that afternoon, but the 'preshow' started weeks or months earlier." A communal sigh of relief was felt as the group no longer had to participate in my aggravating guessing game. I continued to pace in the front of the room, lifting my hand to my chin. "Think about the difference between two invitations to a summer barbeque—one of which has the title 'summer BBQ,' the date, time, location, and clipart of a hot dog. The other invitation says 'grab your flip flops, slip into vacation mode and join us for an afternoon of delicious food, cool drinks, fun, and games at our annual Summer BBQ,' with the same date, time, and location, and a picture of bare feet on fresh cut grass in the background. They're invitations to the exact same event, but you can already picture yourself basking in the warm sun or cool shade, sipping your drink, chatting with friends, and letting someone else worry about who your kids are terrorizing off in the distance."

"OK," Shoshana said. "I get what you're saying, but that's just basic marketing, and I think we do a pretty good job with that. We always use good pictures and descriptive wording. Our marketing is effervescent."

"I do not think that word means what you think it means," JJ said in a poor Spanish accent. The group chuckled at his *Princess Bride* reference.

"Then let's keep going with the preshow! The next opportunity to connect and continue the story is when they RSVP and pay for the barbeque—still weeks from the actual event. What does your RSVP form ask?"

"Name, email, number of guests, and food allergies." JJ felt pretty confident in his response.

"Sure," I said, "You can set up a basic form like that on your website, but what if you threw in a few more questions? What if you asked, 'what are you most looking forward to,' and then offered checkboxes for things like 'reconnecting with friends' or 'not having to cook and do the dishes for one meal?'"

"Or entering my own one-man hotdog eating contest!" Phil said with a big smile.

"Or that," I said. "And maybe another question, like 'of all the events we had this year, which would you most like to attend again next year?'"

Things were starting to make sense to the group. They saw that by adding these sorts of questions, we were doing a few things; the first question would set the stage, getting everyone more excited to be at our barbeque, and pointing out some things they might not have thought about, such as reconnecting with their friends from the community. The question would also build upon the narrative of kicking off shoes and relaxing with a drink, which was introduced in the invitation. What was originally just marketed as a chance to be outdoors and relax is now growing into an on-theme community-building opportunity that may or may not feature a one-man hotdog eating contest. The form and the invitation give a preview of this and other events, just like the posters under the railroad bridge offer a preview of the attractions you will soon ride as you walk onto Main Street!

The second question has absolutely nothing to do with the barbeque but reinforces why they are a part of the community. It makes them think about the times they've spent together—sometimes just for fun, and other times to do good for the community, and it helps them envision spending more time together in the future. It helps connect this event to others and incorporates it into the broader story, chapter, and theme for the year.

As a bonus, those questions help you identify which events people particularly enjoyed, and even give them a little sense of ownership, since their answer will likely help form the calendar for the coming year.

"OK, what happens next in the preshow?" I asked.

Eyes were looking in every direction except mine.

"What happens when they submit the RSVP form?" I hinted. "They get some sort of automated message, right?" Once again, I saw relief to have the answer without a cross examination. "Upon submitting their online RSVP, we have a choice between not sending any email confirmation, sending an email that simply says, 'thank you for your RSVP,' and creating a totally unique and story-progressing auto-response to get them even more psyched about our BBQ! What could we put in it?"

"We can't wait to see you at our annual summer barbeque!" Hector suggested.

"Good. What's the next sentence?"

"We're taking drink requests," Vanessa said as she perked up, "and looking for outdoor games to keep the kids, and maybe even the adults, active. Please reply to this email if you have any thoughts."

Despite this hot/cold thing she has going on, there's a reason why Vanessa is my favorite.

"Perfect! That even adds a human touch to this otherwise fully automated task. But we'll talk about that later. What else?" I could see the wheels spinning, but they weren't quite sure what to say. "Give them another assignment. What else can they do to help you make the event more successful, and also help them have more fun?"

"They can invite their friends!" JJ blurted out with enthusiasm I had not seen from him before.

"Yes! Yes! Yes!" I said, pointing at JJ with a *this guy gets what I'm talking about* gesture. "How much better is that auto-response than the 'your submission has been received' you were going to do?"

I could tell they wanted to clap. They were dying to clap. But they weren't clapping.

"So, we've sent out an invitation to start the story, continued it with the RSVP form and with the RSVP confirmation email, and we've given them something to think about which they'll hopefully act on—sending an email or text to some friends and talking up this awesome event! The story is well underway, and the event itself is still weeks out! You see, the story isn't about hot dogs, and it's certainly not about the organization's history or staff—it's about the 50 different unique stories that will be experienced by the individual attendees during a relaxing afternoon. Not just that, but it's one piece of a larger story and theme about spending time with the community. You could easily make this a part of the annual theme and story by pointing out that the barbeque is an annual tradition, dating back decades, and sharing pictures from past barbecues. Or you can make it work with the second chapter of the campaign story, about the 'current' community, by sharing information about some of the people who will be attending the event, so that the community starts to feel like they know each other. Regardless, either option will feel completely organic. Heck, they might even feel like old friends by the time the event rolls around. You see, when you think about this stuff with the big picture in mind, even by doing the same events you've done year after year, and with almost no extra effort, it can all work together and be so much more impactful!"

The prosecution rests.

***

While we're on the topic of preshow, it would be very remiss of me not to mention the attraction preshows we love to hate—ride queues. Prior to building Disneyland, Walt Disney tasked his Imagineers with learning everything they could about the amusement park business. They visited dozens of parks around the country, in some cases covertly tracking attendance and ride capacity, and in other cases, openly interviewing the owners and operators of the attractions.

What they learned was that there is a precise science to ride capacity, queue design, and the psychological effects that queues have on park visitors. Quite simply, it's important to always have people in line because it shows that a ride is popular. Crowds draw more crowds.

Empty queues send a message to passersby that an attraction might not be a good one.

However, there's a fine line (yes, pun intended) between a well-designed attraction queue and one that works poorly. While you want people in line, the more time patrons spend in line, the less time they spend being separated from their money in shops and restaurants. So, it's important that ride queues, and ride capacity, are set up properly to ensure there is always the right amount of energy visible to those nearby.

For a perfect case study of this principle, we can look to the *Carousel of Progress*, a classic attraction that was originally designed for the 1964 World's Fair, a venue that was expected to draw 100,000 visitors per day. The attraction therefore had a theoretical capacity to meet needs that would far exceed any crowds at Disneyland, where it was later installed. Since Disneyland in the 1960s only had a daily capacity of around 60,000 people, and the attraction was designed to handle almost double that volume of visitors, the queue and ride itself often appeared empty. Anyone who has hosted an event for 50 people in a venue that holds 1,000 knows the feeling. To some, the attraction seemed like a failure once it was installed at Disneyland, but in reality, this had nothing to do with a lack of interest in the ride. It was merely the fact that the ride was designed to handle more visitors per hour than Disneyland could possibly supply. The *Carousel of Progress* consistently processed as many, or more visitors per day as any of the other popular Disneyland rides, yet the queue and ride were constantly empty.

Just like a quality queue, your preshow is an opportunity to excite people and create energy that will often boost participation and make your event or campaign even more successful. When done well, the enthusiasm may create a "pre-party" feeling among your guests. Conversely, if you fail to think about the preshow, you might be setting yourself up for failure, whether that failure is authentic or just in the public's perception. Those who have had to cancel or postpone a great event due to lack of interest know this feeling.

Stories Have Wonderful Endings

Without a solid opening or preshow, your guests might not pay attention to the story itself. Your preshow is critical for enticing your members to attend your event, participate in your campaign, or choose to send their child to your school. But just as important as the opening that primes your audience for the amazing upcoming experience, is the big feel-good ending that drives your message home!

Each situation is different, so there's no one way to script your post-show. One situation might call for an email or letter sent afterward thanking your participants, explaining the impact they made or the goal they helped reach. Another might be in the form of a picture posted on social media so that your guests' friends and family can see what they participated in and become jealous that they did not attend the event themselves.

The problem that you'll run into is that while "and they lived happily ever after" is easy to accomplish in a fully scripted environment, such as a book, film, or ride, for all the planning we do, there's no way to know what will happen in the real world. No matter how well you plan, every once in a while, your campaign or event will start off as a romance and end as a horror.

But, as we know—a problem is really just an opportunity to be creative!

Since you have the opportunity to write your postshow *after* the event or campaign is over, you can turn any outcome into a positive! Didn't have the turnout you hoped? Thank your participants for attending the "intimate" gathering. Didn't raise as much money as you expected? That means each donor's contribution was that much more meaningful. It also means that what you had originally hoped would be your "happily ever after" message is actually "to be continued ...," turning your donors into your story's heroes as they spread your message and help rally more support.

Just as you did with your preshow, don't look at your postshow messaging as a painful process. Once again—this is your chance to turn something that many see as an obligation, or choose to skip entirely, into a positive! This is your chance to leave your constituents with smiles on their faces and a good feeling that will stay with them long after the event is over.

At theme parks, there are some attractions where you step away from the ride vehicle already planning what ride to visit next, and then there are those rides that turn the exit into an attraction of its own.

Disneyland's *Haunted Mansion* show building was built outside the berm that visually separates the guests in the park from the "real world," and thus requires transporting guests from the queue entrance to the ride itself. Rather than using the queue itself to do the job, a "stretching room" elevator brings visitors down below the level of the berm, and a corridor of creepy paintings and sculptures delivers visitors to the loading zone. Following the conclusion of the ride, guests are brought back to the open air of New Orleans Square via an escalator ride. Imagineers took advantage of these necessary transportation hurdles by beginning the story as a preshow during the walk to the "doom buggy" ride vehicles and by adding a small character named Little Leota to the escalator ride out, inviting guests to "hurry back, and don't forget to bring your death certificate." The preshow and postshow elements are so well done that guests who aren't aware of the ride's blueprint don't realize that these pieces are solutions to problems. In fact, the stretching room elevator and Little Leota are highlights of the attraction rather than feeling like filler. There's no reason why your preshow and postshow can't be as enjoyable as these!

Even better are attractions like *Splash Mountain* and *Buzz Lightyear Astro Blasters*, which give riders something personalized to look forward to in the exit queue. Guests can often be seen running toward the video screens as they disembark, where they can see pictures of themselves screaming in terror as they plummet down a huge plume, or in deep concentration as they take aim at another target. Of course, those riders in-the-know have fun posing for these otherwise candid shots, adding an entirely different element to the ride photos.

Imagine the excitement guests will feel when they see the photos from your event posted the next day, or when they are announced as the winner of a raffle following your event. And imagine the surprise the next week when the postal carrier delivers a picture of their family in a magnetic picture frame with your logo on it, and a hand-written note thanking them for participating in your incredibly successful program, with an invitation to join you at the next one.

Even more than the excitement of seeing themselves in pictures or videos is the feeling of accomplishment they'll share knowing that they helped you meet your goal. Your postshow will not only give them the "happily ever after" they were looking for but will reinforce the important role they played in making that happen.

Stories Can Turn Negatives Into Positives

In the example of the barbeque, you'll notice that not only did we begin the story with the first event publicity and could use a postshow to continue it all the way past the event itself, but we turned what is normally a formality, and sometimes a tedious process of informing, RSVPing, and reminding, into a playful and hopefully enjoyable experience for the guest and for you—the employee who is always looking for new creative outlets!

Disney Imagineers take advantage of this opportunity all the time with ride queues. Standing in long lines is a necessity that no guest looks forward to, but in addition to potentially adding or zapping energy from the park, lines serve as crowd control, and in some cases, as a means of transporting guests from the main thoroughfare to the ride loading zone.

Similar to the challenge faced with the *Haunted Mansion*, when they wanted to add a new attraction to Adventureland in California's Disneyland, Imagineers were faced with the harsh reality that there was simply no more room inside the berm that separates the park from the outside world. They took a page from the *Haunted Mansion* and *Pirates of the Caribbean* playbooks by placing the *Indiana Jones Adventure* show building, in which the ride itself is housed, outside the berm. However, they still faced the challenge of the nearly half-mile walk from the ride entrance near the *Jungle Cruise*, to the loading platform.

Where many would see the long distance as a potential deal breaker, Imagineers saw opportunity. The design team was given the gift of a long, winding corridor in which to tell a lengthy preshow story, setting the stage as the visitor meanders through an archeological dig site, explores caves, passes ropes and equipment, comes across boobie traps, and even discovers a few Easter eggs. The queue literally begins telling the ride's story from the moment the guests enter, and on days when the park is not crowded, and the line doesn't stretch through the entire half-mile cave, guests who don't spend time slowly exploring the cave can feel like they're missing out on an important part of the attraction. This same concept is used in *Expedition Everest* and *Avatar, Flight of Passage* in Disney World's Animal Kingdom (among many other attractions at parks around the world), where long queues are unavoidable. Imagineers see these challenges as opportunities, and so should you!

We're often presented with challenges in our nonprofit environment, whether it be the need to constantly remind our members why they are supposed to love us, or in dealing with changes and restrictions brought on by something like a global pandemic. Look at these as opportunities rather than drawbacks! When you have no choice but to overcome the odds, you have a chance to try something new and different. Just like the queue designers for *Indiana Jones Adventure*, you can think of challenges as blank slates to put your creative imprint on. Sure, you can do the bare minimum (as most amusement parks do, by constructing an hour-long ride queue that's nothing more than metal chains leading you left, then right, then left again), but if there's one thing you should have picked up on by reading this book, it's that you should look at every choice as an opportunity to do more!

***

"OK," Shoshana said, somewhat confrontationally, "so, our job moving forward is to basically, at the beginning of each year, pick a creative intent, and theme, and figure out the overall story for the year—which may or may not be an actual story—separate it into 'chapters' that each have their own focuses, and then make sure every program and campaign fits into that theme and story, while also potentially having their own independent stories, and preshows, and postshows. That sounds like a lot of work. Right?"

"Yes, it is a lot of work," I responded. "And it's going to take time to get comfortable with that sort of thinking and master planning. It's going to take a lot of dedication at first, but eventually, it will become second nature to phrase things in ways that make your members the heroes, and take them on some sort of quest. But as you saw with the barbeque example, you don't necessarily have to change everything to make it work. You're basically here to do two things—raise money and serve the community. Fundraising always involves some sort of story that explains the reason people should support us. So, you aren't changing anything there, other than making that story connect to the master plan. And the programming itself—you're also not changing. You're just getting creative about how it connects to your theme, so that it all feels cohesive."

Shoshana rolled her eyes, but I could tell I was getting through to her.

"But I want to mention one more thing, since not everyone works at a small nonprofit like this one: In this chapter, you might have noticed the use of 'campaign' and 'event' when describing how each of the story elements fit into the nonprofit landscape. It's important to realize that even though these facets of the organizational calendar are prime opportunities to work with stories, they aren't the only times to tell stories. Even if your organization has no physical events and your mission is raising money to build wells in Africa, or providing mental health support to those in poverty, everything you do can incorporate some or all of what you learned here.

"For example, schools can use preshow to attract new students. Themes, guides, and heroes can make a student's trip through elementary or high school more meaningful. And postshow concepts can be used to maintain relationships with alumni. If properly planned, and with the support of everyone, including the admissions director, teachers, fundraisers and head of school, a child's experience over the course of many years can be told as a single story! How magical is that!"

"Very magical," Vanessa said. "But what did you mean by 'in this chapter?'"

The Takeaways

- Stories are the best way to connect with people and retain their attention.
- A theme is important to help keep your story focused from start to finish and to make sure it aligns with your goals.
- Your story should feel organic—as if the event or campaign was built into the story, rather than feeling like pieces of the story were added as an afterthought.
- Use the idea of chapters to define the beginning and end of different pieces of the story and prevent mistakes such as having multiple fundraisers overlapping each other, or too many events scheduled at the same time. Be sure that each chapter is distinct but also that all chapters are connected to one another.

- Stories should have a challenge (something your guests need to accomplish), a guide (your organization, who will help them accomplish the challenge), and most importantly, a hero (the guest themselves).
- Your organization is not the hero—always make the guest the hero. By making it their story, not yours, they will feel more connected.
- Stories are not always linear tales—sometimes a story can be the hero's transformation or a new understanding by participating in a number of events.
- Use preshow to set up your story and get people excited before your event or campaign begins.
- Postshow is a good way to keep people engaged, prepare them for what comes next, and turn a negative, such as a failed event or fundraiser, into a positive.

Next Steps

- The concepts in this chapter might have been confusing, since they were all thrown at you at once. Visit thenonprofitimagineers.com to download resources and worksheets that will help you use stories for your campaign and events.

CHAPTER 6

Imagineering Principles

Anna and Rico immigrated to the United States shortly after they married and chose the serene and charming streets of Anytown, USA, to raise their three children. Hector, the eldest of their three children, rarely saw his father, who, as a career Air Force officer, was often away. In many ways, Hector helped raise his younger sisters, and always had a serious and deliberate nature to his actions.

With a thick head of hair, short beard, and horn-rimmed glasses, Hector, now in his early 30s, takes pride in his work as office manager at the NCC, but is careful to never speak of his ties to Anytown. He confided in me that once he referred to a "groaner" as a "dad joke," but he doesn't think anyone noticed and has been careful not to do it again.

I gave Hector a firm pat on the back as I declared, "Today is field trip day! Enough sitting in a room. We need to move our bodies. Let's see things we don't normally get to see. Where should we go?"

JJ, Shoshana, Hector, Phil, and Vanessa stood outside the NCC lobby as the sun peeked through the leafless clattering branches of the birch trees, wondering why we had to leave the comfort of the conference room on a frigid and windy morning such as this.

"How about if we walk to that thing at the other end of Main Street. The tall gold thing."

"The pretzel."

"That's a pretzel?" I asked JJ.

"That's what we call it. It's not really a pretzel."

"It's not really anything," Shoshana added. "Around fifteen years ago, they wanted to build a big 'destination' sculpture in Town Square Park—sort of like the giant bean in Chicago. But they totally overthought it. They commissioned an artist to create a huge knot—you know—because we're Nottatown …"

"Ahh," I said. "But that's not a knot."

"No—so he made these models and the town voted on the design, and then the guy installed the giant knot, but it looked like a huge pretzel. So we all started calling it the pretzel," Shoshana explained.

"That guy was a hack," Vanessa said.

"Total hack. And there's speculation that he was from Anytown," JJ said, looking in Hector's direction. "But anyway, it was such an embarrassment to the city council that they decided to untie the knot."

"You're not serious," I said in disbelief.

"Nice groaner," Vanessa chuckled. "And yes, we're serious. They spent a ton of money literally untying the knot with a crane and two tractors. Channel 4 reported live from it daily. Took almost a week. Now it looks more like a McDonald's french fry than a pretzel, but the name stuck."

"Why don't they just get rid of it?"

"Well, they string lights from it to make it a giant Christmas tree, and each Memorial Day they do these fireman races where they have to climb the french fry," Hector explained. "So, it's actually become somewhat utilitarian."

"Well, let's head that way. I want to see it up close," I said.

We continued walking toward the pretzel, window shopping along the way. "I love your Main Street," I said. "It's so authentic."

"Yeah—So much better than Anytown's Main Street," JJ said, looking again in Hector's general direction. Hector didn't look up. "Have you been there?" JJ asked. I shook my head. "Theirs is basically one of those fake Disneyfied outdoor malls where it's actually just one big structure designed to look like different storefronts. Our buildings are real—some dating back to the 1700s."

"I do love your store names. You really leaned into the whole pun thing."

We walked by Sew It Seems, Buy the Way, and a sandwich shop named Pita Pan. Vanessa stopped to admire the new iPhone in Tech It Easy as we shivered in the chilly shadow of the building. Eventually, we completed the three block trek from the NCC to The Pretzel, schmoozing about weekend plans and complaining about how every other day that week had been 10° warmer.

When we finally reached our destination, a figure emerged from behind The Pretzel. The middle-aged gentleman in a Hawaiian shirt, jeans, and a leather jacket greeted us with a warm smile.

"JJ, Hector, Vanessa, Shoshana, Phil," I said, pointing to each as I said their names, "I'd like you to meet Steve, a former Imagineer." Their eyes widened and their posture improved.

"Pleasure to meet all of you," Steve said as he shook each of their hands.

"Wait, so this 'field trip' was just a very long, drawn out reveal? We could have done this in the warmth of the building."

"That might be true, Vanessa, but just like the cemetery thing, there's a reason why we're here."

"The cemetery thing?" Steve asked.

"You're finally going to tell us why you did the cemetery thing?" JJ said, perking up.

"Nevermind," I said.

We sat around a picnic table for a couple of minutes, getting to know Steve, and quickly acknowledged that it was far too cold to be sitting around a picnic table on a day like today. "Did you notice how while we were moving, our bodies were warm and the conversation flowed," Steve said. "As soon as we lost that kinetic energy, the mood shifted."

"Oh god," Phil said. "Steve's doing it too. This was all just a setup for a lesson."

"Yup!" I said with a big grin, as Steve pulled out a binder, opened it up to a diagram labeled "kinetics" and pointed at it using a short pointer with a Mickey Mouse hand at the end.

Imagineering 101: Kinetics

Picture yourself walking down Main Street at Disneyland. Ahead of you is a horse-drawn carriage and behind you a double decker bus, both moving at a slow and steady pace. In each storefront are displays filled with small figures representing classic Disney films, dancing, flying, and swimming through vibrant scenery. Lively and unmistakably-Disney music fills the air, along with the smell of fudge wafting from the candy shop where a cast member in a red and white striped shirt is dipping enormous green apples in caramel. At the far end of Main Street, rocket ships rise and fall hypnotically, a balloon vendor carries an impossibly large bouquet of Mickey-shaped helium balloons, and gas-powered street lamps flicker with warm orange flames. You could be the only person walking down Main Street, yet the setting still feels alive! That's the power of kinetics.

Simply put, kinetics is the energy of motion. Although technically it's a physics term that you probably first learned from an old episode of *Sesame Street*, kinetics has its place in the Imagineering world because of the psychological energy that comes from interacting with things in motion.

Odds are you're already using kinetics in a variety of ways at your organization.

If you have a physical building that guests visit, you probably have a TV screen playing a slideshow (hopefully with pictures that they or someone they know are in). It's something that visitors see that creates motion, drawing attention to it, and giving a little bit of visual stimulation, just like a spinning barbershop pole or an inflatable figure that dances in the wind outside a shop.

But kinetics doesn't have to literally be motion—sometimes we can add this sort of energy by making changes. Disney Imagineers discovered long ago that by incorporating temporary themes and overlays into their parks and attractions, they can generate significant interest, enthusiasm, and most importantly, crowds. Transforming *It's a Small World* into *It's a Small World Holiday* by adding Christmas decorations and adjusting the music to include *Jingle Bells* and *Deck the Halls*, draws massive crowds at the end of each calendar year. The same is true for a number of other attractions, including *The Haunted Mansion* and *Jungle Cruise*, as well as fireworks and parades.

You can do the same! Add bright colors where normally things are dull, such as on the name placard outside your door, which most people ignore as they walk by your office. Put graphics on floors using vinyl stickers, or near your reception desk, where normally all you see is a blank space. Make small but dramatic changes that will cause your repeat visitors to say, "hey—something's different! I like it!" And prompt your new visitors to say, "That's clever! Why don't we do that where I work?"

You might even add invigorating music rather than elevator muzak to your lobby or outdoor space.

Kinetics doesn't need to be limited to your actual building. You might not realize it, but you've already used kinetics very effectively at past events. Traditional galas—the most "because we've always done it that way" of all events—almost always take advantage of kinetics. The evening begins in one space for drinks and hors d'oeuvres. Everyone is then ushered into another space for dinner. As the meal concludes, the lighting dims, the music increases in decibels, and the energy of the room changes once again. Three hours in one room, around one table, with the same set of eight tablemates, might be excruciating. But, when changes of space, lighting, sound, and even forced movement from one location to another are involved, attendees are reinvigorated.

Similarly, you can use kinetics in your extended campaigns by making changes to keep them fresh. The best campaigns are constantly in motion. They change over time. They don't get stale and lifeless. They are kinetic. Hopefully, when you remind people about your annual campaign every few months, you send out a slightly different e-mail or print mailing with an update in order to keep a sense of momentum—a sense of kinetic energy. Each update tells a different part of your story or contains new information that attracts attention and helps your supporters feel something new. That change might even encourage a donor to give a second or third donation.

Keep in mind, though, constant motion isn't necessarily better than standing still, especially if you're just doing the same thing over and over. You're in constant motion during your drive home, yet there are plenty of times where you leave work, end up at home, and are so completely zoned out that you don't remember the ride at all. If you're concerned that people are losing interest, even though your campaign is chugging along in autodrive, take a page from *Splash Mountain*! (Author's Note: Between the time this book was written and the time it was published, Disney announced plans to retheme *Splash Mountain* as *Tiana's Bayou Adventure*. The new attraction is set to open more than a year after publication. Although the story and theme will be different, it is my expectation that the floorplan of the attraction will remain the same, and the ideas discussed will continue to apply.)

Personally, I hate drops. I love *Splash Mountain*, but the horrid drop that comes just before the end of the ride is nerve-wracking every time. Disney Imagineers know this about me, so they do something very tricky. They make me stand in a queue overlooking the largest drop and force me to hear the screams of the riders repeatedly plummeting to their demise.

But that's not all! Once we're finally on the ride, they continue to build dread with a few evil tricks. Not long after we launch, a lift hill takes us up a moderate climb, then drops us down a small flume. Two more lifts take us higher and higher, as we again get glimpses of riders in other logs plummeting down inevitable drops. Just when we settle in to observe the light-hearted scenery of the dark ride, we experience a drop, and then when we least expect it, another drop. Neither of these are "the" drop, but to a first-time rider, or one who hates drops in general, each of these fake-outs sends us through a cycle of fear, dread, relief, and then more dread that the biggest drop is yet to come. They are playful tricks that keep us engaged and remind us that this isn't your standard dark ride.

Ultimately, when we get to "the" hill, there's no doubt about it. We once again climb up and up and up, slowly summit the apex, and then experience a drop that, to the best of my recollection, lasts at least eight minutes. It's truly, truly awful. But once the anxiety melts away, there's a treat waiting for us! A grand finale with a jubilant rendition of zippity-do-da celebrates our triumphant achievement and dozens of animatronic animals sing and dance for us. The reward for a solid effort.

Many campaigns—especially annual campaigns—are like a drive home after a long day. People start to tune them out after a while, either because they already donated or because they didn't care to donate from the start. If your campaign will be running for a long period of time, and you fear people might start tuning it out, consider breaking it into multiple pieces, each with their own goals and rewards. Add playful milestones or challenges along the way for your community to overcome and to keep them on their heels and having fun. Create moments of urgency as you near each milestone, as a way of attracting attention and bringing in new donations. Use creative videos (not just your CEO doing a talking head) to share your progress and remind people why their participation is important. Send out print materials and e-mails with new headlines and information that fits within the overall theme and story of your campaign but that haven't been spotlighted yet. Just as with *Splash Mountain*, develop a few cycles of fear, dread, and relief ... or something more appropriate for your goals, to keep the kinetic energy and attention of your members.

***

"OK—So, you marched us all the way out here through the bitter cold in order to drive this kinetics-warms-us-up point home," Vanessa said very matter-of-factly, zipping up her hoodie as high as it would go. I looked at Steve and he looked back at me as we nodded in agreement that it worked just as expected. "You do realize," Vanessa continued, "that kinetic energy doesn't warm you—heat is actually *thermal* energy, and it's what is lost when you're forced to be outside on a cold day, using up your potential energy."

We stopped nodding at each other.

"You marched us out here in order for us to use up our potential energy, and not produce enough thermal heat to overcome the heat lost through convection when the wind blows against our skin." I wasn't sure she was totally correct, but she said it so quickly, and with such conviction!

"Oh snap!" JJ gloated. "The student becomes the teacher." He held out his fist but Vanessa refused to bump it, choosing instead to keep both hands in her warm pockets. "Maybe Vanessa should teach the next thing. What topic are we talking about next? How we can still get sunburns even on freezing cold days?" JJ said, turning to Steve.

"Actually, I was going to talk about weenies," Steve said with a completely straight face.

I could see everyone's mind racing to find the perfect joke but also weighing the HR consequences of saying anything inappropriate out loud.

"Vanessa," Steve continued, knowing that he had very little sexual harassment liability in this particular scenario, "what can you tell us about weenies?" Everyone giggled, not just at the question itself, and the seriousness that Steve presented it with, but at the thought of Vanessa sharing this story with her girlfriend later that night over dinner. Vanessa was a good sport and let Steve sheppard the conversation back to a more serious place.

"How about if we start walking back toward the nice, warm Community Center down there at the other end of Main Street and I'll fill all of you in." Steve pointed toward the art deco building with the American flag waving in front of it as he began to slowly walk toward it.

Imagineering 101: Weenies

There's some debate about how the name came about. Some believe a weenie refers to a hot dog cart placed far away, luring crowds from one side of a street to another. Others claim weenies are hot dogs that Walt Disney used to dangle in front of his dog in order to attract her attention. Regardless, weenies have been in the lexicon of Disney Imagineers since Walt first envisioned building Disneyland and continue to be used today.

A weenie attracts your attention, bringing your eye, and hopefully your entire body and those of your family, in a particular direction.

Once again, picture yourself walking down Disneyland's Main Street. This time, dodging horse-drawn carriages and a herd of people with no sense of social etiquette or awareness of anything around them. What keeps you moving from the train station toward the hub? The castle!

Once you reach the hub, what beckons you toward your next destination? Perhaps, the elevated rock work of *Big Thunder Mountain Railroad* in Frontierland, a rocket ship at the far end of Tomorrowland or the carousel that you can see through the gate of the castle. All of these are weenies.

After you visit a land, and you decide that you are ready to move on to the next adventure, the castle is once again there as a visual magnet to help you get your bearings and center you as you choose where to go next.

Walt spent a great deal of time analyzing Disneyland's design with regard to sight lines. He walked the orange groves that would soon be replaced by pirate ships and flying elephants and envisioned not just what it would look like to enter the park and walk toward the castle in the morning, but what it would look like to walk down Main Street toward the exit that same evening. He wanted to ensure that in each direction there was a visual weenie to draw you forward, regardless of whether you were coming or going. This is one of the reasons why the Main Street *Disneyland Railroad* station is elevated and centered in front of the entrance plaza for those entering, and right at the end of Main Street for those leaving.

Weenies aren't just architectural features—they exist in almost everything we do. The cover art of this book is a weenie, attracting you to read it (thank you, by the way—really appreciate it!). Video games use weenies, such as rays of light or tall buildings in their three-dimensional landscapes, to draw you from a starting point, through a level, in the direction you need to go to complete the challenge.

When thinking about a layout, whether it be for day-to-day operations, or for a large (or small) event, take a moment to visualize the space as it is and what it could be. Stand at the end of your main hallway—is there something interesting to draw you in as you walk toward a meeting room or office? As you (and your guests) leave the meeting, does anything draw you back out toward the main entrance, giving you a pleasant and energetic "farewell"? Is there anything welcoming your guests from the street to your parking lot, or from the parking lot to your front door? Does anything thank them for visiting as they leave? These things might seem superfluous, but Imagineering is about doing what others don't bother doing, and every detail makes a difference in telling our stories and improving our guests' experiences.

Now picture yourself in the center of a large hall or beautiful courtyard—the location of your next major fundraising event. Look in each direction. Is there a focal point on each wall, ensuring that your visitors are stimulated, energized and reminded of why they are there? Photobooth backdrops, balloon arches, large pictures of your members in action, or even just your logo projected on a wall are all ways to jazz up what would otherwise be dark, wasted space.

Weenies help establish a visual language for an area or for your organization. Using pictures, colors, and large descriptive words in your organization's font, all help set the tone for what's ahead. At a large event, the visual language might set the stage for an evening of unmitigated fun, which is very different from the visual language that your normally serious organization uses the rest of the year.

In some cases, where your building or event has different spaces for different purposes, weenies help identify what a space is used for and draw different types of people to the directions that will suit them best. If you work at a school that ranges from kindergarten through 12th grade, a large jungle gym draws children toward the playground and establishes that area as the elementary-school zone, while a more sophisticated series of signs and wall art might set the tone for areas reserved for high schoolers.

In the nonprofit world, weenies don't always have to be a physical element. Your fundraising goal can be a weenie, drawing your donors in the direction that you want them to go. Adding a "thermometer" or visual representation of your current progress toward your goal will help people understand how their donation will impact your fundraising effort. Knowing that you might not make it through the year unless you raise an additional $100,000 and need their help now more than ever, or letting them know that their contribution can help put you over the top, can be weenies that lead to a donation. A raffle or giveaway can be a weenie to draw donors in and encourage them to give more. Friendly pictures and language on your website are weenies that lead online visitors toward valuable information.

Weenies can be invaluable in making your campus and organization more exciting and appealing; however, there is one important point to clarify—"weenies" and "signs" are not the same thing. There is a distinction between a directional arrow and a weenie. While a large sign might draw your attention, it is only a weenie if there is some sort of payoff. Just as Walt's dog received a tasty treat when she approached Walt and was given the hot dog dangling in his grasp, people who go through the effort of approaching the weenie at the end of a long walk, or donating to your campaign because you made it interesting to them, should be rewarded.

At Disneyland, the reward is a new experience, whether it's visiting an attraction, seeing a site that otherwise might not have been seen, or unveiling a part of the park the visitor might not have otherwise noticed. How will your community members be rewarded? Perhaps, it's something as simple as a good feeling when your fundraising thermometer reaches the 100 percent mark thanks to their donation, made even more special by a handwritten thank you note sent in the mail. Or maybe they are rewarded with a gift or invitation to an event that is reserved for committed volunteers or major donors. Make sure your weenies, and the rewards that they represent, are worth reaching in order to keep your constituents interested in making the trek to reach the next one.

Imagineering 101: Forced Perspective

Weenies might give you and your members something to focus on in the distance, but there's more to keeping them looking in the right direction and seeing things the way you want them to be seen.

Cinematographers will tell you the only thing that matters is what's in the frame. It doesn't matter what kind of chaotic mess happens behind the camera—the only thing the audience sees is what is in the camera's frame.

During the COVID-19 pandemic, when business became virtual, and all meetings were held in video conference apps, we learned that we could have our colleagues believe the story that our homes were clean and tidy, and our kids were perfect homeschooled angels, simply by closing the door and keeping the camera pointed at a small, organized frame of reference in the corner of the room, rather than the side of the room that looked like it had been hit by a tornado.

The problem that we eventually realized when restrictions were lifted and friends were once again able to visit in person, much like Walt Disney's realization when he built his first theme park that allowed guests to step into his three-dimensional cartoon and movie settings, is that in real life, people can look in every direction. Painted plywood facades angled in one direction won't convince a tourist that they are walking inside a movie any more than a few clean bookshelves will convince friends of your cleanliness once they come over and see the garbage overflowing with empty bottles of wine. Spaces need to look every bit as realistic facing north as they do east. Buildings and mountains need to be as convincing looking up, as bodies of water do looking down.

Even though we know the lands aren't real, in order to make Disney theme parks as convincing as possible, Imagineers use a technique called forced perspective.

The most shared example of forced perspective is found on Main Street, where the exterior facade of the buildings is full scale on the first floor, two-thirds scale on the second floor, and one-half scale on the third floor. By making the top floors slightly smaller, it gives the impression of height that isn't actually there. Had they built Main Street to full scale, the buildings would tower 50-feet on both sides of the visitor, making it feel like a cavernous canyon rather than a pleasant turn-of-the-century town.

At the end of Main Street is the iconic castle, which again uses forced perspective to make it appear taller than it actually is. In some cases, such as Anaheim's Disneyland, the castle's height was determined mainly by budget—the larger the castle, the more it would cost, and Walt Disney ran out of money many times during construction. In other Disneylands and Magic Kingdoms, the height was determined by building codes or the goal of not having to place a red blinking light atop the spire, which is a requirement in Florida for any structure over 200 feet. How do you make a 198-foot castle appear taller than it is? Forced perspective.

Forced perspective isn't always about tricking the eye. By only having one entrance to Disneyland—a practice that wasn't common to amusement parks prior to the building of Disneyland, Imagineers forced visitors down a specific path—past the train station, through town square, up Main Street, eventually to the hub and castle. Walt could set the stage and tell the story that he wanted to tell prior to visitors continuing in the direction of their choosing.

By controlling sightlines with trees, signs, buildings, and even mountains, Imagineers force guests to explore each land and discover what it has to offer. The story is revealed piece by piece as the visitor is immersed in the land.

Ultimately, at the end of the day, families are forced to once again make their way down Main Street, where smells of chocolate fudge are pumped into the air, enticing one more treat for the road. Large window displays draw children to stuffed animals and light-up wands, and parents have no choice but to buy overpriced souvenirs for their little ones. There's no way around it. There's only one exit.

So, how can you use this Imagineering trick to your advantage, when your board won't let you tear down and rebuild your campus at two-thirds scale, even if it'll help tell your story? Never fear—there's still forced perspective in your future!

At its core, forced perspective is all about controlling information, having people look where you want them to look and see what you want them to see.

Revisiting our discussion about *Splash Mountain*—forced perspective was used by Imagineers when they forced us to stand in a queue overlooking the largest drop. It was again used when they added smaller lift hills that resembled the final, horrible, 45,000ish-foot lift hill. They revealed the information to us that they wanted us to have, in order to build suspense and tell the story that they wanted to tell. You can do the same!

For example, you don't need to reveal your entire brilliant annual campaign concept all at once. You might tease a small piece of your campaign at first, to entice your donors and build suspense. Over the campaign's 9-month lifecycle, reveal one element at a time, building upon the last, until the entire story is revealed. You might do this to keep people excited about what comes next, or use this technique if your campaign has so many details and moving parts that your constituents will be confused if given all of the information at once.

Forced perspective could also be effective in situations where you start off vague or broad, and then focus more and more with each iteration. A series of progressive event notifications, first with a general "Save the date," then with a slightly more detailed invitation, and then progressive messages with details about the event and honorees, is a good way to provide new information and keep people interested over the course of several months leading up to an event. With this form of forced perspective, by focusing only on one element at a time, you can keep your marketing fresh—maintaining kinetic energy over the course of a campaign that might last months.

Even if your broader campaign doesn't employ forced perspective, you can take advantage of this technique with individual donors. For example, when speaking with a supporter who has preschool-aged children at home, you might focus on the programming available for young families. When speaking with a different donor who loves nature, you might tell her about your goals of adding more outdoor programming, "should the funding be available…." Odds are you already do this without realizing that you are using an Imagineering technique similar to what Walt used to build his park 70 years ago!

In its most basic form, forced perspective is about having people see something the way you want them to see it. That might mean hiding things you don't necessarily want them to see, or framing things a certain way, the same way bright lights might attract your attention to your right, in hopes that you don't see the electrical panel on the wall to your left.

Forced perspective helps you disguise less-sexy uses of contributions, such as organizational overhead, when soliciting donations. As much as your donors would love for 100 percent of their donation to go toward your program, it's simply not possible. But by offering to have someone's entire donation go toward "youth programming," you can please that donor and cover things like your youth director's salary or the cost of having maintenance and security available during youth programs at your building. There's no need to point this out, though. Simply force your donor's perspective away from the overhead and infrastructure that their donation might help cover, and toward the game night itself that is now possible, thanks to their generosity.

Imagineering 101: Environmental Storytelling

Disneyland's Main Street is more than 800-feet long and takes close to ten minutes to walk from one end to the other. Visitors might be drawn toward the castle at the far end of the street, and they might be fooled by the scaled-down facades, but there's much more to Main Street than weenies and forced perspective. Deep down, Imagineers want you to absorb the entire story they spent so much time writing.

Disney theme park lands and attractions are fully immersive experiences. A complete story is told through the environment in which the visitor is placed. As folks walk through the property, each person will respond to different aspects of the theme and story. Some fall in love with the plants and trees, which are different in each land. Others will notice the architecture, signage, stonework on the ground, or the sounds and music heard over hundreds of hidden speakers. Because of the extensive effort put into the layers of detail, each time someone walks through the space, they will notice different things. Each visit to the Magic Kingdom tells a different story, and each direction a guest glances or meanders reveals new details. Over time, even on the hundredth visit, rather than becoming monotonous and boring, the land becomes even more meaningful and incredible.

Just like *Pirates of the Caribbean* or *It's a Small World*, themed lands tell a nonlinear story. Each person will start in a different spot of the story and absorb certain details while missing others. Some will enter from the north, and others from the south. Some will be so focused on pushing a stroller that they'll miss huge details but discover them later on. Children will see some details and adults will see others. Since environmental storytelling is nonlinear, it's not about beginning with "Once upon a time" and ending with "they lived happily ever after"—it's about making the visitor feel as if he is a character in a scene, with the opportunity to write his own story.

Your campaign certainly might be a linear story, with pieces purposely revealed one after another to transport the donor from beginning to end, but even if it isn't, as you tell your story, think about how environmental storytelling can help you connect with your members. By using different techniques to share your story, you can reach people in an assortment of ways. One person might first notice your social media post, another might see your print materials, and yet another might pause to take in the large banner you placed near the entrance to your building. As your campaign continues, and these members are exposed to different layers of your theme, they will form a stronger connection to your organization and campaign. By creating an immersive environment with unique ways to reach people, every direction they turn they will see a different piece of your story, and grow to love it more and more.

Environmental storytelling can be especially helpful when you have a major announcement or event to publicize. Rather than sending three emails each week for an entire month in hopes that they will pay attention to at least one of them, think about all of the different approaches you can take to telling that story. Use email, social media, phone calls, text messages, banners at your building, printed hand outs and updates to your website. Rather than feeling like they are being bombarded by endless, annoying emails, your constituents will receive the information from an assortment of environmental angles, and probably pay more attention than they would to incessantly repeating email messages.

Importantly, though, that doesn't mean that you should simply repeat the same advertisement in 15 different locations and mediums. A crucial part of environmental storytelling is that everything should feel organic, logical, and tell a *different* piece of the story. As you walk down Main Street, you might see advertisements for Disney's latest film release in every shop window, but at the candy shop, you will see a bag of lollipops with the hungriest of the movie's characters on it, in the magic shop, there might be a cutout of the smartest character performing a trick, and the *Main Street Cinema* might feature a trailer that you can't see on tv. Each piece of the story is designed to fit within that environment and target a specific segment of guests.

Think also about the way that large corporations use sponsorships. When Pepsi pays to have their ad inside a basketball arena, on a billboard next to the freeway and in a gossip magazine, they are building an immersive story. The ad that they play on television during a basketball game will be different from an ad that is run during Saturday morning cartoons. They're making themselves an integrated part of your environment, subconsciously making them a part of your story, whether that story includes the need for a cool drink while running errands with the kids in the back seat or the feeling of holding a cool bottle to your forehead after playing volleyball at the beach on a hot day. You can do the same thing by dropping subtle, targeted hints about your events, campaigns, or simply about your organization in various locations, with different mediums, and by sending different messages.

Environmental storytelling also makes your campaign more relatable to a larger number of people. If you only approached your campaign from one direction—only through social media or only with a paper mailer—you might be missing entire market segments who simply don't respond to that style of engagement. If your campaign advertisements only describe one way that you support the community, you might be missing the mark with important donors. By coming at them from all angles, you make your environment more immersive and increase your chances of connecting in at least one way with a much larger audience. Walking down Main Street, a child will respond to a plush toy and an adult will respond to a 1000-piece *Star Wars* jigsaw puzzle. A wealthy patron will be interested in purchasing a $5,000 crystal castle while a different visitor will only have the budget for a magnet. By having different options for different audiences, each person can form a connection in their own way. At your organization, one donor might be interested in making a small donation in honor of a friend's birthday, while another is mainly interested in a gift so large their name will end up on a building. Some might learn about your needs through Facebook and others by reading a postcard left on a friend's coffee table. Some will find out from their child, who begs to go to an event because he heard there will be free boba drinks there, and others might be enticed by details shared during a sermon by your clergy, or a short video by your executive director. Be sure you are coming at them from all angles, with a unified but creative approach created specifically for different target audiences, so that regardless of which direction they're looking, they see what you have to offer.

***

"OK, so, didn't you just basically say the same thing three different ways? Weenies, forced perspective and environmental storytelling? They're all basically just about making people look at what you're doing."

Steve gave me a "did I really come all this way to be criticized nonstop by this woman" look. I gave him an "I don't know. She's not always like this" look back.

"Look, Vanessa," I started, "there are some similarities, but this is a sort of layered approach. Each of these concepts—weenies, forced perspective and environmental storytelling - add layers to the experience that you're trying to build. Sure, you can just use one concept and do something that's OK, but that's not what Disney does, and that's not why we're here."

"Yeah," Steve continued, "There's a reason why Disney Imagineering is the gold standard of creativity. They don't take shortcuts. They don't fast track things. They are detail oriented. They look at everything from every angle. They do everything they can to get it right from the start, and then they look at it all again, and again, and again to make it even better. They plus everything, as often as possible."

"Nice segway," I said.

"Thanks," Steve replied, with a grin.

Imagineering 101: Plussing

Amusement parks in the 1950s tended to be dirty and loud. Disneyland, which most people thought would be yet another dirty and loud amusement park, was an expensive undertaking and banks didn't want to risk lending millions of dollars to help Walt build it. In fact, many funders were convinced that Disneyland, which originally had no ferris wheel or roller coasters, would fail simply because it was so different from anything that existed at the time.

Attempting to build something that no one had ever built before meant traditional lenders were reluctant to give Walt Disney anywhere near what he needed to fully fund construction. In the end, Walt agreed to produce a television show for ABC in exchange for their underwriting of a loan large enough to get started. Walt then used his personal savings, life insurance, and vacation home as collateral for other loans, and made agreements with an assortment of other lenders and sponsors to cobble together enough to cover the cost of construction. As opening day neared, and vendors began to go unpaid, things were so bad that some speculated that had opening day been delayed by a few months, the entire project might have gone bankrupt.

Barely able to make payroll, and still owing money to tradespeople and vendors who provided construction materials, revenue finally started flowing during the months after Disneyland's grand opening. While some businesspeople would immediately begin paying down their debts to lenders who were skeptical from the beginning, Walt had other ideas. He insisted on using a large portion of his profits to add more to his brand new park and improve the attractions that were already there. He insisted on plussing.

Plussing is the act of making something better. In blue sky meetings, plussing is common practice, building upon an idea and improving it incrementally rather than shooting it down and starting from scratch. In day-to-day life, plussing can happen anytime, anywhere. As I walk from my car to my office, I constantly notice areas where improvements can be made. Some require a note for maintenance, but others can be done right then and there. Picking up trash and straightening up materials in your lobby are both quick ways to plus your facility, as are purchasing an additional trash can to help prevent littering and adding brochure holders and display cases to keep materials looking organized.

Plussing keeps things looking and feeling fresh! It gets new people excited and keeps existing participants coming back.

Not all plussing is physical—it can happen during the process of developing a program or campaign too. Just as we learned earlier, innovation and progress happen more often when people talk and ideas mingle. Don't be afraid to bring your raw ideas to co-workers with different perspectives and disciplines to find out how they might plus them.

Their feedback might help fill gaps in your environmental storytelling or add kinetics to a campaign that would otherwise turn stale.

In situations where the same program repeats on a regular basis, plussing is a natural way to ensure you are constantly improving. Whether you hold a class that repeats every fiscal quarter for a new set of participants, or a religious service that repeats every week, if you make a concerted effort to improve one thing with each iteration, imagine the possibilities!

Keep in mind, plussing isn't restricted to the actual program or service itself. Clergy members shouldn't feel obligated to improve on the liturgy each week. Plussing can occur during the preshow (publicity and marketing), postshow (outreach and follow-up), and everywhere in between. At a church service, for example, you might plus the advertising, parking lot signage, security and greeting procedure at the front door, materials handed to the visitor as they enter, materials handed to the visitor as they exit, or message sent to visitors following the service (if information was collected), none of which have anything to do with the clergy and contents of the service itself. By making one small, incremental tweak each week or month, the visitor's experience will get better and better without any significant effort, and without making any change to the prayers, music, or sermon.

At a school, think about plussing the drop-off and pick-up routines. Plus your strategy for forming connections with parents during these sorts of moments that normally go ignored. Plus weekly e-mails that get sent home by teachers or your communications staff. Plus your students' experiences, so that they go home whistling your tunes and telling everyone they know that they love going to your school.

Having a tough time plussing what you already feel is a beautiful campus and a top-notch experience? Vibrant graphics and glossy card stock are nice, but have you considered the emotional impact? Do your signage, promotional materials, and even the art on the walls tell a story that your visitors truly connect with? Do they tell *their* story? Are *they* the hero? Are you the guide, standing by, ready to help them on their journey? Do you provide them with questions to think about while they are with you; questions that they'll continue to ponder long after they leave; questions that will lead them once again to your organization and build a lasting relationship?

Your answer might be "yes," in which case I ask you, when was the last time you updated those questions, challenges, or journey? Has it been there so long that it has become white noise that your lifelong, committed members walk right by? Are they still feeling challenged and motivated? Plussing isn't always about making something better. Sometimes it's about changing what's not necessarily broken but has run its course.

Imagineering 101: Hidden Mickeys

Walt Disney loved trains. He loved them so much that, when he purchased his 5-acre Holmby Hills estate, he purposely set aside 2 acres of hillside to build a 1:8 scale miniature train that he named the Carolwood Pacific Railroad. There was just one problem with his planned 2,600 foot track—a section of it ran through a piece of the property that his wife planned to use for a flower bed. Rather than change the route, Walt decided to build an s-shaped tunnel under the flower bed and to ensure everyone would be happy with the decision, he had a member of his legal team write up a contract giving his railway the right of way under the garden. His wife Lilian signed it, with his two daughters as witnesses, and he framed and hung the contract on a wall in their home.

Of course, there was absolutely no reason to have a lawyer write up a contract, but sometimes, it's the little extras that few, if any people, will see or know about, that make stories more fun and meaningful.

As Nonprofit Imagineers, this is not only something we have the opportunity to do—it's our obligation! We get to make everything more exciting by adding in little details, just like Walt did with his railroad, and just like Disney Imagineers do when designing most attractions and lands in theme parks.

In the case of *Big Thunder Mountain Railroad*, the Imagineers designed a western town near the queue, created signage corresponding to the characters and plot lines in the story, and planted small details along the ride track as well. In Anaheim Disneyland's ride, for example, the story tells of an earthquake that hit the region, leading to the abandonment of one of the mines. This story element is used to dress up one of the lift hills, during which falling debris surrounds the train, and the rider's narrow escape adds excitement to what is normally a slow and boring section of roller coaster track.

Even if your event or campaign doesn't have an obvious story line, or, at least, not one that is explained to the public, it can be a lot of fun to add special elements to your "show." In the non-Disney world, this practice is sometimes called "Easter eggs." When in the movie *Cars*, Lightning McQueen raced against a competitor with the number 84 and an Apple logo on its hood, that was an Easter egg paying homage to Pixar's former leader, Steve Jobs, who founded Apple in 1984. When in the film *Coco*, the characters walk by a wall containing a poster of the family from *The Incredibles*, drawn in the skeleton-style of Coco's Land of the Dead, that too was an Easter egg. And in the cathedral in Disney's animated version of the *Hunchback of Notre Dame*, where the shape of a Mickey Mouse head is used as the pattern of the building's railing, that was a special Easter egg, more commonly referred to as a hidden Mickey.

In the Disney world, hidden Mickeys are everywhere. Next time you're at a Disney park, keep an eye out for ordinary objects arranged in three circles to form the shape of Mickey's head. This can be anything from three plates on a table, to an electric guitar cable wound in just the right way. Sometimes hidden Mickeys require a keen eye, and sometimes, they're in plain sight. Ultimately, though, hidden Mickeys are an extra opportunity for creativity by the designers and add an extra layer of magic that neither enhances nor detracts from the story and theme. They are the kinds of things that, when noticed, make you think "that's clever."

I enjoy incorporating small details that no one will notice, but help me feel creative during a time when there might not be much room for creativity. It's my way of plussing something that might not otherwise need plussing, or putting my stamp on something that I have little control over. Working quite a bit in the Jewish community, I'm reluctant to call them Easter eggs … so let's just say these special touches are my own "hidden Mickeys."

Regardless of how you do it, the bottom line is that your goal is to provide the best possible guest experience in everything you do. Each interaction with your members or prospective donors should build upon the central theme and story that you predetermine before you launch your campaign or begin marketing your event, and should carry through to the post-show and beyond.

Guest experience is central, and while each of the ideas we've discussed might have a very small, almost imperceptible impact on your story, adding up all of these "magical moments," as Disney executives might call them, will make a dramatic difference in your product.

"It is this plethora of little wows, many of which seem fairly insignificant at the time, on which Quality Service depends," *Be Our Guest— Perfecting the Art of Customer Service*, an official publication of The Walt Disney Institute, explains, "If the little wows are delivered consistently and continuously, they add up to a big WOW!"

***

"So ... do more?" Vanessa was still unimpressed by Steve's presentation. "You're basically saying we just need to keep doing more? Every time we think we've done enough ... do more. That's the big, groundbreaking, drove-all-the-way-out-here-to-preach advice?"

Steve and I were both approaching our limit. I wasn't sure what was going on with Vanessa today—she could often get snippy in a playful way, but this seemed different.

We continued walking toward the building in silence, arms crossed, blowing into our hands, eager to get back to somewhere a bit warmer. Few words were spoken, for fear of Vanessa's unexplainable wrath.

I finally built up the courage. "Vanessa—despite what you might think, there really was a reason for what we did today. This 'Imagineering 101 chapter' of our workshop demonstrated exactly how kinetics and forced perspective work in real life. The Pretzel and the NCC building aren't fictional landmarks that some clever author just made up—they're real-life weenies that drew us from one end of the street to the other. The silly shop names and the backstory of The Pretzel—they might have seemed like extraneous non sequiturs—but they were actually little hidden Mickeys that, if you really think about it, cleverly go all the way back to the time that we first met. This whole town is one big, very, very clever exercise in environmental storytelling!"

The scowl on Vanessa's face began to soften.

"This!" I said, raising my arms dramatically, as Steve, clearly still thinking like a true Imagineer, started playing inspirational cinematic royalty-free music on his phone, "This is the big culminating moment—the crescendo—the end of our very clever story arc, that brought together so many concepts we've been exploring together! We've addressed our concerns, dug deep to tap into our innovative spirit, blue skied together, wrote stories together, plussed together, and now, as we reach the end of this one last session, this is your time to spread your wings and be great! To shoot for the moon! To make lemonade from lemons! To dance like nobody is watching!"

Vanessa still seemed unimpressed. Had I not thrown enough clichés at her?

"What, Vanessa?" I yelled. "This is your graduation! From here you launch into a world of magic and imagination where the only limit is the infinite blue sky! This is a good day! What could you possibly be so upset about?"

After a very long, tense pause, JJ broke the silence and spiritedly jumped in. "Well, as 'clever' as you clearly think it all was, I still don't understand half of what you were telling us yesterday about storytelling! I wouldn't say I'm 'upset,' but maybe that's part of it?"

"I still don't get the Innovator's Dilemma!" Phil yelled more loudly, with a grin on his face.

"I don't know what effervescent really means! I just love the way it sounds!" Shoshana screamed toward the sky, raising her arms to the heavens as if she was celebrating her freedom after breaking out of Shawshank Prison.

"I'm from Anytown!" Hector yelled in a somewhat subdued manner. "And yes—my father-in-law helped plan 'the pretzel prank' on you guys."

"I'm moving away!" Vanessa finally revealed in a gentle voice that seemed louder than any revelations that preceded it.

The group fell silent.

"Jen got a new job. We're moving to the East Coast. Just found out last night. I won't be here to do any of the fun stuff we've talked about this week. It's so not fair!" Nobody knew what to say as they looked around at one another. "Also, I hate puns!" Vanessa screamed cathartically toward the sky. "Even the smart ones are just soooooo stupid."

We walked toward the NCC front doors as each member of the team took their turn wishing Vanessa well.

"That was a weird couple of minutes," Steve said quietly to me under his breath. "And, honestly, after all that build up, I would have thought the big revelation was going to be something better than that she's moving to the East Coast. Kind of anticlimactic if you ask me."

"You wanna hear weird," JJ said, turning to Steve, "this guy held his first video conference with us from a cemetery."

"I was trying to do something new that would capture your attention! Clearly it did."

"Yeah. Very *clever*," JJ said with a wink.

We finally arrived back inside the NCC lobby and huddled around the floor heater on the side of the room. The mood of the group, just like our body temperatures, was noticeably warmer.

"OK. Can we get real for a minute?" Vanessa sincerely asked with a bit more levity, but still quite seriously. "Blue sky, story, kinetics, hidden Mickeys ... You've talked a lot about some very pie-in-the-sky topics—the kinds of things that sound good on paper, or to talk about in theory, but let's get real—It's 4PM and this is your last day here. Tomorrow, you're gone. A few weeks from now, I'm gone. And let's face it, I'm the glue that holds this place together." Vanessa brilliantly didn't break from her straight face. "I really want this to work, but everyone will have all their normal work to do without you pushing us and coaching us and without me covering for all of them. There will still be almost no budget. Realistically, what happens next? It's not like the story can just end here ... How do we actually do it?"

The Takeaways

- **Kinetics** is the Imagineering principle of adding energy by keeping things moving. This might mean literally adding motion to a space through video slideshows or upbeat music but can also be used to keep your campaign and events fresh and keep supporters interested over time.

- **Weenies** attract your supporters' attention. In physical spaces, weenies can draw people toward a destination or give them something inspiring to look at as they explore your campus or event. In fundraising campaigns, weenies can give donors a goal to reach.
- In Disney parks, **forced perspective** is a trick to make something appear differently than it actually is (a building that is only 25-feet tall, appearing to be three full stories). At your nonprofit, you can use forced perspective to have your supporters see information the way you want it to be seen—direct your supporters' attention toward the information most useful to them, in a way that will also benefit your organization.
- **Environmental storytelling** takes into account all of the different ways that people absorb information. Put your message out to different groups in ways that they will find useful and make sure that supporters absorb your story regardless which direction they are "facing."
- **Plussing** is the most basic Imagineering principle to start utilizing right away—always look for ways to improve what you are already doing, whether it is quick and simple tweaks, or requires planning, funding, and manpower.
- **Hidden Mickeys** are a fun way to flex your creative muscles by adding little, often unnoticed touches in your publicity, campaign, or event. They keep you motivated and provide layers of interest for your supporters to be surprised by.

Next Steps

- Head over to thenonprofitimagineers.com for more examples of each of the Imagineering principles we've covered and ideas to help you incorporate them into your planning and operations.

CHAPTER 7

Yes, But How Do We Actually Do It?

Each of our nonprofits performs different functions, and we're all in slightly different positions at our respective organizations—some of us are volunteers, some are board members, some are executives trying to inspire our staff, and some are the grunt workers trying to be more creative. But in a sense, we all have 40 hours of work to do each week, a budget that barely covers what we are already trying to do, and co-workers that mean well, but have their own drama to deal with. Let's set aside the previous six chapters of pie-in-the-sky, best-case scenario, so-optimistic-it-borders-on-unrealistic, pun-filled narrative that was, all things considered, really very clever and well done by the author, because it helped us understand how the principles of this book could be applied to our business … and look at some real-world, non-best-case-scenario ideas that might be helpful to anyone who doesn't live in a nonprofit fantasy land.

Begin the Conversation

If you're overworked, underpaid, and still want to make a lasting difference at your organization, a discussion with your boss never hurts. I guarantee, they will appreciate your enthusiasm and desire to improve the organization. They might not share your eagerness to make big, radical changes, but that's something we can address a little later on. Assuming they're open to new ideas, begin by discussing the mission, vision, and creative intent of your organization and the projects you're working on. Come into the meeting with recommendations for a few small adjustments to the organization or to your job description that will add value without making big waves. Explain to them how your suggestions will benefit them personally, and the organization as a whole. Start small, prove you know what you're talking about, and keep the conversation going from there. Perhaps, buy your boss a copy of this book so that she understands where you're coming from and what the underlying principles are behind your motivations.

Keep in mind, trust is earned. You need to prove that you're capable of thinking big *and* delivering on your promises. Don't expect the keys to the castle right away, but keep pursuing that goal, and little by little, you'll get there.

Identify your wants and needs on a personal level (you're someone who wants to do good and be successful, and needs support), and your wants and needs for your organization (you want the organization to use creativity to do more than it does right now, and be a model of how your industry should progress in the near future). It's possible that your boss or co-workers haven't thought about things the way you do and will gladly be on board with your suggestions once they understand them.

Of course, it's possible they won't understand your vision. Walt used to say, "If management likes my projects, I seriously question proceeding. If they disdain them totally, I proceed immediately." He was a firm believer that if his idea easily gained the approval of others, he wasn't dreaming big enough. Hopefully, if you share an idea that's easily agreed to, it's just the first step of a much grander plan that you're holding in your back pocket until a later date.

If they agree to your suggestions immediately, that's a wonderful start! But be prepared for some pushback or be ready to accept that you might only be able to accomplish a piece of your goal at first. Still, don't feel like you need to temper your bold ideas just to gain approval or to have the courage to bring them up in the first place. That's not how we Nonprofit Imagineers do things! Author and motivational speaker Pat Williams put it best—"Remove the limits from your imagination. Most of our limitations are actually self-imposed. We limit ourselves by worrying about the 'right' or 'proper' way to do things. The moment we place limits on imagination, creativity shuts down."

If you are the boss, and you're trying to inspire your crew to do more and think bigger, start with the same conversation as above. Explain what you're trying to do, get everyone a copy of this book, and take small steps toward your goal.

Have your team read a chapter every couple of weeks, and then discuss how you might integrate the concepts into your own habits. Utilize the discussion questions, worksheets, and resources at thenonprofitimagineers.com to turn theoretical concepts into real-world steps and sign up for my newsletter to continue to be motivated and creative on a regular basis.

As you start to transform your organization, explain that big changes happen slowly and that you expect a combination of small improvements through plussing, and up-front planning of the creative intent, theme, and story for the year. These alone will make a big difference to the organization without adding a significant amount of work to each employee's portfolio.

Ultimately, though, you—the boss—will need to keep your foot on the gas pedal and keep pushing your employees. Just be sure to do so in a respectful and realistic way. Lead by example. After all, they work at a nonprofit, which most likely means they are doing the job of 10 for-profit employees, for half the salary. Don't try to guilt them into doing more work than they already do with the old "make sacrifices for the greater good of the community" shtick. That's not fair to them and will lead to resentment. Rather, have an honest conversation and agree to be a partner and leader in guiding them in the right direction.

Create a Plan for Dealing With Concerns

Remember all those concerns from Chapter 2? Each one had a solution, and many of them, when properly addressed, were actually opportunities rather than hindrances. Here are some quick ideas to help you navigate those choppy waters.

Create a Test Environment and Make Mistakes in It

If there's one thing to take away from the first half of the book, it's that Innovation happens through experimentation, learning from our mistakes, and always trying again and again until we make progress. Perhaps, the best way to frame your Nonprofit Imagineering goals is to point out ahead of time that what you're about to try is just a test and is probably going to fail … or, at least, might not succeed the way you want it to.

Had you visited Google's homepage when it first launched in 1998, you would have noticed that the Google logo contained the word "beta." That's right—the official logo of what is now one of the largest companies in the world literally had "beta" in it.

In 2019, Disney fan discussion boards were abuzz when they heard that Disney was testing a beta version of their previously unreleased Disney+ streaming platform. What started as an invitation-only experiment generated a great deal of attention, organically spreading the word and getting Disney fans excited, even though beta testers noted an assortment of difficulties using the platform. Rather than complaining about the terrible new platform, they were eager to report the issues and help Disney improve the product before it launched to the public. There's something exciting and special about knowing that you're testing an experimental new system that the public does not have access to and that your input might help shape the product.

As a Nonprofit Imagineer, you can do the same! Before you launch your next groundbreaking, original idea—the one that may upset traditionalists, or possibly fail miserably—prepare a marketing campaign that points out that this is just a beta test. Preface your marketing by specifically stating that you are excited to try something new, that it is a work in progress, and feedback is encouraged. You might even require that anyone participating in your never-been-done-before program sign up ahead of time to gain access to the program and fill out a survey after.

Internally, be sure to remind your board, management, and co-workers that the greatest Innovations came from those who experimented over and over again. The best-known innovators aren't the most brilliant minds but rather are the ones who had the courage and persistence to try and fail 999 times before finally succeeding on the 1000th try. Thomas Edison was spot on when he said, "Genius is 1 percent inspiration and 99 percent perspiration."

By getting out ahead of the new idea and broadcasting that it's a beta, and by explicitly stating that making mistakes is part of the trajectory toward the final product, we free ourselves from feeling the need to hide our mistakes. We can openly discuss them, even be proud of them, and in having conversations about what went wrong, we can have impromptu blue sky meetings with participants who were not involved in the original planning, to figure out what to try next.

Being open about your beta does one more thing for your organization—it tells the world that you're creative and innovative! That little "beta" label that you add to your program or your skunkworks proudly declares that you are actively trying new things for the express purpose of effecting change! And because you're doing it in a relatively passive way (you're not taking out an ad that says "Look at us! We're innovative!"), people will see that it is genuine and authentic, and respect you even more than those who spend millions of dollars each year on ad buys to try to convince the public of it.

Utilize Existing Information to Defend Your Ideas

Part of your job as a Nonprofit Imagineer is to do the work to unlock the adjacent possible—shepherding your organization, door by door, room by room, to places they've never been. Sometimes, you'll have to pull them kicking and screaming, but more often than not, this will be a natural and easy progression over a long period of time.

When Walt first proposed the idea of a feature-length motion picture, some critics questioned whether adults were capable of sitting through 90 minutes of cartoons. They thought that adult attention spans couldn't handle extended cartoons and that they would get up and leave halfway through. Cynics were wrong, and even before releasing *Snow White*, Walt had the data to prove it. "As a matter of fact, that question had been settled as early as 1935, when European audiences lined up in long queues to see a two-hour bill of our shorts," Walt explained in an article he published in 1940. "This bill ran for seventeen weeks in Stockholm, and similar all-cartoon bills have been quite successful in this country."

In this case, Walt proved that 90-minute cartoon features would work, given that 120 minutes of animated shorts had been combined and successfully sold to European audiences in the past. Walt was using existing information to unlock adjacent possibilities between 90+ minutes of cartoon shorts and a single 90-minute feature-length movie that he wanted to produce.

These days, nearly a century after Walt Disney used shorts to prove *Snow White* would succeed, Pixar animators continue to experiment with shorts in order to prove their technology. If you've ever watched a Pixar short prior to the feature at a movie theater, it wasn't created just for fun—that short was created to give animators a chance to test new technology and prove that something theoretical will succeed as a feature.

Using existing information is a valuable resource at your disposal when you try to explain your new ideas. In many cases, there will be plenty of evidence from other organizations using similar, "adjacent" tactics to successfully achieve their goals.

It is even possible that you'll find evidence at your own organization. When trying to explain your concept for a fundraising campaign that might sound new and scary to those who fear change, take the time to explain the similarities to previous campaigns that your predecessors have run. If those previous campaigns were successful, use a little bit of forced perspective to point out that yours isn't that different. If they weren't successful, explain what you learned and how yours will be different and therefore more successful.

Another existing resource at your disposal is demographics information. Sometimes, traditionalists are hesitant to acknowledge that the world is changing at a dramatic pace. Using published information from organizations such as Pew Research Center can help explain the need for your organization to keep up with that change. Share information about your current demographics and those of the ages or markets you are trying to reach. Explain that change is necessary to keep up with the trends and, ultimately, to grow and reach new markets. Give examples of other organizations, similar to yours, who are succeeding thanks to their willingness to adapt. Apprehensions will quickly melt away once naysayers understand that your suggestions might be new to your organization but are already successful for others.

But, for every piece of useful research that helps prove your point, there will be just as many pieces of information floating around that will disprove your point. We often use demographics information, Pew Research reports, and internal surveys and questionnaires to plan for the future. The problem is all of these are snapshots of the past and don't reflect the future. Sometimes, the data are months or years old, and in our constantly changing world, some of that information can become outdated very quickly. Don't feel obligated to try to innovate based on backward-facing information!

Additionally, being innovative means doing things no one has ever done. How can you conduct a poll and get relevant data about something the poll participants have never experienced?

Michael Eisner, former CEO of The Walt Disney Company, explained in an interview with ABC, "For some reason, a lot of people in the creative industries think that you should come up with lots of great ideas and then subject them to audience research. But most audience—or customer—research is useless. Exit research is fine, even helpful, and a good thing. Audiences are honest generally on what they have just seen, but prospective research is ridiculous."

I'm not saying to throw out all the data that you don't agree with, or to recklessly update your mission in spite of conflicting data you are presented with, but there will be times to use a little bit of forced perspective and guide your naysayers toward the information that supports your arguments for innovation while downplaying any backward-facing data that prevents you from moving forward. Keep this approach in your back pocket when a board member says, "But we sent out a questionnaire a few years ago, and people are OK with black and white copies on pastel paper being mailed to them once a month with an RSVP form and check request on the bottom."

Be Ready to Adapt

There's a great story about a groundskeeper who bumped into Walt Disney a few months after Disneyland opened and pointed to a patch of grass that had been trampled by tourists wanting to take pictures in front of the castle. "We should put up a fence around this grass to protect it from being trampled," the groundskeeper suggested, to which Walt responded, "No—we should take out the grass and put a sign that says 'stand here for the best picture in front of the castle.'"

We already know that certain things that we try will fail. Disneyland's history is filled with failures. Google "yesterland" and you'll find dozens of attractions and shows that either failed for one reason or another, or simply became too outdated to remain in the parks. The key is listening to what people are saying and being ready to let go of those mistakes, failures, and relics of times gone by. If you aren't ready to cover that patch of trampled grass, or demolish attractions that have outlived their usefulness, you're going to run out of real estate pretty quickly.

One of the most notable failures in Walt Disney's life was actually the reason for his biggest success! Had Charles Mintz, the distributor that Walt worked with on his early *Oswald the Lucky Rabbit* cartoons, not stolen the idea and copyright from the Disney brothers, Walt never would have come up with Mickey Mouse! Pat Williams points out:

> Charlie Mintz actually did Walt a favor by taking Oswald away. If Walt hadn't lost Oswald, we never would have heard of Mickey Mouse—and Walt Disney might never have become a household name. Mickey was not merely the right idea at the right time; he was the creative solution to a crisis in Walt's life.

We need to not only be ready to adapt following failure but also be on the lookout for opportunities for adaptation. There's a saying that "no crisis should go unused." As Nonprofit Imagineers, who spend our time trying to counteract the "because we've always done it that way" critics, crises present golden opportunities. During the financial crisis of 2008, when the biggest donors couldn't be counted on to prop up insolvent organizations, there was no choice but to try new approaches to fundraising. Some might have called them "last ditch efforts," but you and I know that it was in those moments that the creative among us saw opportunities to shine. During the pandemic of 2020, when nearly every location-based organization (synagogues, schools, etc.) had to cancel all in-person classes, programs, and services, rather than spelling disaster, you and I saw it as an opportunity to try new technologies and reach new audiences that never attended in-person events to begin with.

The key with all crises is that rather than sticking our heads in the sand at the moment that a crisis hits, we need to be ready to adapt! Be ready to pave over that patch of trampled grass and give it a better use! Be prepared to stand up in front of your peers and proclaim "This is our opportunity to do something great!"

Start Brainstorming ... and Don't Stop!

Ideas come from everywhere! In fact, the best ideas come along out of the blue, when you're washing your car, watching a baseball game, or trying to fall asleep. Small and large blue sky meetings, and impromptu solitary blue sky moments can happen anytime, anywhere. They can be scheduled months in advance, or they can be on the walk out to the car after a long day at work. They can be focused on coming up with solutions to a specific problem, or they can simply be opportunities to burn the box and daydream together. The important thing is to always be on the lookout for inspiration, be ready for nuggets of ideas to drop at any moment, and know what to do when that happens. Above all, remember that you should never be looking for just one idea to solve a problem—you should be assembling hundreds of ideas. As chemist and author Linus Pauling said, "The way to get good ideas is to get lots of ideas and throw the bad ones away."

Create an Ideas Folder

Just as we learned in the opening chapters of this book, Walt understood that a fundamental catalyst for innovation is "ideas meeting opportunity." He put great value into pseudo-serendipitous blue sky meetings, during which ideas mingle in a somewhat engineered environment. Sometimes, ideas instantly spark great change, but other times, ideas need to lay low as slow hunches deep in the catacombs of your digital or literal desk drawers, waiting for their moment to shine.

In the late 1930s, a Disney artist named Joe Grant pitched an idea for an animated short told from the perspective of a cocker spaniel. Disney animation knew it was the start of something promising and wanted to develop the project, but it was put on hold during the War, and when they resumed production in 1943, they couldn't get past the feeling that their story was missing something. Fortunately, it was around that time that Walt read a story about Happy Dan, a clever mutt created by Ward Greene. Walt realized that Happy Dan was exactly what Joe Grant's short needed, and by merging their two short stories, his team ended up with the beloved feature-length film, *Lady and the Tramp*.

Looking back, the story could have ended in a number of ways. Walt could have pushed for the original short about the cocker spaniel to be made before the war. Or he could have scrapped it completely when the war started and he knew he didn't have time to produce it. But Walt had the foresight to put it in his ideas folder and wait for the right time—to wait for serendipity. The decade-long delay might not have been intentional, but by putting the idea for the original short into his ideas folder, Walt was able to wait for the idea to mingle with another and form something great.

Just as Walt patiently kept story ideas slowly simmering until the time was right to produce and distribute them as films, we must keep ideas percolating on a back burner, ready to bubble up. The most important thing is that we write them down! Don't count on an idea being "good enough that I'll remember it when the time is right."

Interestingly, shortly after Disneyland was built, an article in the *Long Beach Independent-Press-Telegram* noted that "plans for this wonderland first began to go on paper as far back as 1932 when Walt's magnificent dream began to take form. In cleaning files at the Burbank studio recently, original Disneyland sketches, bearing the 1932 date, were found." As you may recall, construction on Disneyland began in 1954. 1932 was more than 20 years before Walt put shovels in the ground! It was well before Walt sat on a park bench watching his daughters ride the carousel in Griffith Park, which is commonly known to be the moment when Walt Disney first envisioned a park where adults and children could enjoy attractions together (his daughter, Diane, wasn't born until 1933). The idea for Disneyland (or, more accurately, for a concept that eventually evolved into Disneyland) was in the back of Walt's mind for more than 20 years before the time was right. Not just in the back of his mind—but sketched on paper and filed into his ideas folder.

As a Nonprofit Imagineer, you need to develop a system for allowing ideas to find their time. Like me, you might want to create a physical "ideas folder" on your desk, a virtual one in the cloud, and a folder in your e-mail inbox for anything that seems clever, but has no immediate, clear use. I save pictures of clever signs, notes about places I visit, or e-mails with punchy subject lines that I might want to feel inspired by in the future. Sometimes, these ideas come from our competitors, and sometimes, they are completely random. Just recently, I heard the phrase "not everyone thinks in words." I don't know how I might use it—whether in a campaign about the importance of art in school, or an article about effective communication. I probably don't even fully understand how meaningful this phrase is right now. So, it will sit in an e-mail, in my "ideas folder," awaiting its moment to shine.

Or, it will just sit there and never shine.

Not all ideas are good ideas. Not every story is worth telling. More than two million cells were painted for *Snow White*, but only 250,000 were used in the actual movie! Some sequences were cut from the story because they didn't contribute to the final story that Walt wanted to tell, and others were complete and signed off by Walt, and then with the invention of the multiplane camera, were redone from scratch in order to gain the more realistic three-dimensional movement that this invention unlocked. Can you imagine being the animator who just put a year into animating thousands of cells, only to throw them all away and start from scratch? Can you imagine how those animators must have fought Walt, crying "you approved this work! It's not worth throwing out just to try a new technique!" It might hurt to do work that won't be used, or to nurture a hunch that never sees the light of day, but be prepared to let ideas or work go in order to make room for something better. Sometimes it's easier to start from scratch with a better foundation than to try to continue pursuing an idea that isn't coming together, or isn't the best that it can be.

Of course, sometimes, "the right time" won't come along without a little bit of a nudge. After all, we're in the *pseudo*-serendipity business.... Sometimes, we realize that an idea will never see its time if we don't get proactive and purposely unlock a few adjacent possibles. After producing dozens of shorts, including very successful and critically acclaimed *Silly Symphonies* and the *Three Little Pigs* series, Walt and his team realized they had hit a creative roadblock and pushing into the adjacent possible was the only way to get past it. "I used to feel at times that there wasn't another good story idea left in the world which could be told in eight hundred feet," Walt said. "The length limitation of the *Symphony* became more and more galling ... Our files were filled with abandoned stories on which we had spent thousands. It was inevitable that we should go into feature-length pictures if only for the unlimited new story material this field held for us."

At a time when no one had animated a feature-length film, Walt certainly could have remained a slave to the glass ceiling and continued to make shorts. He likely would have been very successful, but at a certain point, something had to change. There had to be a catalyst that enabled opening the door and moving to the next adjacent possible room. For Walt, that catalyst was the personal decision to no longer wait for the world around him to change, and instead, to invest a considerable amount of money and manpower to try something that had never quite been done—the production of an animated feature length film.

What is your glass ceiling? What brilliant ideas are in your folder, waiting for the right time that may never come without a nudge in the right direction? How can you make that time arrive on your schedule rather than leaving it up to Madam Serendipity?

Identify Your Competitors

We've discussed the idea that innovation often happens when we take two unrelated things that have been done before in different environments and combine them to make something new. Disneyland—the combination of an amusement park and a themed film set—is a prime example of this. If you feel like you are all out of creative ideas (which, really, should never happen, but let's pretend ...), take a moment to evaluate who you think your competitors are and what you can learn from them. If you work for a church, you probably think the other churches in your neighborhood, who are trying to appeal to the same set of local families, are your direct competitors. If you work for an elementary school, you probably assume your competition is other private and public schools in the area.

You're not wrong. But, you're also not completely right. You need to think broader.

Our competitors might not be who we think they are. Pepsi might be Coke's biggest competitor, but Coke isn't Pepsi's. The Coca-Cola company only produces drinks, so other drink manufacturers are their competitors. Pepsi, on the other hand, also owns Frito-Lay, Quaker, and a number of other brands that manufacture an assortment of products. To Pepsi, Coke just competes with a small segment of their products. If Pepsi were to focus on competing with Coca-Cola, they would need to abandon a large number of their products and would be missing a huge market!

So, I ask again, who are your top competitors? If you work for a school, who, other than local schools, are competing for your students/ families attention and money? Who are you competing with on individual programs, such as summer camp or after school sports? Who are you competing with for the attention of parents? Who are you competing with for donations or volunteer time? If you are a community center, what sorts of organizations offer similar programs that draw your market base away from you?

Once you identify who all of your competitors are, evaluate what they do similarly and differently from you, and what you can learn from them. If you are a synagogue trying to create family programming every Sunday afternoon, look around the community at other nonprofit organizations, such as schools, libraries, and neighborhood parks, as well as small and large businesses, such as professional sports teams, miniature golf centers, and toy stores, to see what they have planned on Sundays. What are they doing to successfully draw in families from your neighborhood? What have they tried recently that failed? What can you learn from their successes and failures? There's no reason why a school or community center can't mimic and improve upon a program that your local minor league baseball team did with families last year. Innovation isn't always creating something completely new from scratch—innovation often happens by taking something that already exists and applying it to a completely new field.

While you're identifying and learning from your competitor's programs, take a stroll through their property. How do you feel walking into that storefront, playground or arena? Does it make you happy to be there? Is it dark or bright? Does it feel cluttered or clean? Outdated or modern? Does it smell good or bad? Did they find creative new ways to display signage? Are they playing music that brings the space to life?

Visit their website. Try to make a donation or learn about their mission. Try to RSVP for an event or buy a ticket to a home game. What makes you feel comfortable? What makes you feel uneasy? What stands out as something you'd like to mimic? What mistakes are they making that you should avoid? Odds are that if you're critical of someone else's space, others are equally critical of yours.

Now walk through your property or browse your website. Try to see it the same way that a prospective family or a current member or a volunteer or a donor would see it. Is it easier to donate to your organization than to buy a ticket to a Disney park or sports game? How does your website or property make you feel? Is it setting the stage for the experience that you want visitors to have? Is it telling the story that you want told? Do you fall in love with it again and again, each time you see it? How does it look through the eyes of a child who can't read yet? Or through the eyes of an elderly person who has trouble seeing? How does moving through your property feel to someone in a wheelchair? Is the wheelchair-friendly entrance as inviting as the main entrance? Does your signage speak to all of the different audiences that you were trying to speak to? Would you be able to find support if you were in need? If someone wanted to contact you, would they be able to talk to a real person quickly and easily, like speaking to a cast member at Disneyland, or is contacting your organization reminiscent of trying to cancel your cable subscription? Make a list of actionable items, and start checking them off your list! Start plussing! Your goal should be to do everything better than your competition ... Even better than Disney.

Identify Your Role Models

As nonprofits, we need to remember that although we're competing with other nonprofits for the same eyeballs and shekels, competitors shouldn't be viewed negatively. We strive to be the best in the biz, but that is not done in an attempt to beat down the competition. We don't want other social goods to suffer. Our goal is to be so good that we rise above them!

Realistically, though, it's not possible to be better than everyone else, especially if we start comparing ourselves to professional baseball teams or Disney. In those scenarios, it's best to look at competitors as role models rather than competition.

Wait! I understand how other organizations in my neighborhood are "competitors," and I can even see the connection between my organization and local businesses, but are you really trying to convince us that Disney is our nonprofit's competition?

Yes—believe it or not, we are in competition with Disney! That might terrify you or it might energize you, but when you think about it, your nonprofit and Disney entertainment are both in competition for disposable income. You'd like people to donate it to you, and Disney would like it to be spent at their theme parks, at the box office to see their latest release, or on a subscription to Disney+. You would like people to attend your events and Disney would like those same people to be at Disneyland or on a Disney cruise. As a synagogue Creative Director, part of my job was to convince people to pay for membership, which is sometimes thousands of dollars per year. It just so happens that Disney Annual Passports for the entire family could be purchased for less money. If you were an average Joe, spending most of your income on your mortgage, car payment, insurance, taxes and food, what would you rather do with your extra money—pay for membership at an organization that you feel is important but you only connect with a couple of times per year, or take the family to Disneyland a couple of times each month?

So … what can we learn from this? For starters, rather than thinking of Disney as our competitors (because, really, we don't stand a chance), let's look at them as our role models, which, I remind you, is literally what we've been doing since page 1.

Just like us, Walt Disney's goal was never to make money. Deep down, he was not a capitalistic person. He never aimed to raise his stock price by 5 percent per quarter or to make money for angel investors. Uncle Walt's goal was to unite the world and make it a better place. Walt wanted to build a utopia, first as a theme park, and eventually, as a residential city (had he lived longer, it's possible that EPCOT, which stands for Experimental Prototype Community of Tomorrow, would have been an urban development rather than theme park). He wanted the message of *It's a Small World* to not just be a tune we whistle as we head home, but to be what we all believe and strive for, deep in our hearts. Sounds a lot like what we do every day at our organizations, right?

Even today, decades after Walt Disney passed away, at its core, The Disney Company's goal is to earn the trust of each parent and each person who buys a Disney product, visits a Disney park, or watches a Disney film. The Disney Company wants us to know that by spending a dollar at Disney World, or by telling our children that they have our permission to watch the Disney Channel, we can trust that they will provide only the highest quality, family friendly products.

Nonprofits function under that same strict code. We want our members to know that in donating to our cause, they are contributing to something worthy of their attention and that their money will be spent responsibly to fulfill our mission. They need to know that we are worthy of their trust, the same way that Uncle Walt was worthy of ours.

Billy Graham, the popular evangelist, visited Disneyland in 1962 and had a conversation with Walt about the world of fantasy that he had created. Walt replied, "Billy, take a look around you. Look at all the people, representing all nationalities, all colors, all languages. And they are all smiling, all having fun together. Billy, this is the real world. The fantasy is outside."

So, now that we see how Disney (and pretty much every company out there) can be viewed as our competition *or* as a role model, it's time to start treating them as the valuable creativity-inducing resources that they are!

As Walt Disney developed his plans for EPCOT (The city—not the theme park), he researched it, in part, by visiting two of the largest shopping malls in America. What do shopping malls have to do with prototypical communities of tomorrow? Who knows. But Walt saw the benefits of looking beyond the usual models, and I'm sure, had he lived long enough to build EPCOT the way he envisioned, we would have seen some amazing adjacent possibles being unlocked, thanks to a few visits to completely random locations.

In our nonprofit world, visits to seemingly unrelated destinations can prove quite beneficial. For example, like it or not, your nonprofit is in the customer service industry (just like Disney). Disney's customers are "guests," while our customers are "members" or "donors." Regardless of what we call them, we all need to provide a service they value and appreciate, and treat them with respect. Their satisfaction is important, and everyone, from your accountants to your maintenance staff to your CEO, needs to work toward that goal at all times. We can learn a lot from Disney's customer service model and that's just the beginning!

So, head out on official business to the movie theater, a salon, or even the nearest Disney theme park and observe how they treat their customers.

Model your interactions after those companies that have perfected customer service. And while you're there, keep an eye out for everything that makes you think "that's clever," or "I like the way they did that …" and file it away in your ideas folder.

Involve Your "Cast"

As we've discussed, story is the most important element in connecting with our members and donors. Story is more than a point-to-point narrative—it is immersive, nonlinear, and requires the efforts of our entire staff (aka "cast") to be truly effective. Walt built Disneyland so that children could meet his characters in real life. He wanted them to be able to form a connection beyond that of a child watching a television show. Human interaction is incredibly important! You might be able to create a beautiful flier and an amazing promotional video, but after you draw them in for that first personal contact, if your guest's interaction with your organization comes up short, it might mean failure.

Communicate Your Common Purpose

We've discussed simplifying mission statements in order to expand our organization's horizons, and the use of themes to tie our campaigns together, but there's one more Disney Imagineering principle that might be even more easily understood and more impactful to our fellow employees and volunteers: understanding our common purpose.

At Disney, they define their common purpose as "We create happiness by providing the finest in entertainment for people of all ages everywhere." Simply put, regardless of what job you do at a theme park, movie studio, or cruise ship, if you work for Disney, your goal is to create happiness. Whether you're steam cleaning Main Street in the middle of the night, writing new-hire training video scripts, or imagineering the next great attraction, the job that you do plays a role in creating happiness.

When a new janitor is hired for a theme park, it's much easier to give them a sense of purpose by explaining that their job is to create happiness by making guests' days more enjoyable than to explain how their duties fit within Disney's mission statement of entertaining the public.

Mission statements and common purpose go hand in hand, but one guides the overall direction of the company, and the other keeps 200,000+ individuals focused on a common, attainable objective. It helps them understand that there's more to their job than the actual tasks on their job description. Each time they use their broom handle to battle in a pretend sword fight with a 4-year old, or simply smile at a guest, they are creating happiness.

Similarly, it might be a challenge to keep your front desk receptionist, who spends eight hours a day forwarding calls and sorting mail, or your accountant who processes credit card after credit card, focused on your mission statement when it has little to do with their day-to-day responsibilities.

Rather, consider what their common purpose is. Is it to build community? Save the whales? Feed the homeless? Remind your co-workers and your community of this. It's too easy to get caught up in the day-to-day minutiae of processing payroll, formatting weekly e-mails or removing stains from commercial-grade carpets that you forget why you do what you do. Your accountant's job might be balancing the books, but she shares the same common purpose as every other team member. She plays a role in your show, and without her, the funds that do so much good might never become available to you. Without your maintenance crew's commitment to keeping your property clean and well maintained, your guests might be distracted by a large stain on a wall rather than having their eyes on the bride's shimmering ivory dress. It never hurts to remind your constituents too. When they call in to complain about their credit card being charged incorrectly or their name being misspelled in your latest donor list, remind them that your goal is to do good in the world, and that while you will absolutely correct the error, you appreciate their partnership in achieving this mission. It's hard for people to remain angry when they are reminded that you're all on the same team.

One way Disney Imagineering keeps everyone on track with the same common purpose during large projects is with a mood board. When designing a land, there might be thousands of people involved, including architects, engineers, lighting directors, composers, chefs, and graphic artists. These people might work on the project from start to finish or might come on board for a few weeks during a multiyear project.

They might work in the same room as those Imagineers that first envisioned the land or might be working thousands of miles away. Mood boards can help bring everyone up to speed and put them on the same page regardless of what point in the process they become involved. Mood boards explain the emotions and underlying concept behind the project. Each person working on the new land might have a different interpretation of how that emotion should be evoked, but as long as they have a common goal and theme in mind, the end product will feel cohesive.

Consider adding a mood board to your office break room or shared cloud drive. Allow co-workers to add their own drawings or images from Google searches to see their interpretation of your common purpose. It will serve as a reminder about why you're there and bring new energy to the staff.

If you work at a school, pictures of your students participating in hands-on learning might be a great reminder to everyone from security guards to PE coaches of why it's important to continue pushing for more than just reading, writing, and arithmetic in classrooms. If you work to build wells in third world countries, a letter and picture from a single child who now has clean water to drink will remind your staff why their perseverance is so important. Whatever method you find most effective, understanding your common purpose will keep your staff focused on more than just the basics.

It's All About the People

You can plus your building, tell a great story, and direct people exactly where you want them to go, but ultimately, at the heart of every story and every interaction, are people.

Human interaction is important and is too-often overlooked. Take a minute to donate $10 to your organization. How did you do it? (Or, how would you have done it, since I know for a fact that you didn't actually do what I asked). You probably would have gone online to your website, clicked a few buttons, entered your credit card information, hit submit, and received an automated response. At what point in that process did a real person interact with you?

There are many times when people are using your website to make a donation or find information, and the only human in that interaction is the visitor to your website. Is there a way to make it personal?

In the business world, there's often discussion about hi-tech versus hi-touch. At what point does the quest to increase automation become counter to our organization's mission? At what point do we become so focused on streamlining our processes and lowering our operating costs that we take all human interaction out of the equation?

Disney works very hard to find balance between hi-tech and hi-touch. As you walk through a Disney theme park, you'll notice staff members everywhere. At boards that tell the approximate wait times for popular attractions, there is always a cast member standing by to answer questions. At the entrance to nearly every attraction, regardless of whether it's open or closed at that moment, you'll find a cast member welcoming you. As you wait for a parade to begin, you'll see dozens of cast members who seem to have nothing to do—that's because their job is to connect with you on a human level, to answer questions, provide support, and make sure everyone is having a great time. There's no requirement for humans to be greeting guests at each of these locations. Signage is already in place to tell visitors what they need to know. Yet, Disney places cast members at these spots anyway.

How can you create the same welcoming, personal atmosphere in an online interaction? Create prompts for donors and prospective members to contact you. Provide real names, e-mail addresses, and phone extensions for your staff members so that guests who need assistance don't feel like they're on the outside of a humanless organization. Following an interaction such as an online donation or RSVP, have someone contact them directly to show your appreciation and answer any questions they might have. Maybe even change the generic "contact us" link in your website footer to "Click here to email Ben. He's happy to help!"

I use a promotional items company to purchase "swag" with our logo on it that we give away at events for free, or sell as spiritwear to our supporters. Following my first purchase, I received an e-mail from the CEO himself asking if there was anything he could help with, and thanking me for using their services. It was surely automated, so I tested the system by hitting reply and letting him know about a concern I had. Within a few hours, I received a response from a real person, letting me know he would do what he could to help with my concerns as he forwarded my e-mail to the appropriate department to expedite the shipping and meet my deadline. I am fairly certain the CEO never saw my response. It was more likely an overseas customer service representative trained to impersonate the CEO's right-hand man. But either way, I felt a human touch and it clearly has stuck with me to this day.

Take a moment to think about what sorts of human interactions happen for your donors or members. How much does someone need to contribute to get a call from a member of your staff or a personal e-mail from a real person—not an automated e-mail from your info@ e-mail address?

In the world of Nonprofit Imagineering, we understand the importance of the little touches—where the smallest details can make the biggest difference. And where several tiny details can be world-changing. What would it be like to give every donor and every supporter a personal, human touch? Don't tell me why it's not possible. Don't ask yourself if it's possible. Ask your cohort to blue sky how to make it possible.

Encourage Role Play!

At the end of each day, a line forms outside Disneyland's City Hall. Early in the day, the line is short, but as the sun sets, more and more unhappy visitors await their turn to explain to a customer service representative why their visit to The Happiest Place on Earth wasn't perfect. Complaints range from the obnoxious "I didn't get to ride my favorite ride because it was broken down for an hour, I demand you give me a ticket to come back another day for free" to the sincere "someone stole a bag out of my stroller, please help me recover it." Always with a smile on their faces and the utmost patience, the people behind the counter do everything they can to meet the needs and expectations of the customer, regardless of how ridiculous their demand might be.

After all, to Disney employees, customers are "guests" and must be treated just as a guest in your home should be treated. "Cast Members" have their "roles to play" in the "show" that is Disney theme parks. While "on stage," in "costume," it is the job of the "host/hostess" to ensure all guests are well taken care of.

I know it's going to seem silly, but giving your fellow employees "a role to play in your show," rather than "a task to do in the office," might help them understand the overall goal of your common purpose. Tell them that from the time they arrive in your parking lot, to the time they leave for home, they are "inside the berm," and each guest's experience should be unlike anything in the real world. Some will scoff at the suggestion and completely ignore it, but others might meet the challenge with delight. There's something liberating about making customer service your top priority. For a brief moment, when on the phone or face to face with a member or donor, their focus is not on making copies or entering data— it's to be the reason someone smiles today, or to be the reason they fall in love with your organization over and over.

When you ask them to be a cast member, give them a single, specific instruction to help them play the role you need them to play. At Disney theme parks, each cast member has a role to play in making the guest experience exceptional, and often, the most enthusiastic feedback from guests relates to a positive experience with a passionate cast member. Those cast members who dive deep into their character, truly becoming the adventurer on the jungle river or the spooky proprietor of the haunted mansion, create the best memories for guests. What role can your co-workers play in greeting guests and sharing your message? What single line or catch phrase can they repeat as they meet new people to remind them of your common purpose and goals?

Empower the Lay

Did you know that you can use the same proprietary software that Pixar animators use? You can play around with their PTex software, which adds textures to computer-generated animation. You can even download and manipulate the exact data set that they used to sculpt the island in *Moana*. Even better—you can use it for free! What's the catch? There isn't one! This is all available through the Disney Open Source project, which gives everyone free access to some of their most cutting-edge software, with the hope that if you find a way to make it better, or a creative new use for the software, you'll share that knowledge with Disney.

Open source is nothing new or novel. WordPress—the framework that 455 million websites are built on—is completely open source.

Anyone can download the software, make any changes they want, and use it however they want. This is the reason it's so successful! By giving a useful tool to the masses, and empowering people to make changes and play around with the system, each day new capabilities are built and shared through plugins and updates to the operating code.

Similar to the flexibility that enables small startups to be more innovative than large corporations, by using open source concepts, individuals can experiment with powerful new ideas without having to get the permission of boards, managers, and bean counters. A third grader can come up with the next great idea and implement it using open source software, and the company that provided that free framework can learn from the third grader and use her creativity and success to improve on their own work.

Even if you aren't familiar with Disney Open Source or WordPress, perhaps you've heard of the Apple App Store and Google Play Store. Nearly all of the apps you use on your phone and tablet are created by companies other than Apple and Google. Thanks to free APIs, which allow developers to connect their applications to data and code from Google and Apple, the sky is the limit when it comes to new, creative applications that Google and Apple pay $0 in development fees to produce for you. In fact, Google and Apple bring in millions of dollars each year for doing little more than enabling other companies to make apps.

Take a page from these open source programs and APIs and develop an open source program of your own. Rally your supporters to come up with ideas for programs and classes, and invite them to use your resources to help them get going. For some, a room that holds 30 people is all that's standing in their way (you probably have that …). For others, they simply need help spreading the word about their great idea by posting about it on social media or sending the idea to a few hundred people (you probably have that ability too …). By becoming an incubator for community programming, you can invest very little time and money in programs that can add great value to your organization and get community members excited about grassroots efforts.

It's entirely possible that the ideas you are presented with are already in your ideas folder, and you've simply been waiting for the right moment, when someone other than you would be available to provide the manpower.

Of course, you need to be the gatekeeper, and institute an approval process similar to app stores. You can't promote every idea. You can't provide funding and resources to everyone. But by cultivating an environment that encourages collaboration with those beyond your staff and board members, you turn your community into an army of passionate and invested supporters. And you do it all without having to get board approval for every new idea, or having to give up countless hours of your own time.

Engage Your Army

As we've learned, immersive environmental storytelling means that your message needs to come from all directions, in all shapes and sizes. There's no better way to have it come from all directions than by turning your members and your staff into your army of campaigners. Ask people to help share your message, to personally invite people to your event, or post on social media. Most people won't do it unless you specifically ask them to, even though this sort of outreach can be the most effective!

This is made easier when the message you're trying to spread is viral in nature. Create graphics that your members *want* to share. Make them fun and impactful. You might not pay attention to, and are unlikely to share a graphic advertising an event at someone else's organization, but a meme about a topic you can relate to, with a reference to the event in the description of the picture, can garner a significant number of shares and likes.

As you walk through a Disney theme park, you will notice a number of signs telling you "this is the best spot to take a picture." This gentle nudge reminds you to stop, take a picture, and as we all know, to post that picture to social media. In reality, these signs have less to do with helping you create memories and more to do with promoting all things Disney. It's sneaky, but it works! And it will work for you too!

Find a spot on your campus where you can set up a photo op—anything from a brightly painted wall to a large banner with the word "love" will do the trick. Ideally, the photo op will be loosely connected to your mission, but it's more important that people want to use it than that it informs people about what you do. Set up photo ops at events, on the first day of school, or just because…. Be sure and hang a small sign reminding people to take selfies at the photo op and share them with your hashtag.

Shareable moments don't have to be in person. It's easy to create social media filters that can be applied to pictures on Facebook, Instagram, and other platforms, allowing supporters to share your message. You might also want to create and share a small printable item at important times of year. On the first day of school, encourage families to take a picture holding your branded "first day of school" sign. On Holocaust Remembrance Day, supporters can share selfies holding a sign that says "I will never forget."

Keep in mind, not everything needs to be an advertisement for your organization. There's great value in someone taking a picture at your event and sharing it, even if there's no mention of your organization. If something is worthy of their attention, close friends will often ask follow up questions about where the picture was taken, and even if there's no promotional value to it, your supporter will be reminded of your event and their connection to your cause each time they see their own picture.

Always Be Plussing!

We're here to make your organization the best it can be and that means improving everything! But, just as Innovation happens over time, through slow and steady progress, your goal shouldn't just be huge leaps forward—it should be steady growth.

When it comes to making improvements, don't try to do it all at once. With each project, every step of the way, ask yourself "Is this the best I can do?" Plus it, and then plus it again. Each day, ask the same question. Make small improvements, many of which might only take one to two minutes. Constantly evaluate how things are going, and what can be done to make it better.

During a long campaign, you should be asking how to plus it many times! Just because you established a plan in September, that doesn't mean it shouldn't be tweaked throughout the next nine months. Disneyland will never be complete, and neither should your work.

Most importantly—don't get lazy, and don't expect someone else to improve on your idea. Your campaign lives and dies with you—always be plussing. When your campaign or event ends up being one of the most creative in the history of your organization, and when that campaign gets noticeably better with each passing month, it will be worth the extra effort and will open the door to the next adjacent possible!

Plus Using the 70-20-10 Model

While some might find it invigorating to always be plussing, others will find it challenging and exhausting. It can be difficult to generate the creative energy to brainstorm and implement big ideas while also plussing existing ones. Oh—and also while doing the 40 hours of work you already have on your plate.

One approach to balance everyday work with creative goals is the 70-20-10 model. You've probably heard variations on this, such as Google's requirement that all employees commit 20 percent of their time to personal projects. In the 70-20-10 model, you spend 70 percent of your time doing your day-to-day work. You know, the work you were hired to do. 20 percent of your time should be spent plussing and working on new programs that are already in the pipeline or are easy to accomplish—in other words, the things that are somewhat creative and new but aren't going to ruffle feathers. The last 10 percent of your time should be spent on the fringes of what's possible, opening new doors to new adjacent rooms. Ideally, some of the concepts that you work on during that 10 percent will become more and more realistic as you develop them, and will eventually move over to the 20 percent category, and then eventually, to the 70 percent. Nearly everything we do today was at one point part of that 10 percent! When I was a teenager, had I said that I want to produce videos and broadcast information around the world in microseconds, I would have been laughed at. But, because someone was committing 10 percent of their time to developing the Internet, envisioning phones with cameras on them, and making personal computers so powerful they can edit videos better than any technology that existed in 1990, those tasks are the meat and potatoes of 70 percent of my day job.

Reconsider Your Idea of Success

I think we can all agree that Disneyland is the quintessential success story. Walt Disney, however, might not see it that way.

As soon as Disneyland opened, the surrounding streets became flooded with cheap motels and restaurants, taking advantage of visiting tourists. The roads were dirty and busy—a stark contrast to the idyllic land of imagination within. While Walt could control the sites and sounds inside his berm, he could do nothing about what guests saw immediately outside it. To us, Disneyland is perfect. To him, Disneyland was in some ways a failure. He knew he could do better and soon began buying what would eventually total 27,000 acres of land in Florida—a piece of land so large that he could control everything within and outside of his future theme parks. Walt's metrics for determining the success of Disneyland were different from what we use. Some things that we might have thought of as failures, such as the chaotic opening day fiasco, were probably in many ways a success to Walt. And some things that we see as successes were clearly failures to him.

What metrics are you using to measure success and failure? Is your campaign only successful if it raises more money than last year's? Is your school only successful if this year's student body is larger than in the past? Is a program only successful if you bring in a certain number of attendees?

I challenge you to think about other metrics to measure success by, and plus your organization, programs, and campaigns with those in mind. Are religious services all about bodies in the pews? Or are they about friends reconnecting once a week? What are you doing to make it easier for those friends to reconnect and for service participants to make new friends?

Is your fundraiser only about a dollar amount, or have you factored in the number of people who became more committed to helping your organization because of the story you told? If you gained one new supporter, isn't that a success story? What are you doing to gain one new supporter this week, regardless of whether they donate or not? And what will you do next week, and the week after?

Sometimes, we form tunnel vision and end up missing 10 opportunities for success because we're too focused on one way that we don't want to fail. If you're out of ideas for plussing toward one goal, figure out the other goals that you should be aiming for and start plussing toward those!

Plus in All Five Senses

Disney theme parks are fully immersive storytelling models—not just because we can look in every direction, but because we can touch, taste, hear, and smell the story around us! As we walk down Main Street, we can smell the scent of fudge and candy canes. As we ride the *Jungle Cruise*, we can feel the mist on our faces. Years or decades after our last visit, just thinking about churros and popcorn makes our mouths water and instantly takes us back to the vendor selling treats in front of the castle. Smell and taste are some of our most important senses, yet we hardly ever try to appeal to them! Your immersive storytelling should be about much more than just sights and sounds.

Look at a picture of crayons and tell me you can't smell that picture. Walk under a peppertree and tell me it doesn't remind you of your childhood summer camp.

What can you do to stimulate an extra sense or two around your property? Perhaps, a very specific candy can be available at reception—one that brings back fond childhood memories for your supporters, or one that children and adults will instantly tie to your organization if they ever happen upon it at a specialty store 10 years later. Maybe star jasmine can be planted around your courtyard so that each time someone smells the fragrance as they walk through their neighborhood they think of you. Perhaps tactile, experiential objects can be added to your office desk—toys and fidgets with your logo on them that will bring a little bit of hands-on whimsy to your guest's day. School administrators and therapists use this approach all the time to help people feel more comfortable—why shouldn't it also work for adults coming in for financial support? Encourage them to take those items home after your meeting! That's what branded items are for!

And perhaps most importantly, always be on the lookout for opportunities to create visuals that add interest to your physical space. Projectors, televisions, and computer screens can be placed almost anywhere, and used for an infinite number of creative purposes beyond showing videos and slideshows. Plants and fountains can be indoors. Couches, lamps, and rugs can be in your courtyard, under a tree on the lawn, or even in the middle of the parking lot! If Imagineers can make ride vehicles move from room to room without a track and can use projection mapping to make a castle or mountain come to life, I have faith you can find creative new ways to breathe new life into your spaces.

Perhaps, the simplest way to plus your office, building, brochure, or website is through color. Walt Disney was one of the first to create television series in color—even before color televisions were ubiquitous in American households, because he understood the power that it held. A splash of red can make you feel passionate while a wall of blues can be calming. Colors can exhilarate or make you feel nostalgic. Color is so important that when Walt Disney was looking for a new show to bring to NBC—a network that was struggling to produce color broadcasts in the early 1960s, he suggested adding the word "color" to the series name and include a new character whose songs celebrated color. The *Wonderful World of Color*, with Professor Ludwig Von Drake, a kooky anthropomorphized duck teaching about an assortment of scientific topics, including color, was an instant hit when it debuted in 1961.

Our goal is to make your organization stand out from the rest! Always be on the lookout for smells, tastes, sounds, objects, and visuals that can be used to plus your visitor's day.

Do It on a Budget

There's always a budget.... Even companies with seemingly endless rivers of money have budgets. Disney does its best to come up with the money to do incredible things, but once that budget is established, Imagineers have to stick to it!

The problem is your nonprofit budget is probably less like a flowing river and more like a tiny puddle on a hot, dry day. The great news is, if you've ever had to attempt to fix your own wobbly desk chair because there wasn't a budget to buy a new one, or make do with twinkle lights that don't all light up, you and Walt have something in common! Walt once explained, "My first motion picture camera was 'ad libbed' out of spare parts and a dry goods box swiped from an alley off Hollywood Boulevard." If he can start an empire with recycled scraps, I promise, there's plenty you can do with your budget.

Look, for example, to the crew as they built Disney Springs—a shopping, dining, and entertainment complex in Florida's Walt Disney World. The story that Imagineers developed for the complex was that it was a century-old town that grew around a natural spring. The central focus of this massive three-zone complex, as you might expect, is a large water feature that Imagineers created using various types of colored cement and colored glass. Since the process of layering colors and materials was so intensive, they had to come up with a way to keep the cement from fully drying before they could incorporate all of the materials into it. To solve this problem, Imagineers didn't turn to scientists or high-priced experts, they turned to their housekeepers! They found that by borrowing sheets from one of the Disney World hotels, dampening them and laying them over the fresh cement, it gave them the extra drying time to perfect the design they were after! By coming up with a creative, and practically free solution, they were able to save themselves from going over budget, thus freeing up money to use elsewhere.

Sound familiar?

In another example, when tasked with creating a relatively standard "flume" ride, in which artificial hollow logs would ride along a water flume, Imagineers took advantage of the closing of *America Sings*, a Tomorrow-land attraction featuring a cast of audio-animatronic animals, to create something spectacular on a budget. They were able to reuse nearly every animatronic animal for their new attraction, *Splash Mountain*, thus saving what might have been millions of dollars, while simultaneously creating an imaginative and beloved E-ticket attraction.

I'll give you one more example, then I promise we'll keep going: Walt Disney was the first to produce a movie with surround sound at a time when no theater was equipped to play films with more than one channel of audio. This proved to be a problem, since the movie *Fantasia*, and the "fantasound" setup that it required, could only be played in a small number of theaters willing to invest in the surround sound system. The final product was very cool, but because so few theaters were playing it, only a tiny portion of the population was able to see the movie in all of its glory.

When Walt wanted to air the first television show in stereo, he learned from his mistake with fantasound, and rather than requiring viewers to purchase new hardware, he came up with a brilliant, creative, and budget-friendly solution. Those who had two radios at home, and lived in participating cities, could tune one radio to a station broadcasting the "left," and a second radio to a different station broadcasting the "right," and as such, listen to *Walt Disney Presents* in stereo without spending a dime on new technology!

You can do that too! My first suggestion is to start by owning your own lights. This might sound like a strange suggestion, but in an environment where budgets are tight and you need to be creative in your problem-solving, having some basic, flexible resources in your tool chest is important. Having to rent items for each use will drain your tiny budget puddle very quickly. Invest in things like LED uplights capable of changing to any color, generic photo booth backdrops without specific event information, and stands for different sized signs and banners. By having versatile infrastructure pieces like these, you can spend smaller amounts of money on add-ons and set a different tone for each event with minimal cost. Use lights and a backdrop to create a weenie for a small event that normally wouldn't have any special features because of the lack of budget, or use multiple signs and banners in different parts of your campus to tell a story that will entice your visitors to explore and learn about your organization or campaign.

You can also enlarge your budget puddle by being proactive. When we nonprofit employees budget, it's generally reactive—we are given a certain amount of money to spend in a year, generally determined by the executive director and a couple of board members, and we do the best we can with it. But by being proactive, and finding new sources of funding, we can expand our possibilities greatly.

When organizers for the 1964 World's Fair approached Walt Disney with the request that he create several attractions, Walt jumped at the opportunity because he recognized the potential to push his creative boundaries using someone else's money. *It's a Small World, Great Moments with Mr. Lincoln, The Carousel of Progress*, and an attraction for Ford that developed the technology for *The People Mover* attraction were all built for the 1964 World's Fair using sponsors' money, with the intent of installing them in Disneyland shortly after the fair closed. The technological advances made while imagineering those attractions catapulted Disney through adjacent possibles that might have taken decades had it not been for the outside funding he received.

Similarly, the Imagineers who built Walt Disney World later realized that they were wrong in their original assumptions that their visitors would mostly be composed of an older demographic. They had to quickly pivot and cater to a younger crowd, like that of Disneyland in California. Imagineers were not only challenged to build a thrill ride as quickly as possible but to find the money to do so. Since it wasn't in their annual budget, that money had to come from an outside source. Marty Sklar explained:

> RCA agreed to consider sponsorship of a major attraction in the Magic Kingdom Park after its opening, if (that was the keyword) we Imagineers could develop an attraction that they would be proud to be associated with. Ten million dollars, the equivalent of about $90 million today, was on the line.

Rather than start from scratch, the Imagineers began with a concept that Walt himself had been excited about—a rocket ship ride through space. To have precise control over lighting and sound, this roller coaster would be the first of its kind—one that was to be built entirely indoors. The problem that Walt Disney faced years earlier, when he first envisioned the attraction, was that technology did not exist to make the roller coaster possible. In order to ensure the safety of all riders, a sophisticated series of braking mechanisms was needed to prevent ride vehicles from becoming too close to one another. At the time, computers capable of doing this simply didn't exist. Unfortunately, Walt Disney passed away before enough technological adjacent possibles were opened for the attraction to be built.

Finally, with RCA's sponsorship interest years later, Imagineers were able to revisit the original idea, develop new ride controls that would enable them to build and operate it indoors, and come up with a storyline that pleased RCA by including vignettes in the entry and exit queues showing RCA's "space-aged" technology being used in this futuristic environment. The result is one of Disney's most popular attractions—*Space Mountain*.

By using an existing idea and making small tweaks to it, Disney Imagineers were able to unlock millions of dollars in funding! You can do that too! There are countless grants available to all sorts of nonprofits. Where some might think "we can't apply for that grant because that doesn't apply to us," hopefully you think "it's not something we'd normally apply for, but how can I make this work for us?" Can you loosen up your mission statement and expand your existing programs and services to fit the grant specifications? Can you do exactly what you've already been doing, but target a different audience.… One covered by the grant? Odds are, by looking at what you already do from a different angle, or dipping into your ideas folder for exciting possibilities that you originally nixed because of your small budget, you can open yourself up to all sorts of new funding options.

Even if you can't find more money, there's one more way to look at your budget shortfall. "Zilch is what drives us to be more innovative, more passionate, more creative." Nancy Lublin explains in her book *Zilch: The Power of Zero in Business*. "Stop whining about your budget cuts and start asking yourself what you would do if you had zilch. You'll be surprised to discover just how powerful that is."

This last chapter was just the beginning of your journey as a Nonprofit Imagineer—it just barely scratched the surface of what is possible by a passionate, caring, and creative person like yourself. Even with no budget, no time, and no support, you are capable of doing amazing things!

We started this discussion on a theoretical level—simply understanding what creativity and innovation are. As we moved forward, section by section, chapter by chapter, we became more and more detail-oriented. And now, as we come to the final chapter, it's time to talk about the most important detail of Nonprofit Imagineering—You.

The Takeaways

- Now that you're ready to put some of what you learned from this book into action, the first step is to have conversations with your team and get them on board.
- Create a "beta" environment in order to be innovative without fear of failure.

- Use previous successes and statistical data to help convince people that your new idea should work. However, don't get too caught up on data, since it rarely helps you prove the success of a brand new idea.
- Create an "ideas folder" and fill it with interesting things that you see—regardless of where you see them. Look at companies and organizations completely unrelated to you for inspiration, and treat everyone both as a competitor and as a role model to help you come up with new ideas.
- Involve your co-workers and volunteers to help accomplish your mission. Make sure they're all on the same page by establishing a common purpose, and give them roles to play in your story. Empower people to come up with ideas by turning your organization into an incubator, and give your supporters the tools they need to properly disseminate your information.
- Always Be Plussing. Use the 70-20-10 approach to commit a small amount of time each week to innovative concepts, and try to find ways to plus your organization that you might not previously have considered.
- You can be creative and bring "wow" elements to your events and facility on a budget by owning versatile infrastructure pieces such as multi-color lighting and banner/sign holders.
- Be proactive and look for ways to earn grant money or approach new donors by adjusting existing programs in ways that open your organization up to new sources of funding without having to make significant changes.

Next Steps

- How are you using the concepts in this book to bring out your Nonprofit Imagineering best? See how others are doing, and share your success stories, your struggles and your questions at thenonprofitimagineers.com.

CHAPTER 8

Did I Ever Tell You You're My Hero?

Every good story has three key elements: a hero, a challenge to overcome, and a guide to lead the way. I'd like to think that I've proven myself to be a knowledgeable guide as we tackle this challenge of unharnessing our inner creativity and innovative spirit to benefit the nonprofit world. But regardless of what you think of me, without question, you are the hero of this story.

You need to understand this, because even though we are nearing the final pages of this book, our story doesn't end here. What happens next is up to you. Either you'll internalize the concepts we've discussed and start to make things happen, or you'll finish out the last chapter, drop this book off at a neighbor's Little Free Library, and start reading *The Queen's Gambit*, because you saw the miniseries on Netflix and just found out it was based on a novel. I hope it's the former, and I hope you'll send me an e-mail at ben@thenonprofitimagineers.com to let me know what happens in Chapter 9.

We've spent seven chapters preparing you for your quest ahead, and I promise to end this on an inspiring note, but before we do that, let's talk about expectations.

Managing Expectations

As Walt Disney and his Imagineers were planning Disneyland, Walt knew that traffic from Los Angeles to the resort would be a problem. He didn't know what the solution was, however, until a serendipitous moment while traveling through Germany with his family, when a monorail car zipped by above the road on which he was driving. At that moment, a slow hunch collided with new information and Walt knew that a monorail train would not just be a convenient way to transport guests to Disneyland, but would enable his preshow to begin on the scenic ride, miles before reaching the front gate. Unfortunately, city planners did not see eye to eye with Walt. They could not wrap their heads around the idea of a monorail being a part of the city's mass transportation plan. Ultimately, Walt Disney took it upon himself to create the first daily operating monorail in the western hemisphere at Disneyland, in part, to prove a point to city planners everywhere and proactively unlock an adjacent possible. In 2022, the city of Los Angeles was considering adding a monorail as part of its mass transit system, in part because 60 years earlier, Walt Disney built his monorail at Disneyland.

Walt was the head of a company, with millions of dollars, a huge staff of artists, and a certain amount of celebrity, all of which helped get Disneyland off the ground, a monorail built, and movies made to his exact specifications. Even with all of that, it took an immense amount of gumption and decades of perseverance to do what he did.

You, on the other hand, are an employee, volunteer, or board member at a nonprofit. You can't build a monorail just to prove a point. You—the same person that keeps a screwdriver in your desk drawer because the key to the display case went missing years ago—think you'll read one book and suddenly have what it takes to change the world?

Let's be real for a minute. You dream big—about guiding our industry into a 21st century nonprofit renaissance, but is that even possible? Walt's vision of a utopian community that would one day change the world ended up being a theme park with a giant geodescent sphere in the middle. What chance do you really have at leading us to nonprofit 3.0? The best that you can hope for is to painstakingly unlock a few doors to adjacent possibles in order to bring your organization to something resembling your ultimate vision, and even that might take your entire career.

It's wonderful to dream big—to spend our time floating around as blue sky fantasizers, but there are limits to what we can accomplish. We need to be Realists, and we need to be Spoilers. No matter how much we might want it, we can't organically grow our e-mail list by 1,000 percent overnight, just like Disney Imagineers can't fit 10,000 actuators in the head of a mannequin.

Actuators, as you may recall, are what make animatronics move. Each actuator can only do two things—move up and move down. With enough actuators, very sophisticated things can be done; however, inside a space the size of a human head, there is a finite volume that can only fit a certain number of mechanisms. Imagineers must do as much as they can with as little as possible to achieve the motion and emotion they're looking for. They have limits imposed on them, and they must use creativity to make the best of the situation.

Sound familiar? You and I don't work with actuators, but trying to do a lot within limitations that we have no control over is fairly common in our world. Sometimes, our job is to manage our own expectations, or those of our co-workers. It's about finding balance—dreaming big and spoiling just the right amount. Remember—innovation happens right on the edge, between what's been done and what seems impossible. Sometimes, we need to push until we arrive at the right point in development, then leave it at that … for now … as we prepare for the next battle.

Doing the Grunt Work

Progress isn't always sexy. Not everyone can be making 7-figure handshake deals with huge donors to guarantee your organization's survival over the next 10 years.

When Disney Imagineers were tasked with reimagining their Florida Downtown Disney complex into Disney Springs, they solicited feedback about how the existing Downtown Disney site was being used by guests. What did visitors love? What did they want to see improved? Much to Imagineers' surprise, a great deal of feedback wasn't about the experience in the shopping center, but rather about getting to it! Guests—especially local residents—hated sitting in traffic to get from the edge of the Disney World property into the Downtown Disney parking lot, and hated even more the stress of locating and sometimes fighting for spots in the undersized parking lot.

Ultimately, Imagineers realized that to expand Downtown Disney into Disney Springs, they would need to widen the road leading to it and build a much larger parking structure.

Imagine being the Imagineer who was asked to spend the next year of her life overseeing the widening of a street, or the building of a parking structure, while all of her fellow Imagineers got to write the story of Disney Springs. Imagine having to focus on asphalt, concrete, and lane lines while others were sourcing century-old bricks to line the themed streets, and designing terracotta molds for the walls of the outdoor shopping center.

The truth is we all have a to-do list filled with mundane, unexciting tasks that we've been putting off for weeks, months, or even years. From updating that outdated thank you note template to making the parking lot a little more welcoming, there are all sorts of things that can and should be done to improve your organization, and which no one is going to volunteer for, especially when updating pictures on your website and setting lunches with big donors is much more interesting. Prepare yourself now to do the grunt work as you transform what others feel is "good enough" into something great!

Being a Solo Act

Even after you communicate your common purpose, get your co-workers and volunteers to role play, and develop your army of lay programmers, at times, it might still feel like you're going it alone. Everyone you work with has their own set of problems to deal with each day, and their own personal and professional goals that don't necessarily align with yours. Sure, they're happy to participate in a blue sky meeting with you, and they'll feign a smile when you ask them to act a certain role in your show, but when it comes time to put your groundbreaking plan into action, most of the work is going to fall on your shoulders. So, how can you get it done as an army of one?

You're the hero—it's time for your training montage set to 80's music!

Start by making sure you're at the top of your game. Before you plus the world around you, plus yourself. Read everything you can, watch educational TV shows (not just *The Real Housewives* …), see movies, visit landmarks and tourist attractions, and talk to people from all backgrounds, demographics, and with different interests than yours. Inspiration will come from all sorts of sources and topics.

As Greg Satell explained in *Mapping Innovation: A Playbook for Navigating a Disruptive Age*:

> It's hard to see how Darwin could ever have come up with his famous theory if he had confined his interests to biology. It was, in fact, a book on geology that first got the ball rolling. And his breakthrough moment came while reading the work of Thomas Malthus, an economist. Biology, geology, and economics are three very different fields with relatively little in common. But by combining them Darwin was able to attain groundbreaking new insights. Without any one of those three elements, it is doubtful he would have achieved what he did.

You need to be at the top of your game because *you* are the reason change is about to happen! You are the one who read this book, and you understand that the reason Disneyland is so special isn't because they use kinetics, or weenies, or stories, or forced perspective—it's because they use *all of them, all the time!*

It's very likely that as you read this book, you identified with at least some of the concepts because you already do them. You've brainstormed. You've plussed. You've told a story. But have you done all of them at the same time? Have you pushed back when a board member said, "that's not how we do things around here." Have you given your supporters the opportunity to taste, smell, and hear your organization?

"Don't wait for someone to give you a sign," Beth Comstock tells us in *Imagine It forward*. "Give yourself permission to make change happen and to fail. Don't let fear suck your confidence out of you. Do this for you, and do it for your organization."

You are the one who read this book, and it's up to you to disseminate the information and to keep pushing! No one else is going to share your vision and your passion! You didn't just skim this book—you read it, absorbed it, and folded the corners of so many pages because you had to keep putting it down to envision how you might put the ideas into action! You are the hero who will keep trying and failing and trying again. And you'll do it because you know that if you don't, then who will?

And if not now, when?

Will It—It Is Not a Dream

When Walt Disney had the idea to create the first full-length, fully animated motion picture, he knew the industry would instantly criticize him and call him crazy. He knew that if he couldn't properly express his idea, and sell his staff, his brother, and even his wife, he had no chance of gaining their support for spending the hundreds of thousands of dollars and committing years of studio time that would be necessary to produce the movie. "At first, Walt told no one about his plans," Pat Williams explains in *How to Be Like Walt: Capturing the Disney Magic Every Day in Your Life*. "He spent several weeks in secret, reading, researching, making notes, and blocking out a storyline for the film. Finally, he was ready to tell his two closest confidants, [his wife] Lillian and [brother] Roy—and he knew exactly how they would react."

Their response, similar to the response you'd expect to a new, untested idea, was that Walt should continue doing what was working. Cartoon shorts paid the bills, and there was no need for the Disney animation studio to be industry disruptors by creating a feature-length film when they could still do a lot to make their shorts better and better.

But Walt didn't want to create better shorts. He wanted to do things nobody was even thinking about. He wanted to change the world of animation and motion pictures.

He patiently continued to develop the story of *Snow White* until finally, one day he invited his animators to a live, one-man show, during which he acted out every sequence of the film with great enthusiasm, earning the support of his team.

Patience and perseverance, or stick-to-it-ivity, as the old song goes, were driving forces behind many of his motion pictures. *Bambi* was supposed to immediately follow *Snow White* but instead took more than nine years to properly prepare, produce, and release. The first storyboards for *Alice in Wonderland* were produced in 1931, but Disney didn't start working on it in earnest until 1939 and wasn't able to release it until 1951. Walt acquired the rights to *Peter Pan* in 1939 but didn't begin production until 1950 and didn't release it until 1953.

Not only did timing delays frustrate Walt, but poor box office performance nearly bankrupted his studio many times. The head of any other animation studio would have thought long and hard about producing yet another animated feature after losing millions on *Bambi* and *Fantasia*, but Walt not only insisted that they continue to produce features, he demanded the highest quality in animation and story.

Walt understood what he was aiming at. He understood that the ultimate goal was bigger than just producing a single animated movie. He wasn't just interested in the present—he always had his eye on the adjacent possibles that he could open in the future. Walt explained:

> We were growing as craftsmen, through study, self-criticism, and experiment. In this way, the inherent possibilities in our medium were dug into and brought to light … It is the way men build a sound business of any kind-sweat, intelligence, and love of the job. Viewed in this light of steady, intelligent growth, there is nothing remarkable about the 'Three Little Pigs' or even 'Fantasia'—they become inevitable.

In Walt's own words—by simply sticking to it and continuing the drive forward, innovation was "inevitable."

Roy often argued with his brother, Walt, about the amount of time and money being spent on ventures that Roy didn't understand. In the end, though, he admitted that despite digging in as best he could, he was no match for Walt's stick-to-it-ivity, in part because he knew that Walt was generally right. He might not have understood Walt's dreams, but he knew that Walt always had a vision.

Similarly, the bigger your dream, the more legwork it'll take to develop your idea to the point where others will understand it. And that's just the beginning of the long road ahead. But as political activist and visionary Theodor Herzl said, "If you will it, it is no dream."

Hopefully, you won't be rejected time and time again as you pursue change, but it's going to require a lot of elbow grease on your part. This is even truer if you're working against a small budget, little free time, and limited support staff to do the legwork. Even with the support of thousands of skilled laborers, Walt could still be seen painting the walls of a Tomorrowland attraction at midnight, hours before Disneyland opened for the first time on July 17, 1955. Be prepared for the long, hard road ahead. But keep at it—it's not just a dream!

Remember, This Is Bigger Than You or Me

Some problems can't be solved by one person, or even by one organization. No matter how much effort you put into it, and how forward thinking and creative you are, it's possible that your organization, or even the entire industry, is heading toward a dead end and needs to try an entirely different approach.

"Most of the public problems we face these days stretch beyond any one organization's boundaries," Dr. John M. Bryson, author and professor, points out. "Our big challenges in education, health, employment, poverty, the environment—you name it—typically need to be conceptualized at the supraorganizational or system level, not the organizational level. Those systems are what really need to work better if our lives and the world are to be made better and broadly based public value is to be created."

Do you remember the "Got Milk" campaign? Or "Pork—the other white meat?" These were not advertisements for specific companies—they were coordinated efforts by entire industries that noticed that without intervention, they were all doomed. "Beef—it's what's for dinner" and "The incredible edible egg" addressed trends that had nothing to do with individual owners, boards, or managers. Society wasn't eating as much meat and eggs as it used to. Something had to be done to fix that.

Nonprofits, especially faith-based organizations, are facing a similar challenge today. The older demographics that value attending services and belonging to a synagogue or church are declining, and young adults don't feel the same obligation. No amount of social media marketing or street-light banners by any one organization will change their minds. A successful campaign might fill the pews or increase donations temporarily, but the problem is bigger than you or me and must be addressed globally.

It requires a completely new way of thinking. It might even require leaving behind what has traditionally worked in the past—what we're comfortable with and have grown to rely on—to prepare for the future.

It requires being ready to dismiss anything that we do strictly "because we've always done it that way." That means making changes from the core—from deep inside, out. It means asking the same question Alpha-GoZero's programmers asked—If we started from scratch with no institutional history, how would we approach the problem differently? What could change the next time around?

For many nonprofits who are aware that the road that we as a society are on is leading toward a dead end for our specific types of organizations, this is the time for the Nonprofit Imagineers to step up and be heard! It's time to improve what's working, discard what isn't, and above all, to try new things. This is the time to acknowledge the dead end (or maybe even the cliff) ahead, and to start something new together, before we are in a state of triage. If we can do something visionary right now, it's possible that 1+1 can equal 3, rather than equaling 1½.

But for you and me, right here, right now—If we know that the problem is too big for any one of us to solve on our own, why do we do what we do? If we're fighting a battle we know we can't win, why continue to fight?

Our job descriptions might have us thinking that we fight the fight to try to raise more money to support our mission or get more people to attend programs … But as Nonprofit Imagineers, we know that we keep showing up because what we're doing today might lead to newer and greater things in the future. What we do, even in failure, might be what's necessary to start our organization, or the world, on a new trail that didn't exist before we just now started blazing it. Through our work, we will enable those who come after us to reach a higher peak.

We do what we do for the same reason that Ruth Shellhorn took pride in her job planting trees throughout Disneyland in 1955. She might only have received limited enjoyment from the young trees' shade, but with each passing year, those trees continue to grow, and more and more visitors are able to benefit from her contribution.

We do this *because* it's bigger than us, and that's exciting! The small improvements we make today, and even more importantly, the sometimes-brutal failures we experience today, might end up being important milestones in monumental success stories they write about decades from now. Where others might see "this is bigger than you or me" as a roadblock preventing us from achieving our goals, we Nonprofit

Imagineers see it as a launchpad. "This is the promise of the next few years," Walt Disney once concluded. "Beyond that is the future which we can not see, today. We, the last of the pioneers and the first of the moderns, will not live to see this future realized. We are happy in the job of building its foundations."

Just Keep Swimming

This book began with a detour along the road to Neverland. But, I have to ask—why were we heading to Neverland to begin with?

Neverland is a place where no one grows up. No one evolves. Nothing changes.

You and I are the kind of people that would wither away in Neverland. Maybe we'd be OK for a short visit—but it's not the kind of place you want to raise a family.

We would never find happiness there—in a land of status-quo. A land that celebrates "how we've always done it."

Some will find contentment there, but to us, it's actually all about the journey—not the destination. The destination is irrelevant. "Second star to the right, and straight on till morning." Deep down, we don't even want to get there!

We will set long-term goals to give us something to aim for, but with each passing year, as everything around us changes—sometimes quickly, sometimes imperceptibly—we will be forced into a dance of constantly changing those goals. As soon as we get close, we Nonprofit Imagineers must set the bar higher, the endgame farther, or else there's nothing left to strive for. As soon as we feel like victory is within our grasp, we realize that we can do even better! That we *must* do better!

After all, our goal isn't just to make people fall in love with what we offer—it's to have them fall in love with us over and over again! Each interaction must be different. Each must be better.

Each step that we take reveals new roads in new directions and unlocks new possibilities that we couldn't see before. Because of that, the destination we put into our GPS 10 years ago and the destination that we are driving toward today are two completely different places. The destination is irrelevant.

All that matters is the path—the foggy road to anywhere but where we are right now, and the trust that whatever direction we're headed will take us somewhere we've never been. With each passing day, we, the temporary stewards of the drive for innovation, trudge along, one foot in front of the other, moving ourselves and everyone around us adjacent by adjacent by adjacent. Whether we feel we're making progress or not, we have to heed the words of Dory from *Finding Nemo* and "just keep swimming."

"Everyone who's ever taken a shower has had an idea. It's the person who gets out of the shower, dries off and does something about it who makes a difference," Nolan Bushnell, the creator of Atari, once said.

In the grand scheme of things, we each get to hold the baton for a very short amount of time. During that brief time, we can't sit idly by—we must learn from those who came before us and figure out what the next step is to move civilization a mile, or a foot, or an inch, before our time is up and we pass the baton to the next generation. We must act! We need to just keep swimming. We need to keep opening doors to see where they take us. In any direction. In every direction. The destination is irrelevant.

Some of us might be lucky enough to be holding the baton at just the right time in history to lend our face and name to our brilliant communal Innovation. But for the other 999 of us, our contributions will be in the boxes we burn, the pseudo-serendipitous connections we form, and in our magnificent failures.

In time, every challenge can be overcome. Every idea can be made a reality. Everything that should be an Innovation, will be. And, whether it feels like it or not, every one of us can make a significant and lasting difference in this world, as long as we do one thing:

Just. Keep. Swimming.

The Postshow

There was probably a part of you that found the Nottatown narrative odd or extraneous at times, but there was another part of you that formed a connection to the characters, finding a piece of yourself in them and identifying with their struggles as nonprofit professionals and as human beings. This book certainly could have been written without the narrative, but would you have identified with the information the same way? Would you have understood how to use the information at your organization? Would you have seen how your greatest ideas will come from putting the video game enthusiast, chalk artist, army brat, and *South Park* fan in a room together and telling them that there are no limits?

JJ, Hector, Shoshana, Phil, and Vanessa's struggles were, in many ways, our own struggles, and after cutting the story off so abruptly at the end of Chapter 6, it would be unfair to leave you without a fitting end to our story.

In a perfect world, there would be a perfect ending. Maybe it would be something with the pomp and fanfare of an Olympics closing ceremony—dramatically tying together this series of carefully curated stories and setting ourselves up for the next ones four years from now. Or perhaps a romantic-comedy ending is the way to go, which you can read curled up under a cozy blanket with a glass of wine and a bowl of homemade kettle corn, leaving you with a feeling like everything is right with the world.

But this isn't a perfect world, and no single ending will make everyone happy, so I'll leave you with three possible endings. Choose your own adventure.

The Sad Ending

"It's so weird that Hellman's and Best Foods have basically the same logo," Phil said.

"Are you asking why, or are you just making an observation?" Shoshana responded.

"Just making an observation, I guess," Phil said, flipping through his Instagram feed on his phone.

Three years had passed since I completed my workshops with the Nottatown Community Center. Shoshana and Phil were the only two staff members remaining from the original group that I worked so closely with.

Vanessa was the first to leave, just a few weeks after our final meeting, when her soon-to-be fiancé took a job on the East Coast. She and I continue to text each other—no hard feelings from her salty attitude on our last day together.

During the months that followed our sessions, I continued to be in touch with the rest of the group as they brainstormed, put together a plan for the future, and plussed smaller things along the way.

It wasn't long before the NCC Board of Directors hired a new executive director to replace Jonathan. They chose not to list the job publicly, and rather to hire one of their own—giving the executive director position to Aaron, a longtime board member, and semiretired former executive director of a different nonprofit organization, who left his previous position because he felt burnt out.

Although, at first, they were optimistic that Aaron would be an ally in continuing the work that we had started together, they found that he had his own vision and agenda that looked very similar to what he had accomplished years before at his previous post. While he spoke about innovation quite a bit, it quickly became clear that his idea of innovation was actually to do what they had always done. Under those circumstances, the idea of "The Hub" was put on hold, never to be resurrected.

He spent his first six months interviewing the existing staff and analyzing what each person's strengths and weaknesses were. Rather than push for expansion to bring in more funding, he laid off some of the administrative staff to cut costs, with the expectation that each remaining staff member could absorb a little bit more into their portfolio of duties. He thought that appealing to their sense of duty to the social good would push his team to happily do more than their share of work while still being underpaid. He was wrong.

Hector soon left, followed by JJ. Shoshana and Phil tried to fly under the radar as they pushed for more creativity and "burn the box" thinking, but they were met by roadblocks every step of the way, primarily by Aaron, who wanted more than anything else, to return the NCC to its glory days, and often micromanaged the team rather than trusting them to do the jobs they were hired to do.

Aaron was a good person who meant well and wanted what was best for the organization, but was also an out-of-touch manager who thought that mimicking the greatest successes from the past would rejuvenate the organization.

The NCC continues to do what it has always done, with an overworked and uninspired staff that sees a high turnover rate.

Just one relic of my time at Nottatown remains visible—pinned to the wall above Shoshana's desk, amidst family photos and graphics of clever puns, is a picture of *Finding Nemo's* Dory, and the words "Just keep swimming."

The Happy Ending

"It's so weird that Hardees and Carl's Jr. have basically the same logo," Phil said.

"Are you asking why, or are you just making an observation?" Shoshana responded.

"Sure, if you know why," Phil said, as he printed a picture of a Carl's Jr. advertisement for his mood board.

"They were two totally separate companies on the east and west coasts, and then rather than trying to expand into other markets, Carl's Jr. ended up buying Hardees and making the two brands match," Shoshana explained, matter-of-factly.

"Is that the innovator's dilemma?"

"No."

Three years had passed since I finished my workshops with the Nottatown Community Center.

After I left, the Board of Directors recognized that since the organization had been running smoothly in Jonathan's absence, they would promote from within, making JJ the interim executive director for one year while they decided whether to list the position officially or give him the permanent role. In addition to taking managerial courses at the community college, and offering continued education opportunities to any staff members interested, he implemented weekly blue sky meetings to keep their creative muscles well-toned, and required that everyone spend at least 10 percent of their time exploring anything they were interested in, or mapping out pet projects that could one day benefit the organization.

The first thing they did after I left was go back and evaluate what their biggest problems were, and whether they were asking the right questions. I received an e-mail from Shoshana shortly after I left. She explained that in their discussions, they realized that no matter what changes they made, their reach within the community was extremely limited, and it would take a long time to gain traction and organically grow on their own. They were concerned that if they couldn't show measurable results quickly, the board might bring in a new executive director who might not share their vision.

In my response, I drew upon my time as a real estate agent, when I was taught that rather than trying to personally publicize a new listing to 100,000 individual people, all I really had to do was share the information with my network of a few hundred agents, and let them share it with their 100,000 collective clients. With this nugget of inspiration as a starting point, they continued the blue sky process and came up with a four-part strategy for growing their influence within the community using their network of businesses and organizations as intermediaries.

Part 1: In their effort to bring "The Hub" concept to life, the NCC solicited partnerships with organizations and businesses around Nottatown. They decided to create "The Nottatown Loop"—based on the idea of the Freedom Trail in Boston that gives tourists the opportunity to explore a number of historic sites as they walk along a designated 2.5-mile path through the city. Two dozen historic businesses, schools, and organizations were added to a five-mile long loop through Nottatown. Tourists and locals alike were encouraged to visit each of these organizations to learn about Nottatown's history, pick up a small charm for a bracelet, and eventually end up at the final stop—The Nottatown Community Center, where a Nottatown History display was set up in the halls and along the outdoor walkways of the building. Most of the information and pictures for the display came from the town's residents, giving them a sense of ownership and pride for the celebration of their town.

Part 2: Ten organizations, including three religious organizations, three small businesses, three educational institutions, and the NCC, made an agreement to install special bulletin boards that would cross-promote each other's mutually beneficial programs and offers that would be available to all community members. Beautiful four foot by four foot magnetic boards with "The Nottatown Hub" imprinted along the top were hung at each location, and on the first of each month, Phil and Shoshana made their rounds to update each of the boards with identical, professionally designed fliers (not a single one was printed in black and white on colored paper). Additionally, special "passport" books were created so that event attendees could receive points for each program they attended, regardless of which organization was the host. Amazon was brought on as a sponsor for the Nottatown Hub program, offering incentives and prizes when attendees collected certain increments of points. Future plans include replacing the magnetic boards with flat panel television displays that can be easily updated remotely, and creating an app to replace the passport booklet, and make it easier to find events and offers.

Part 3: With numerous organizations fully invested in the community-wide efforts of The Hub at The NCC, a large celebration and street fair was planned for the 4th of July, featuring a chalk walk. Each organization on The Loop was asked to select an artist to represent their organization and solicit donations to fully cover the costs associated with their chalk art display and a booth at the street fair. They spent months prior to the event discussing and brainstorming what their organization was all about, and what creative intent the artwork should represent. Artists were then given the creative license to design their own art, enabling each piece to be unique and vibrant while having impactful common purposes.

The chalk walk and fair, which was held on the block of Main Street immediately in front of the NCC, was a huge success, not just for the community, but for the NCC, which increased their recognition and attracted new energy.

Part 4: At the chalk walk festival, the NCC unveiled its plans for their new incubator program—offering free space and modest resources for anyone who wanted to develop a new program or small business that would benefit the community. Within six months, they had more applications than they could accommodate. Their once-empty classrooms now house 10 different start-ups, including a resource center for abused women, a saltwater taffy distributor that donates 50 percent of their profits to different charities, a ballet studio, and a for-profit technical training school that gives free classes to all NCC members.

Once the "beta" testing of the Loop proved successful, advertisements were placed along the main highway to Neverland, attracting new visitors who previously only stopped for gas and snacks. The town's businesses and the NCC have generated considerably more sales and donations, thanks to the fresh flow of patrons. Additionally, the NCC now reaches a much larger audience of passionate patrons who not only attend events but contribute financial support as well.

Each year the NCC organizes their annual Nottatown Chalk Fest, which grows and changes based on new themes and stories. As new ideas form, the Loop and the Hub are also renewed and rejuvenated, keeping the businesses and the townspeople enthusiastic for this community-wide effort.

I still receive text messages from Phil, Hector, JJ, Shoshana, and even Vanessa (who still works part time remotely for the NCC after moving away with her fiancé) every so often with pictures of their blue sky idea boards and Shoshana's chalk art on the walls. My favorite piece of her chalk art, which I printed and pinned to the wall of my office amidst family photos and graphics of clever puns, is a drawing of Dory, smiling among her *Finding Nemo* friends, and the words "just keep swimming."

The *Sandlot* Movie Ending

EXTERIOR, AFTERNOON, DIRT FIELD BEHIND NOTTATOWN
COMMUNITY CENTER

The gang plays catch and fade from the scene one by one.

NARRATOR
JJ, Shoshana, Phil, and Hector all lived
together in the neighborhood for a couple
of more years, and every summer was

great. But none of them ever came close
to that first summer after our workshop.

(as they dissolve:)

I kept in touch with the gang over the
years, and I found out that a friend staying
at Phil's house for the weekend saw the
fully operational miniature Disneyland Tea
Cups replica he had created for his wife
Wendy back in college, and offered him a
job at his company in Pasadena, California
building Rose Parade floats for companies
like Honda, Trader Joe's, and Disney.

Hector followed in his father's footsteps,
joining the Marines, and later married the
love of his life who he met while stationed
in Spain. He now works for a nonprofit
there, as their Creative Director.

After moving away, Vanessa went back
to school and earned her doctorate in
astrophysics (with a solid 3.0 GPA). She now
lives with her wife in Southern California.
If you look closely, you'll see her at the
flight control desk during SpaceX launches.

Shoshana took what she learned at the NCC
and rose to the level of Vice President of
Donor Relations at Harvard University. She
has a 100 percent success rate with big
solicitations when she is able to work the
word "effervescent" into her sales pitch.

JJ stuck around and is now the executive
director of the NCC, which has flourished
under his leadership. Despite its
irreverence, he pushed for a community
production of the Broadway hit "The Book of
Mormon." Even though everyone said community
centers can't put on plays with profanity
in them, thanks to Phil's insistence that
people love *South Park* and all things

that Matt Stone and Trey Parker create,
it ended up being the most successful
amateur production in Nottatown history.

Nobody has seen or heard anything about
Jonathan since he left Nottatown, other
than a Facebook review for a South Carolina
hair salon, left by a private profile with
his name, that many speculate is his.

And as for me,

INT. OFFICE

Computer screen with e-mails being deleted one by one

NARRATOR
Nearly three years after I penned the
first sentences of my memoir about my time
with the fictitious Nottatown Community
Center, I finally finished it. Now, I sit
by my computer, consulting with clients,
reading books on random topics, and weeding
through e-mails, hoping readers will
send flattering, pun-filled messages about
their successes as Nonprofit Imagineers.

CUT TO:

A FADED KODACHROME PHOTO WITH THE WORDS "JUST KEEP SWIMMING"
HANDWRITTEN ON THE EDGE

Six adults of varying ages standing in front of the Nottatown
"Pretzel." All of them are smiling except Vanessa.

END TITLES

FADE OUT.

Inspirational Resources
(aka The Bibliography)

Digital Resources

"All in the Details: Putting the 'Springs' Into Disney Springs." n.d. *Disney Parks Blog.* https://disneyparks.disney.go.com/blog/2016/01/all-in-the-details-putting-the-springs-into-disney-springs/ (accessed April 8, 2022).

Disney California Adventure History and Evolution. n.d. *www.youtube.com.* www.youtube.com/watch?v=vGxtY6AzXoE (accessed April 8, 2022).

Disney Imaginations » About Imagineering. n.d. https://disneyimaginations.com/about-imaginations/about-imagineering/ (accessed May 4, 2022).

Indian Hills Community Sign. n.d. www.facebook.com/IndianHillsCommunitySign/ (accessed April 12, 2022).

"Innovation." n.d. *Econlib.* www.econlib.org/library/Enc/Innovation.html (accessed April 8, 2022).

"Jim Hill Media—Themed Entertainment News, Blogs, Podcasts, and More." n.d. *Jim Hill Media.* https://jimhillmedia.com/ (accessed April 8, 2022).

Location-Based Interactive Storytelling the Walt Disney Imagineering Way. n.d. www.gdcvault.com/play/1019732/Location-Based-Interactive-Storytelling-the (accessed April 8, 2022).

Port Disney: The Forgotten Plans to Bring a Disney Theme Park to Long Beach. n.d. *www.youtube.com.* www.youtube.com/watch?v=VTnX2fPKX-A (accessed April 8, 2022).

SamLand's Disney Adventures. n.d. http://samlanddisney.blogspot.com/ (accessed April 8, 2022).

The Art of Innovation | Guy Kawasaki | TEDxBerkeley. n.d. *www.youtube.com.* www.youtube.com/watch?v=Mtjatz9r-Vc (accessed April 8, 2022).

"You Probably Don't Know This About Disney's Monorail ..." July 14, 2015. *Theme Park Tourist.* www.themeparktourist.com/features/20150711/30416/walt-disney-and-rise-monorail?page=3 (accessed April 1, 2022).

Wikipedia. May 23, 2021. "Nicolson Pavement." *Wikipedia.* https://en.wikipedia.org/w/index.php?title=Nicolson_pavement&oldid=1024698411 (accessed April 8, 2022).

Wikipedia. April 4, 2022. "Walt Disney Imagineering." *Wikipedia.* https://en.wikipedia.org/w/index.php?title=Walt_Disney_Imagineering&oldid=1081027565 (accessed April 8, 2022).

Books About Innovation and Creativity

Berkun, S. 2010. *The Myths of Innovation* 1. Updated and Expanded pbk ed. O'Reilly.

Brabandere, L.D. and I. Alan. 2013. *Thinking in New Boxes: A New Paradigm for Business Creativity.* Random House.

Clarke, C. 2009. *Storytelling for Grant Seekers—A Guide to Creative Nonprofit Fundraising.* Jossey-Bass.

Collins, J. 2001. *Good to Great: Why Some Companies Make the Leap ... and Others Don't.* Random House.

Christensen, C. 2011. *The Innovator's Dilemma.* Harper Business.

Csikszentmihalyi, M. 2013. *Creativity: The Psychology and Discovery of Invention.* Harper Perennial Modern Classics.

DeGraff, J.T. 2011. *Innovation You: Four Steps to Becoming New and Improved,* 1st ed. Ballantine Books.

DeGraff, J. and D. Staney. 2017. *The Innovation Code: The Creative Power of Constructive Conflict.* Open WorldCat,

Du Sautoy, M. 2019. *The Creativity Code.* The Belknap Press of Harvard University Press.

Erixon, F. and W. Björn. 2016. *The Innovation Illusion: How So Little Is Created by So Many Working So Hard.* Yale University Press.

Gallo, C. 2010. *The Innovation Secrets of Steve Jobs.* McGraw Hill.

Gupta, A.K. 2016. *Grassroots Innovation: Minds on the Margin Are Not Marginal Minds.* Penguin Books India.

Imber, A. 2016. *The Innovation Formula: The 14 Science-Based Keys for Creating a Culture Where Innovation Thrives.* Open WorldCat. www.books24x7.com/marc.asp?bookid=113183 (accessed April 8, 2022).

Johnson, S. 2011. *Where Good Ideas Come From.* Riverhead Books.

Johnson, S. 2006. *Everything Bad Is Good for You: How Today's Popular Culture Is Actually Making Us Smarter.* 1st Riverhead trade pbk, ed. Riverhead Books.

Kelly, T. 2001. *The Art of Innovation.* Currency.

Levy, L. 2016. *To Pixar and Beyond: My Unlikely Journey With Steve Jobs to Make Entertainment History.* Houghton Mifflin Harcourt.

Llopis, G, and E. Jim. 2017. *The Innovation Mentality: Six Strategies to Disrupt the Status Quo and Reinvent the Way We Work.* Entrepreneur Press.

May, R. 1994. *The Courage to Create.* W.W. Norton.

Miller, D. 2017. *Building a Story Brand.* Harper Collins.

Penenberg, A.L. 2013. *Play at Work: How Games Inspire Breakthrough Thinking.* Portfolio Hardcover.

Perez-Breva, L. 2016. *Innovating: A Doer's Manifesto for Starting From a Hunch, Prototyping Problems, Scaling Up, and Learning to Be Productively Wrong.* MIT Press.

Ridley, M. 2020. *How Innovation Works.* 4th Estate.

Satell, G. 2017. *Mapping Innovation: A Playbook for Navigating a Disruptive Age.* McGraw-Hill.

Seelig, T. 2017. *Creativity Rules.* HarperOne.

Sturges, T. 2014. *Every Idea Is a Good Idea: Be Creative Anytime, Anywhere.* Jeremy P. Tarcher/Penguin.

Sutton, R.I. 2007. *Weird Ideas That Work: How to Build a Creative Company.* Paperback ed. Free Press.

Webb, N.J. 2019. *The Innovation Mandate—The Growth Secrets of the Best Organizations in the World.* Harper Collins Leadreship.

Wilson, E. 2017. *The Origins of Creativity.* Liveright Publishing Corporation.

Winicot, M. 2015. *Walt Disney: Creativity Lessons—The Great Teachings of a Huge Innovator.* UNITEXTO Digital Publishing.

Books About Innovative and Creative People

Isaacson, W. 2011. *Steve Jobs.* Simon & Schuster.

Jones, B.J. 2013. *Jim Henson: The Biography*, First ed. Ballantine Books.

Vance, A. 2015. *Elon Musk: Tesla, SpaceX, and the Quest for a Fantastic Future*, First ed. Ecco, an imprint of Harper Collins Publishers.

Books About Nonprofits and Fundraising

Bryson, J.M. 2011. *Strategic Planning for Public and Nonprofit Organizations: A Guide to Strengthening and Sustaining Organizational Achievement*, 4th ed. Jossey-Bass.

Lublin, N. 2010. *Zilch: The Power of Zero in Business.* Portfolio.

Books About Disney

Catmull, E. 2020. *Creativity, Inc.*

Disney Institute, ed. 2003. *Be Our Guest: Perfecting the Art of Customer Service.* Disney Editions.

Gabler, N. 2006. *Walt Disney: The Triumph of the American Imagination*, 1st ed. Knopf.

Gennawey, S. 2014. *The Disneyland Story: The Unofficial Guide to the Evolution of Walt Disney's Dream.* Open WorldCat. https://search.ebscohost.com/login.aspx?direct=true&scope=site&db=nlebk&db=nlabk&AN=683552.

Pierce, T.J. 2016. *Three Years in Wonderland: The Disney Brothers, C. V. Wood, and the Making of the Great American Theme Park.* University Press of Mississippi.

Prosperi, L.J. and Imagineers (Group). 2016. *The Imagineering Pyramid: Using Disney Theme Park Design Principles to Develop and Promote Your Creative Ideas.*

Rafferty, K., B. Gordon, the Imagineers, and M.D. Eisner (Foreword). 1996. *Walt Disney Imagineering: A Behind the Dreams Look at Making the Magic Real* 1, paperback ed. Hyperion [u.a.].

Sklar, M, and S. Leslie. 2015. *One Little Spark! Mickey's Ten Commandments and the Road to Imagineering,* First ed. Disney Editions.

Williams, P. and D. Jim. 2004. *How to Be like Walt.* Health Communications.

About the Author

Ben Vorspan has been serving the nonprofit community for more than 20 years and, during that time, has built a reputation for the creativity that he injects into nonprofit marketing, communications, fundraising, programming, and membership engagement.

After graduating from UC Santa Barbara, Ben began working in marketing, communications, and creative roles with an assortment of businesses and organizations, including the Hebrew Union College, The Jewish Federation of Greater Los Angeles, schools, religious organizations and a variety of mission-driven nonprofits.

In 2007, Ben founded Inspired Multimedia, Inc., a consulting firm specializing in working with nonprofit organizations around the world to build websites, improve marketing efforts and provide tools and resources customized to fit this niche. During that time, he also co-founded and ran a thriving nonprofit group for young professionals in the Los Angeles area, receiving national recognition and grants.

Ben is a diehard Disney fan, enjoys playing music, cooking, and working with his hands, and lives in Los Angeles where he is married to Elana, a fellow nonprofit professional, and has two brilliant and creative children, Evan and Judah.

Index

Adapting to change, 155–156
Adjacent Possible, 51–55, 57–58,
    77, 92, 153, 159–160, 174,
    179–180, 184, 189
AlphaGo, 39–41
Animatronics, 51, 75, 107, 185
Annual Campaign, 103, 127–128,
    135

Barbershop music, 63–64
Becket, Welton, *xviii*
Beta testing, 151–153
Blue sky process
    asking questions and reframing,
        76–81
    brilliant stories, 82–89
    creative people types, 71–74
    "Dreamer, Realist and Spoiler",
        72–73
    meetings to brainstorm, 67–69,
        70–71
    problem-solving, 74–76
    team members for meetings,
        67–69, 71–74
Board of Directors, 36, 39–42, 152,
    155, 172
Brainstorming, 68, 70, 81, 157–168,
    199
Budgeting, 177–181

Challenges facing nonprofit sector,
    190–191
Change making
    Economics of, 32–36
    Responsibly, 13
    Through conversation with
        colleagues, 149–151
Christensen, Clayton, 29
Collins, Jim, 22
Common Purpose, 165–167
Communications, 111–118, 137
Competitors, 160–162

Comstock, Beth, 187
Concerns, dealing with, 151–156
Constructive conflict, 71
Creative destruction, 11–13
Creative intent, 9–11

Demographics information, 154
Disneyland's failures and adaptation,
    155–156
Disney's California Adventure (DCA),
    66, 74, 100, 101
Disney, Roy O., 21–22, 34, 188–189
Disney Springs, 177–178, 185–186
Disney Films
    Alice in Wonderland, 188
    Cars, 143
    Coco, 143
    Fantasia, 26, 178, 189
    The Galloping Gauchos, 22
    Hunchback of Notre Dame, 143
    Lady and the Tramp, 157
    Peter Pan, 188
    Plane Crazy, 22
    Snow White and the Seven Dwarfs,
        153–154, 188
Disney Theme Park Attractions
    America Sings, 178
    The Autopia, 102
    Avatar, Flight of Passage, 118
    Big Thunder Mountain Railroad, 94,
        100, 110, 130, 142
    Buzz Lightyear Astro Blasters, 102,
        107, 117
    Carousel, 13, 130
    Carousel of Progress, 115
    Castles, 13, 25, 130, 134, 136, 155,
        176
    Disneyland Railroad, 130
    *DuckTales World Showcase
        Adventure*, 75
    Enchanted Tiki Room, 52
    Expedition Everest, 118

Great Moments with Mr. Lincoln, 179

Haunted Mansion, 108, 109, 117, 118

Indiana Jones Adventure, 77, 107, 118, 119

It's a Small World, 53, 108, 109, 126, 136, 163, 179

Jungle Cruise, 102, 118

Kim Possible World Showcase Adventure, 75

Main Street Cinema, 13, 138

Mark Twain River Boat, 26

Matterhorn Bobsleds, 13

Monorail, 183–184

The People Mover, 179

Peter Pan's Flight, 9–10, 25

Phineas and Ferb Agent P's World Showcase Adventure, 75

Pirates of the Caribbean, 13–15, 108–109, 118, 136

Space Mountain, 102, 180

Splash Mountain, 100, 117, 127–129, 134, 178

Star Tours, 102

Star Wars Rise of the Resistance, 107

Submarine Voyage, 13

Tiana's Bayou Adventure, 127

Disney Theme Park Lands
    Bear Country/Critter Country, 100
    Fantasyland, 102
    Frontierland, 93, 98, 130
    Main Street USA, 112, 125, 126, 130, 131, 133, 134, 136–138, 176
    New Orleans Square, 117
    Pixar Pier, 101
    Tomorrowland, 102

Disney, Walt
    Accomplishments, 4
    Failures, 21–22
    Feelings about Disneyland, 38
    Inevitability of innovation, 189
    Stages of creativity, 72–73
    Willingness to adapt, 155

Disruptive technology, 29–34

Donors
    Addressing concerns, 36–37
    Heroes of campaign, 108
    Relations, 169, 170
    Solicitation, 36, 135–136, 138

Edison, Thomas, 22, 28, 152

Eisner, Michael, 66, 73–74, 155

Environmental storytelling, 136–139

Event planning, 38, 103, 111–114, 131, 172
    Galas, 127

Experimental Prototype Community of Tomorrow (EPCOT), 75, 75, 163, 164

Experimentation, 151–153

Failure, dealing with, 21–22, 37, 115, 156, 175

False positives and negatives, 25–27

Fantasound system, 178

Forced perspective, 133–136

Ford, Henry, 58

Fundraising, 12, 38, 95, 103, 119, 131, 132, 154, 156, xvii
    See "annual campaign"
    See "donors"

Grants, 181

Great By Choice, 22

Gregersen, Hal, 77

Gurr, Bob, 76

Hidden Mickeys, *see "Imagineering principles"*

High tech vs. high touch, 168–169

Hilsen, Don, xix

How Innovation Works, 7

Ideas folder, 157–160

Imagineering principles
    See "common purpose"
    See "creative intent"
    environmental storytelling, 136–139
    forced perspective, 133–136
    hidden mickeys, 142–146
    kinetics, 125–130
    plussing, 139–141
    weenies, 130–132

Innovation, 14–16
    adjacent possibles, 51–55

animatronics, 51–53
attempting change, 24–25
"Big I versus small I" innovations,
    54–55
board approval issue, 39–42
competitors, 160–162
existing information and new ideas,
    153–155
experimentation, 151–153
failures, 21–24
false positives and negatives, 25–27
innovator's dilemma, 29–32
Internet and GPS, 50
iPhone, 51, 58
laser, 50, 57
light bulb, 28
Luis Perez-Breva's explanation, 49
Nicolson pavement, 49–50
problem-solving, 57–61
role models, 162–165
in schools, 56–57
successes and failures, 37–38
test/beta environment, 151–153
tradition, 55–57
The innovator's dilemma, 29–31
Iwerks, Ub, 21

Johnson, Steven, 52 56, 67
Jobs, Steve, 26, 51, 56, 57, 58, 143

Kimball, Ward, 35
Kinetics, see "Imagineering principles"

Leadership, 30, 33, 53, 150–151
Lublin, Nancy, 5

Marketing campaigns, 16, 41, 49, 94,
    95, 137–138, 152, 172
Measuring Success, 175
Mission statements, 5–8
Mood board, 167

Narrative storytelling, 94
Neural coupling, 94
Nonprofit Imagineers
    expectation management, 183–185
    long-term goals setting, 192–193
    motivation to do grunt work,
        185–187

solo act, 186–187
timing delays, 189
Nonprofit Organizations
    See "Board of Directors"
    See "Budgeting"
    Capitalism, 38–39
    See "Fundraising"

Online engagement, 168–169
Open source program, 170–172
Oswald the Lucky Rabbit, 21, 156

People
    "cast members", 165–167,
        169–170
    importance of human interactions,
        167–169
    co-worker involvement, xviii–xix,
        169–170
    volunteers, 170–174
Pixar, 26, 33, 82, 154, 170
    Pixar Pitch, 82, 83
Plussing, 139–141, 173–177
    70-20-10 approach, 174
    five senses, 176–177
Postshow, 116–121, 141, 195–200
Preshow, 110–115
Problem-solving, innovation,
    57–61
Prosperi, Louis, 8

Queues, 27, 77, 94, 107, 110,
    114–115, 117–119, 128, 134,
    142

Religious Organizations
    Church, 29–32, 141, 160
    Synagogue, 11, 48, 53, 54, 161,
        163, 190
Ridley, Matt, 7, 12
Role models, 162–165

The Sandlot movie, 200–202
Sandefur, Timothy, 36
Schumpeter, Joseph, 11
Schools, 56–57, 109, 120, 132, 141,
    161
Sklar, Marty, xviii, 70, 180
Skunkworks project, 33–35

Silicon Valley Television Show, 55
Small start-ups, 33
Societal trends, 190–192
Storytelling, 136–139
    Challenges, guides, and heroes,
        106–108
    chapters, 101–106
    in advertising and campaigns,
        92–97
    linear and nonlinear, 108–110
    natural and realistic, 97–101
    negative to positive turn, 118–119
    postshow, 115–118
    preshow, 110–115, 118–119
    in theme parks, 97–98
    themes, 97–99
Stuntronics, 51
Synagogue, see *religious organizations*

Team conversations, 149–151
Team, engagement
    common purpose, 165–167
    message sharing and supporters,
        172–173
    role play, 169–170
Test environment, 151–153
The Imagineering Pyramid, 8

Weenies, 130–132
WestCOT, 73–74
"We've always done it that way", 11–13
Williams, Pat, 188
WordPress framework, 170–171
World's Fair (1964), 115, 179

Zilch: The Power of Zero in Business,
    5, 181

OTHER TITLES IN THE HUMAN RESOURCE MANAGEMENT AND ORGANIZATIONAL BEHAVIOR COLLECTION

Michael J. Provitera, Barry University, Editor

- *The Intrapreneurship Formula* by Sandra Lam
- *Navigating Conflict* by Lynne Curry
- *Innovation Soup* by Sanjay Puligadda and Don Waisanen
- *The Aperture for Modern CEOs* by Sylvana Storey
- *The Future of Human Resources* by Tim Baker
- *Change Fatigue Revisited* by Richard Dool and Tahsin I. Alam
- *Championing the Cause of Leadership* by Ted Meyer
- *Embracing Ambiguity* by Michael Edmondson
- *Breaking the Proactive Paradox* by Tim Baker
- *The Modern Trusted Advisor* by Nancy MacKay and Alan Weiss
- *Achieving Success as a 21st Century Manager* by Dean E. Frost
- *A.I. and Remote Working* by Tony Miller
- *Best Boss!* by Duncan Ferguson, Toni M. Pristo, and John Furcon
- *Managing for Accountability* by Lynne Curry
- *Fundamentals of Level Three Leadership* by James G.S. Clawson

Concise and Applied Business Books

The Collection listed above is one of 30 business subject collections that Business Expert Press has grown to make BEP a premiere publisher of print and digital books. Our concise and applied books are for...

- Professionals and Practitioners
- Faculty who adopt our books for courses
- Librarians who know that BEP's Digital Libraries are a unique way to offer students ebooks to download, not restricted with any digital rights management
- Executive Training Course Leaders
- Business Seminar Organizers

Business Expert Press books are for anyone who needs to dig deeper on business ideas, goals, and solutions to everyday problems. Whether one print book, one ebook, or buying a digital library of 110 ebooks, we remain the affordable and smart way to be business smart. For more information, please visit www.businessexpertpress.com, or contact sales@businessexpertpress.com.

Printed in the USA
CPSIA information can be obtained
at www.ICGtesting.com
JSHW012056060823
46055JS00002B/67